Contextual Anger Regulation Therapy

D1593542

Anger is a natural human emotion that can serve important survival functions, but the excessive presence of anger and its associated negative outcomes—such as aggression and violence—can lead to significant interpersonal, intrapersonal, occupational, legal, familial, societal, and physical health problems. Unfortunately, clinical anger clients haven't historically been helped in truly sustainable ways, and loved ones and society at large are often left to simply watch as these individuals struggle to overcome their anger and the noxious behaviors that often emanate from this troubling condition.

Contextual Anger Regulation Therapy gives clinicians the power to change this. The book presents an exciting nine-module mindfulness and acceptance-based behavioral treatment program that has been effectively utilized in formal clinical settings with clinical anger clients, including those mandated for treatment following both non-domestic and domestic violence. Treatment success has not only been demonstrated in observable ways, including significant reductions in violence recidivism and marked improvements in quality of life; it has also been seen in scientific data both in the laboratory and with large numbers of mandated clinical anger clients.

Frank L. Gardner, PhD, ABPP, is professor and director of the PsyD program in school and clinical psychology at Kean University in Union, New Jersey. He has founded two of the premier centers for the treatment and study of anger and violence in the United States. In addition, he is codeveloper of the Mindfulness–Acceptance–Commitment (MAC) approach to performance enhancement and is the founding editor-in-chief of the *Journal of Clinical Sport Psychology (JCSP)*.

Zella E. Moore, PsyD, is an associate professor of psychology at Manhattan College in New York, where she is dedicated to teaching and mentoring undergraduate psychology students. Zella is also codeveloper of the Mindfulness–Acceptance–Commitment (MAC) approach to enhancing human performance and is the founding senior associate editor of the *Journal of Clinical Sport Psychology (JCSP)*.

Practical Clinical Guidebooks Series

Contextual Anger Regulation Therapy

A Mindfulness and Acceptance-Based Approach

Frank L. Gardner and
Zella E. Moore

Routledge
Taylor & Francis Group

NEW YORK AND LONDON

First published 2014
by Routledge
711 Third Avenue, New York, NY 10017

Simultaneously published in the UK
by Routledge
27 Church Road, Hove, East Sussex BN3 2FA

© 2014 by Taylor & Francis

Routledge is an imprint of the Taylor & Francis Group, an informa business

Library of Congress Cataloging in Publication Data
Gardner, Frank L., 1953-
  Contextual anger regulation therapy :
  a mindfulness and acceptance-based approach /
  Frank L. Gardner and Zella E. Moore.
  pages cm.—(Practical clinical guidebooks)
  Includes bibliographical references and index.
  1. Anger—Treatment. 2. Acceptance and commitment therapy.
  I. Moore, Zella E., 1975- II. Title.
  RC569.5.A53.G37 2013
  616.89'1425—dc23
  2013008573

ISBN: 978–0–415–87297–3 (hbk)
ISBN: 978–0–415–87298–0 (pbk)
ISBN: 978–0–203–86491–3 (ebk)

Typeset in Sabon
by Swales & Willis Ltd, Exeter, Devon

Printed and bound in the United States of America by Sheridan Books, Inc. (a Sheridan Group Company).

A professional life has very little meaning without being embedded in something greater. To my absolutely perfect wife who has taught me how to live a life and not simply have one; to my unbelievable new son who fills me with joy and wonderment every single day, and to my older son who fills me with immense pride; thank you all for giving me the energy and desire to make a difference every day. You are all at the center of what I value.

—Frank

To my unbelievable husband—I am so tremendously blessed to have you as the love of my life. And to our beautiful new baby boy—I sit in amazement of my love for you, and promise to cherish every single moment of your precious life. I love you both with every inch of my heart.

—Zella

Contents

List of Figures and Tables

Figures

Tables

Preface

The development of this text as a vehicle for the dissemination of the Contextual Anger Regulation Therapy (CART) protocol for the treatment of clinical anger and associated behavioral difficulties is a testament to the science–practice connection in professional psychology that we so vehemently support. From the outset, we envisioned that this text would provide clinicians and researchers with an empirically informed and integrated approach to studying and working with this population so in need of direct attention, and we now hope that this text is successful in promoting discussion, providing a model for effective practice, spurring future research endeavors, and creating newfound interest in clinical anger work. We envision that practice should guide scientific inquiry, which subsequently should directly inform innovative empirically derived treatment approaches capable of being applied in real-world clinical settings. We think clients are owed our commitment to that reciprocal relationship.

We can't help but think of all the clinically angry individuals who have deserved improvements in their various life domains so impacted by their emotional and behavioral upheaval. Clinical patients struggling with other forms of psychopathology, from depression to anxiety and beyond, are able to improve following scientifically informed, empirically grounded interventions. Do those struggling with the emotion of anger deserve less? Of course not.

Yet, clinical anger patients haven't seemed to be helped in truly sustainable ways based on the common treatments provided to date, and loved ones and society at large are often left to simply watch as these individuals struggle to overcome their anger and the noxious behaviors that often emanate from this troubling condition. Did these individuals really have to remain relegated to maintaining such high anger pathology throughout their entire lives; struggle with the resultant behavioral difficulties that lead to interpersonal, intrapersonal, occupational, legal, familial, and societal problems; and succumb to the physical health risks associated with clinical levels of anger and hostility? We certainly didn't want that to be the case. Yet, analyses have for some time suggested a concerning absence of empirical evidence for the efficacy of anger-related treatments. There simply had to be something better. So, we decided it was time to do our small part to aid in the understanding and treatment of this challenging clinical phenomenon. We put great effort into the entire process, from the theory-building stage all the way to the development of a new, integrative, acceptance-based behavioral treatment known as Contextual Anger Regulation Therapy.

Our theory-building process (described in Chapters 1 and 2) connected the scientific knowledge base in experimental psychopathology and clinical science, and contemporary findings related to emotion regulation, mindfulness and acceptance, and transdiagnostic processes. Together, this led to the theory and practical application of the nine-module CART protocol. The development of CART from theory to protocol, and from empirical investigation to clinical application, ultimately led to the development of this text. This has been such a rewarding professional endeavor, and we are so excited to share it with you. While we have received welcomed positive feedback regarding the application and effectiveness of this treatment approach, we genuinely hope that this text will encourage researchers to become involved in further investigating the CART program, as this of course is an essential requirement of any true scientific discipline. We likewise hope this text provides clinicians with a fresh perspective and energizes them to utilize this user-friendly guide as a step-by-step treatment manual in their work with clinical anger patients and other clientele who struggle with comorbid anger pathology. Herein, we hope to have provided readers with the theoretical (Anger Avoidance Model—AAM), empirical, and practical (CART) tools necessary to enact substantial and sustainable change with this complex clinical population. Welcome!

Acknowledgments

The development of both the Anger Avoidance Model and Contextual Anger Regulation Therapy were the result of years of hard work on both of our parts. The underserved and poorly understood nature of the clinical anger population, and the fascinating scientific developments within experimental psychopathology and clinical science primed us to reevaluate, reformulate, and finally develop a new theoretical model to understand clinical anger pathology, and a new, empirically informed treatment approach to remediate clinical anger and its toxic behavioral manifestations. Since developing the nine-module CART treatment protocol a number of years ago, we have been struck by how effective it has been in formal clinical settings, and with such highly disturbed clients, including those mandated for treatment for both non-domestic and domestic violence. CART treatment efficacy has not only been demonstrated in obviously observable ways, including significant reductions in violence recidivism and marked improvements in quality of life, but has also been seen in the empirical data collected in our clinical laboratory and in formal empirical studies with large numbers of mandated clinical anger patients. We subsequently found ourselves inspired to write this text in order to turn what we have done in clinical practice, and what we teach in workshops and in-service presentations, into a formal and user-friendly text. We genuinely hope that clinicians will embrace this modular, integrative approach to the treatment of this challenging clinical population, and will equally enjoy seeing their clients improve in core fundamental, extensive, and sustainable ways. We are so excited for your clinical anger patients to begin their new lives, and are thus delighted that you have embarked upon this journey with us.

A number of important people have earned our heartfelt thanks and appreciation. We first offer enormous thanks to our families and friends for their ongoing sacrifice, support, and unconditional love. Second, we extend our gratitude to our professional families. Frank's appreciation goes out to the students and faculty with whom he has worked. Zella would personally like to thank her professional family of undergraduate students, faculty colleagues, and administration at Manhattan College in

Riverdale, New York, who offer amazing support and create such a wonderful environment in which to work. We likewise thank the dedicated staff at Routledge for their willing support, ongoing encouragement, and commitment to this project, and to the scientific advancement of professional psychology. Lastly, we cannot forget to thank our professional colleagues worldwide who are committed to scientific progress and to providing their patients with the most cutting-edge and empirically informed psychological care.

1   Understanding Clinical Anger

Anger is in all of us, from the newborn child to the old and wise, and from the kindest person to the most vengeful tyrant. There's no formula, prescription, or strategy to avoid the actual experience of this powerful emotional state. It is part of who we are, and the propensity for the emotion of anger will follow each of us to the end of our lives. Why? Because the emotion of anger is a natural human emotion that has its roots in the primary evolution-based motive of survival. Although emotion theorists do not agree on whether anger is a primary emotion or emanates secondarily from a more generalized distress state (Camras, 1992; Izard, 1991), they do agree that anger, like all human emotions, serves a variety of basic adaptive functions. From this evolutionary-based perspective, the emotion of anger serves as a signal of impending danger, and as such, organizes and triggers psychological and physiological processes related to goal-seeking and/or self-protection (Izard & Kobak, 1991; Saarni *et al.*, 2006). Anger may also serve as a secondary emotion by functioning as an affective response to other emotional states. For instance, the emotion of fear, which may be experienced as unbearable by some, is frequently associated with strong feelings of uncontrollability and vulnerability, and can in turn serve as a discriminative stimulus for the secondary emotion of anger. This perspective is consistent with recent research, which has demonstrated that anger is in fact associated with both approach behavior (i.e. goal seeking), and avoidance/escape behavior (i.e. protective response to real or perceived threat-oriented behavior; Dettore, Pabian, & Gardner, 2010; Donahue *et al.*, 2009). The capacity to effectively respond to both threatening and goal-related demands from the environment requires the awareness, understanding, and utilization of, and overt behavioral responses to, the subjective experience of anger.

Of course, the experience of anger can be conceptualized as falling on a continuum, upon which anger may range from mild irritation to extreme rage, and includes cognitive, subjective, and physiological elements. We support the conceptualization that emotion (i.e. anger), cognition, physiological responses, and subjective experience are all interacting entities, and should not be seen in a linear fashion in which cognition precedes subjective experience, which in turn precedes physiological responses. In addition, while anger has a clear adaptive function in its preparation of human beings to respond to external threat, it can also certainly pose significant problems, in that the associated action tendencies of anger (its behavioral expression) tend to have a negative impact on others and often result in substantial short- and long-term personal and interpersonal costs. Such expressions can include physical altercations, arguments, non-verbal displays of discontent, and aggression/violence, to name a few, and such costs can include relationship distress, occupational disruption, judicial action, and loneliness, among many others. Thus, since every human being will certainly *feel* the emotion of anger throughout their lifetime, the development of appropriate experience and expression of anger is necessary for optimal functioning and overall wellbeing. Of course, it is important to remember that when we talk about anger, we must always be cognizant of differentiating the healthy, normal, adaptive experiences and functions of anger from the dysfunctional, pathological, self, and interpersonal aspects of the experience and expression of anger. In this text, therefore, we refer to the dysfunctional/pathological variant of anger as *clinical anger*.

This introductory chapter begins the full discussion of clinical anger, its behavioral manifestations, and its remediation by beginning a dialogue on: (a) anger as a clinical problem; (b) diagnostic issues and status with regard to clinical anger; and (c) the theoretical models seeking to describe the relationship between anger and violence. Subsequently, we then present an historical perspective on the theory, research, and treatment of clinical anger so that readers can glean a full picture of where this interesting and important area of study has been, and appears to be progressing in the future.

Anger as a Unique Clinical Problem

Basic to the concept of clinical anger is the idea that excessive anger inevitably results in an individual being in a "fight or flight" mode too frequently. The consequence of this is the expenditure of substantial personal resources to functionally or dysfunctionally monitor and control the external environment, along with one's own internal processes (i.e. cognitions, emotions, and physical sensations), and as a result, the individual all too often acts in an aggressive or violent manner toward friends, foes, or even benign individuals.

Yet while there are clear and present interpersonal costs, possibly the most fundamental long-term cost of clinical anger is its relationship to personal health-related problems, specifically the development of cardiovascular disease. Specifically, anger and hostility—the latter of which is most accurately thought of as a chronic angry ruminative process (Gardner & Moore, 2008), not unlike worry in anxiety (Borkovec, Alcaine, & Behar,

2004) and brooding/rumination in depression (Nolen-Hoeksema, 2000)—have been shown in the professional literature to be consistently related to the development of coronary heart disease (Smith & Ruiz, 2002; Suls & Bunde, 2005). Of particular importance have been several prospective studies that have supported the strong link between anger, hostility, and aggression, and the later development of cardiovascular disease (Smith *et al.*, 2004; Williams *et al.*, 2000). Traditionally, it has been postulated that the cardiovascular risk associated with anger, hostility, and aggressiveness is due to exaggerated cardiovascular and neuroendocrine responses to stressors (Williams, Barefoot, & Shekelle, 1985). On the other hand, more recent explanations have implicated increased peripheral inflammation in response to chronic hostility, which is a known risk factor for atherosclerosis and myocardial infarction (Ridker *et al.*, 2000). While the precise pathogenesis of the relationship between anger and cardiovascular disease is not fully understood at this time, current empirical research strongly suggests that anger poses a substantial health risk, particularly for individuals in the middle stages of life. In fact, a fascinating recent meta-analysis by Mund and Mitte (2012) on more than 6,000 patients found that those who hold back/restrain the expression of anger experience greater likelihood of developing cardiovascular disease, hypertension, and cancer. Additionally, such individuals were found to live an average of two years less than those who adequately expressed the emotion of anger. These direct health consequences are certainly staggering.

In addition to negative personal health outcomes, the often noted dysfunctional behavioral component of anger, which is aggression and/or violent behavior, results in significant personal and societal costs in terms of judicial, correctional, and public health outcomes. For example, a study by Tafrate, Kassinove, and Dundin (2002) suggested that individuals identified as anger prone (that is, individuals identified as experiencing high levels of trait anger) are twice as likely to be arrested and three times as likely to have served time in the prison system than those scoring low on trait anger, with most of the offenses related to violent acts. In addition, it has been argued that anger is a mediator of domestic violence and substance abuse (Barbour *et al.*, 1998). Consistent with this view, a recent meta-analysis by Norlander and Eckhardt (2005) suggested that elevated levels of anger and hostility are in fact distinguishing characteristics of male perpetrators of interpersonal violence.

Additionally, it is well accepted that a substantial number of motor vehicle accidents, costly in terms of personal wellbeing as well as medical and insurance costs, are related to angry/aggressive drivers (US Department of Transportation, 2005). Compared to low-anger motorists, high-anger motorists driving a similar number of miles have been shown to take significantly more driving risks such as speeding, passing unsafely, tailgating, frequently switching driving lanes, running stoplights, making illegal turns, and engaging in both verbal and physical aggression;

and have more vehicular accidents (Deffenbacher *et al.*, 2000, 2003). In another study of aggressive drivers, Deffenbacher *et al.* (2005) found that high-anger drivers were four times more likely to engage in aggressive driving behaviors, twice as likely to engage in high-risk driving behaviors, and were recipients of significantly more moving-violations than low-anger drivers.

Clinical anger in the workplace has also been found to be directly associated with negative occupational outcomes. For example, Carroll (2001) found that anger in the workplace is associated with reduced job performance and lower employee performance evaluations, which in turn culminate in reduced compensation and career advancement. In addition, they found that angry employees demonstrated lower organizational commitment and increased employee turnover, thus having a direct cost to individuals, and an indirect cost to organizations and society at large.

In summary, clinical anger and its related dysfunctional behavioral response of aggression and violence result in a variety of significant health, legal, interpersonal, and occupational outcomes affecting individuals, those close to them, and the world in which they live.

Clinical Anger and Psychological Comorbidities

In addition to being a significant problem in and of itself, clinical anger has also been shown to be associated with numerous other psychological disorders coming to the attention of the practicing psychologist. For example, Fava and Rosenbaum (1998) found that approximately one-third of depressed patients experienced "anger attacks," defined as the sudden and intense experience of anger accompanied by significant autonomic arousal. Additional studies have found that 36% of patients meeting criteria for a *Diagnostic and Statistical Manual of Mental Disorders-IV-TR* (*DSM-IV-TR*; American Psychiatric Association (APA), 2000) diagnosis of major depressive disorder, 61% of patients meeting criteria for a diagnosis of bipolar II disorder (Benazzi, 2003), and 48% of patients meeting criteria for posttraumatic stress disorder (Murphy *et al.*, 2004) reported substantial difficulties with anger that resulted in negative health, vocational, and occupational outcomes. Similarly, it has been found that measures of anger were significantly elevated, even when controlling for severity of PTSD symptoms, and were strongly related to occupational impairment, in combat-related PTSD cases (Frueh *et al.*, 1998).

Anger has likewise been shown to negatively impact the effectiveness of otherwise empirically supported psychological treatments for other psychological disorders. For example, socially anxious patients demonstrated higher levels of experienced anger and demonstrated greater problematic expression of anger than non-anxious controls, and possibly most importantly for those who provide psychological care to anxious patients, elevated levels of anger were associated with premature termination from treatment and a generally less satisfactory response to cognitive behavioral treatment of social anxiety (Erwin *et al.*, 2003). What we are seeing, then, is that while anger in its natural adaptive form is a necessary evolutionary emotional state, the dysfunctional experience and expression of this intense emotion is not only problematic in and of itself, but also co-occurs with other psychopathological conditions and further complicates the subsequent remediation of those conditions.

Diagnostic Issues and Status

Interestingly, although problematic anger has long been associated with dysfunctional behavior, relationship consequences, and negative health outcomes, the concept of an "anger disorder" is not currently recognized as a unique mental disorder by the *DSM-5* (APA, 2013). The closest to an adult "anger disorder" currently found in the *DSM* is intermittent explosive disorder (IED). As a category, IED focuses on dysfunctional aggressive behavior, and is characterized by the following abbreviated criteria.

1. Episodes reflecting a failure to adequately resist verbally or physically aggressive impulses.
2. The level of aggressive behavior is clearly out of proportion to any precipitating psychosocial stressor.
3. The aggressive behavior cannot be better accounted for by another psychiatric disorder (i.e. antisocial personality disorder, borderline personality disorder, bipolar disorder).

A perusal of the criteria for IED leads to the unmistakable conclusion that this category of disorder is actually a disorder specific to violent and aggressive behavior, and the criteria do not even mention *anger* as a sign or symptom necessary for diagnosis.

There was some hope that the new *DSM-5* (APA, 2013) would include an anger diagnosis. However, this has not been the case. The closest new diagnostic addition in the *DSM-5* is a childhood classification known as disruptive mood dysregulation disorder (DMDD). This new diagnosis was born out of the notable increase in diagnoses of bipolar disorder (BD) in children and the need to better represent the developmental precursor to the adult disorder. While not actually seeking to represent clinically angry adult clientele, the DMDD criteria appear staggeringly appropriate for this population. To illustrate this, let's review some of the specifics (although not an exhaustive list) of the DMDD criteria. First, the disorder requires that the individual engage in significant and recurrent verbal and/or behavioral "temper outbursts" that do not proportionally match the situation, which may include aggression toward other people or things. These eruptions in temper typically occur three or more times each week for at least a year. When not in the midst of a temper outburst, the individual's mood is characterized as consistently angry or irritable, which is outwardly visible by others in the environment. Finally, but not exhaustively, the temper outbursts and between-episode anger and irritability should be observable in at least two settings.

Does this sound like the clinically angry client? It most certainly does! However, one catch is that this diagnosis is included in the new *DSM* as a *childhood* diagnosis, requiring a diagnosis after 6 years of age and before 18 years of age. In addition, the onset of the excessive temper outbursts must be prior to age 10.

Unfortunately, at present, individuals with clinical anger are classified under a multitude of psychiatric diagnoses even though these adult clients exhibit a similar symptom and behavior constellation as the DMDD disorder ostensibly established for children. While conceptualizing DMDD as a disorder that extends into adulthood in the form of clinical anger may appear warranted, at present we cannot utilize such a diagnosis with adult clientele.

Based on the ineffectiveness of the then-current *DSM-IV-TR* (APA, 2000) system to capture the clinical anger population, we decided it would be informative to conduct a study evaluating the utility of the then-proposed *DSM-5* DMDD diagnosis as an adult diagnosis for clinical anger patients (Dettore, Kempel, & Gardner, 2010). We actually only needed to modify DMDD age-related criteria in order to allow an adult diagnosis to be given. Data were obtained via review of clinical and actuarial records gleaned from a sample of 86 court-mandated violent offenders undergoing treatment at a university-based anger treatment facility. The sample was 75% male, with a mean age of 32.14. Participants were self-identified as 60.5% African-American, 25.9% Caucasian, 11.1% Hispanic, and 2.4% as "other." Thirty-two (32) different Axis I and Axis II *DSM-IV-TR* disorders were represented within the population, despite a predominant cohesive pattern of presenting pathology. Participants' diagnoses included 26 Axis I diagnoses and 6 Axis II diagnoses. The primary *DSM-IV-TR* diagnoses for Axis I were: 13.5% major depressive disorder, 9.3% alcohol dependence, 6.8% dysthymic disorder, 5.9% posttraumatic stress disorder, 5.1% adjustment disorder, and approximately 59.4% cutting across all other Axis I disorders. Axis II diagnoses were: 6.8% antisocial personality disorder, 5.0% borderline personality disorder, 1.4% narcissistic personality disorder, and 20% personality disorder NOS (not otherwise specified). When DMDD was used as an alternative diagnosis, a whopping 49% of clients met criteria for the proposed diagnosis. With nearly half of the overall sample represented by this then-proposed *DSM-5* disorder, DMDD accounted for a significantly greater proportion of this court-mandated adult clinical anger population than any other single diagnosis.

The fact is that no anger diagnosis exists in the *DSM*. However, this has not been due to a lack of effort. Given the absence of a unique diagnostic entity, Eckhardt and Deffenbacher (1995) long ago proposed a relatively simple new category for future iterations of the *DSM*, which would include three specific anger disorders: (a) *adjustment disorder with angry mood* (a disorder not unlike the old *DSM-IV-TR* adjustment disorder diagnosis, but with an emphasis on anger as a primary emotional manifestation); (b) *situational anger disorder*, which would share some features with IED but would focus more on situation-specificity of an angry response, and would be less dependent on aggressive behavior than IED; and (c) *general anger disorder*, which would be representative of high levels of trait anger and anger reactivity. These previously proposed disorders would be more focused on the experience of anger, although anger expression in the form of aggressive or violent behavior would certainly fall under their umbrellas. One can also readily see a relative similarity between this proposed anger diagnostic classification and the classification of anxiety disorders; adjustment disorder with anxious mood; simple phobia; and generalized anxiety disorder.

As an alternative diagnostic model, DiGiuseppe and Tafrate (2007) presented the most well-developed proposal for an anger disorder category in future *DSM* volumes. They have referred to their proposed anger disorder as *anger regulation-expression disorder* (ARED), and have suggested that individuals could meet criteria for this disorder via two distinct pathways. The first would be through subjective anger experiences as indicated by frequent, intense, and enduring angry affect, with two or more of the following being present either during or immediately following the anger experience: (a) physiological activation, (b) rumination, (c) cognitive distortions, (d) ineffective communication, (e) brooding/withdrawal, or (f) subjective distress. The second pathway would be through expressive patterns of behavior associated with the angry experience. These behavioral patterns must be out of proportion to the triggering stimulus, and at least one of the following must be consistently related to anger experiences: (a) aggressive/aversive verbalizations, (b) physical aggression toward people, (c) property destruction, (d) provocative/threatening bodily expression, or (e) various passive-aggressive behaviors including rumor spreading, secretly interfering with others' tasks or property, or intentionally failing to meet other people's expectations.

A diagnosis of ARED would require one of the above two pathways (experience or expressive), as well as evidence of consistent/repetitive damage to social or vocational relationships, and angry or expressive symptoms not better accounted for by another psychological disorder. Using the proposed ARED classification, clinicians would then be left with three choices based upon symptom presentation: (a) anger disorder, predominantly subjective (i.e. experiencing) type; (b) anger disorder, predominantly expressive type; or (c) anger disorder, combined type.

While it has been suggested that anger-based diagnostic criteria would provide impetus for greater attention to research in the basic science and treatment of clinical anger (DiGiuseppe & Tafrate, 2007), the reality of clinical practice is that anger-related difficulties are a residual aspect of a number of diagnostic conditions such as mood disorders, PTSD, social anxiety, and a variety of personality disorders, and do not often present as a unique and independent symptom cluster. This is not unlike the clinical reality that other emotional disorders (such as depressive and anxiety disorders) are highly co-occurring (Brown & Barlow, 1992). The need to address anger-related difficulties would thus inevitably continue to cut across *DSM* disorders, even if an independent anger disorder existed. Further, the boundary between normal and pathological levels of anger may be seen as somewhat arbitrary, and we do not yet have clear diagnostic measurement tools allowing for formal and accepted clinical anger cutoff scores (such as the Beck Depression Inventory-2 for depression; Beck, Steer, & Brown, 1996). In addition, we have no empirical data to suggest that individuals experiencing clinical anger but not meeting threshold for inclusion in any diagnostic category have any fewer psychosocial difficulties than those who do. In fact, we will argue in subsequent chapters that the ultimate clinical criterion for the determination of an anger-related problem should not be the *level* or *amount* of anger experienced. Rather, it should be the *degree* that the anger experience can be tolerated/accepted, which in turn gives rise to the form and intensity of the *expression* of anger, either in the form of overt behavior (such as violence) or more subtle cognitive processes such as efforts at over-control (i.e. suppression and/or rumination). It is this behavioral *response* to the experience of anger that ultimately interferes with personal, vocational, and/or interpersonal wellbeing. In essence, people generally suffer more consequences from the overt behavioral manifestations of aggressive/violent behavior and/or efforts at over-controlling/suppressing their response to anger, than they do from the actual subjective anger experience itself. Hence, from our perspective, any effort to categorize anger disorders based solely on signs and symptoms is problematic and does not advance the understanding of anger nor aid in the development of effective treatments.

Finally, and possibly most importantly, the field has recently begun moving away from the categorical model of psychological diagnoses, best represented by the *DSM* (Brown & Barlow, 1992). Instead, the field is placing an ever-increasing emphasis on core transdiagnostic processes as a more empirically sound means of understanding psychopathology. From a transdiagnostic perspective, psychopathology is not best understood by the variety of topographical signs and symptoms, which tend to overlap greatly between diagnostic categories. Rather, based upon an ever-growing body of research in experimental psychopathology, processes such as rumination, experiential avoidance, self-focused attention, and broad deficits in emotion regulation appear to be the core processes of many (if not most) diagnostic categories, and thus offer a more effective means of understanding problematic behavior (Aldao, Nolen-Hoeksema, & Schweizer, 2010; Kashdan *et al.*, 2006; Roemer & Orsillo, 2009). Viewing psychopathology from this perspective allows clinicians to tailor treatments to ameliorate pathological processes resulting in enhanced overall wellbeing and behavioral functioning, rather than efforts at direct alteration of diagnostic signs and symptoms. This approach is not unlike the difference between antibiotic treatment for the pathophysiology of a bacterial infection, as opposed to the use of over-the-counter medications for the brief amelioration of the overt signs and symptoms of such conditions. In turn, as psychological treatments are being developed to target the amelioration of these psychological processes rather than the simple treatment of topographical symptom checklists at the heart of the current categorical model of diagnosis (i.e. *DSM-5* and beyond), the need for additional diagnoses in the form of anger disorders appears, to us, as perhaps somewhat unnecessary. In fact, clinicians can expect that individuals referred for anger-related problems will also likely show evidence of depression and anxiety, as their social-interpersonal world is often chaotic and difficult. Although an anger-based diagnostic classification would certainly be a welcomed addition, as the field steadily evolves toward a more transdiagnostic approach to understanding and treating psychopathology, having a cogent and empirically informed theory for understanding the pathological processes underlying clinical anger and violence would appear to be more important than developing new a diagnostic criteria set, and appears critically necessary for adequate treatment development.

The Relationship between Anger and Violence

One of the unfortunate things about anger (especially clinical anger) is that it is often accompanied by nasty little friends, commonly named *aggression* and *violence*. In attempting to understand the relationship between anger and aggressive/violent behavior, it is first necessary to distinguish between instrumental aggression and reactive aggression (also referred to as hostile aggression or affective aggression). *Instrumental aggression* is best conceptualized as calculated and predatory (i.e. emphasizing acquiring another individual's possessions and/or asserting control over their behavior for personal benefit), and it tends to occur independent of the subjective experience of anger. In contrast, violence related to *reactive aggression* has been described as impulsive, situation-focused (i.e. emphasizing physical aggression toward others without a desire for overt personal gain), and related to the subjective experience of anger (Bushman

& Anderson, 2001; DiGiuseppe & Tafrate, 2007; Gardner & Moore, 2008). This text primarily focuses on reactive aggression, which involves aggressive or violent behavior that has a direct relationship to the experience of anger. Now, at this point, one might be wondering why we speak of aggression and violence in somewhat different terms, as they seem rather synonymous. For clarity, we point out that it is common to define and conceptualize aggressive behavior as including behaviors such as yelling, screaming, threatening, and similar verbal and non-verbal behaviors; while violence can be defined and conceptualized as overt motor (physical) acts such as throwing objects, hitting, slapping, kicking, or using weapons against others. Historically, the term "aggressive behavior" has subsumed the term "violent behavior" so that, in effect, they were interchangeable terms. However, we generally find it useful to view them as separate classes of behavior, though often quite intertwined.

Next, let's briefly consider those theories that seek to explain or describe the relationship between anger and aggression/violence. While it is not our intention to offer an exhaustive description, review, or critique of the variety of models offered to date to explain the relationship between anger and aggression/violence, we would like to briefly present the foundation of the most influential models.

The majority of contemporary models of the anger–violence relationship essentially posit that environmental events of some type result in the experience of frustration along with attributions/cognitions of injustice, fairness, and/or appropriateness of others' behavior, which in turn culminates in the experience of anger. This is often known as the frustration-aggression hypothesis (Berkowitz, 1989). According to this model, the emotion of anger thus provides the *motivation* for aggressive or violent behavior, which in turn serves to *relieve* the experience of anger.

Baumeister, Smart, and Boden (1996) have suggested that unstable appraisals of the self and others in response to frustration result in anger, which directly leads to aggressive or violent behavior. Tedeschi and Nessler (1993) have offered a similar model, suggesting that cognitions of external blame and unfairness culminate in aggressive/violent behavior through the arousal of intense anger. Fundamentally, in these models, anger is hypothesized as serving a meditational role in the relationship between negative attributions of self and others, with corresponding frustration and ultimately aggressive/violent behavior. In essence, these negative attributions serve to intensify anger arousal in response to some frustrating stimulus.

Somewhat differently, Beck (1999) has proposed a cognitive theory of anger and related problems, including hostility and violence. Consistent with his cognitive theories of depression and anxiety, his model suggests that environmental events/stimuli trigger specific core beliefs (most typically related to maltreatment, subjugation, and unfairness) and automatic thoughts emanating from these beliefs, which in turn result in angry affect and its behavioral consequences (often taking the form of violence). In yet another example of a cognitive perspective, Kassinove and Tafrate (2002) have proposed a cognitive model for understanding the relationship between anger and aggressive/violent behavior similar to that of Beck's, which essentially postulates that specific thoughts/beliefs, in most cases related to unrealistic demands, expectations, or assumptions about others, result in the emotional experience of anger with associated physiological changes. From this theoretical perspective, heightened anger and the physiological arousal associated with it results in socially constructed (i.e. learned) responses in the form of aggressive/violent behavior, which in turn function to discharge the experienced anger. This process is theorized as being maintained by immediate reinforcing interpersonal outcomes, which is essentially the attainment of desired interpersonal goals.

From a different perspective, one of the most well known models for understanding the relationship between anger and aggression/violence has been proposed by Novaco and colleagues (Novaco & Welsh, 1989; Stokols *et al.*, 1978), who have presented a somewhat less linear approach to understanding the relationship between events, cognition, physiological activation, and anger. From their perspective, the behavioral response to anger must be understood as a function of three interacting factors that function in a reciprocal manner: (a) external anger eliciting events (or stimuli); (b) distorted cognitive processes relating to blame, unfairness, and intentionality; and (c) physiological arousal/activation. From these three interacting factors, a behavioral response follows that may take the form of aggressive/violent behavior or more constructive behavioral responses such as assertiveness. According to the Novaco model, aggressive/violent behavior is still proposed to be the result of high levels of anger.

Berkowitz (1983, 1993, 2003) has proposed an alternative theoretical model for understanding the relationship between anger and aggression/violence. In his model, it is believed that unpleasant stimuli lead to frustration and overall discomfort, which in turn produce negative emotional reactions. It is this general negative emotional state that mediates the relationship between frustration and aggression. From this perspective, while frustration may most often result in the experience of anger, any negative emotion can in fact trigger a simultaneous urge to escape or attack. As such, following the elicitation of general negative affect, cognitive processes determine which specific emotion is experienced and which behavior will be exhibited as a response to that emotion. While the process is somewhat different than those presented previously, in this model, cognitive processes are still assumed to play a central role in determining both which emotion is experienced (i.e. attributions of unfairness result in anger, attributions of physical danger result in anxiety) and in what way it is expressed (i.e. attack or escape).

Anderson and Bushman (2002) have also proposed a model for under-standing the relationship between anger and aggression/violence (the general aggression model) that extends the traditional models presented above to include a number of additional variables. The general aggres-sion model suggests that personal traits, situational variables, and social, biological, and psychological factors all contribute to the occurrence of aggressive behavior. From this theoretical perspective, traits, gender roles, biological propensities, social norms, and cognitive variables all contrib-ute to the elicitation of emotional states such as anger and associated physiological arousal, which in turn leads the individual to a cost–benefit analysis of behavioral options (based upon personal learning histories), including aggressive or violent behavior. While anger plays a central role in this model, it is suggested that many variables may in fact trigger or inhibit the ultimate production of aggressive/violent behavior.

Finally, DiGiuseppe and Tafrate (2007) have proposed a slightly expanded cognitive model in which the presence of frustration, unpleas-ant stimuli, or perception of imminent attack activates a motive to either flee or fight. In turn, based on appraisal of threat and personal resources, the individual experiences anxiety or anger. Anger then generates the motive to aggress, and the stronger the experienced anger, the stronger the motive to aggress will be. In this model, it is hypothesized that the strength of the motive to aggress (which includes the desire for revenge) is based upon social learning experiences and is reinforced by outcomes of the aggressive behavior, including personal enjoyment of that behavior.

While these various theories differ in some minor respects, when looked at closely they all suggest some distinct and basic commonalities. These include an emphasis on factors such as cognitive appraisals and attributions of events; aggressive behavioral reactions as a response to the experience of anger/negative affect; and subsequent maintaining/rein-forcing consequences. From this common viewpoint, cognitive appraisal is viewed as the essential vehicle through which external events result in anger, and aggressive or violent behavior is thus seen as a frequent con-sequence of that emotion. While often not directly stated, the conclusion that directly follows from this perspective is that *reducing* the experi-ence of anger is necessary for the reduction of aggressive responses, and in turn, modification of cognitive processes would be necessary for the reduction of anger.

Yet, empirical research has been at best inconsistent in its support for these various models (DiGiuseppe & Tafrate, 2007). We personally sug-gest herein that there are four significant problems with these models as a means of understanding the relationship between anger and aggressive/violent behavior.

1. These traditional models, and the empirical data that have been gen-erated from them, have failed to allow for a clear basis by which to

predict aggressive behavior. That is, when will anger result in aggressive behavior and when won't it?

2. While there is some evidence that specific cognitive content (i.e. thoughts of unfairness, revenge) and anger are in fact correlated with one another, there is little evidence to suggest that specific cognitions precede and/or intensify the experience of anger. In fact, there is as much evidence that the experience of anger directs the content of cognitions as there is for the reverse (Lemerise & Dodge, 2008). It would seem that the best interpretation of the existing empirical data is that cognition, the subjective experience of emotion, physiological arousal, and learned action tendencies that occur as overt behavioral responses to emotion are inextricably tied together in a reciprocal relationship, and thus, any effort to assume a linear, causal role of one to another is essentially oversimplified and inaccurate (Barlow *et al.*, 2010; Kring & Werner, 2004).

3. Based on these traditional models, psychological treatments focusing on core components of these models (such as modification of specific cognitions and physiological relaxation) should result in substantial reductions in anger and in turn aggressive/violent behavior in clinical populations; yet, as we will discuss in greater detail later in this chapter, the efficacy data for treatments based upon these theoretical models have been less than compelling (Olatunji & Lohr, 2005).

4. The traditional models presented above all suggest, in some way, that aggressive/violent behavior is generally the inevitable product of internal processes that culminate in high levels of anger. However, studies have suggested that high inhibition of anger (i.e. lack of experience of anger) is as likely to be related to violent behavior as the more theoretically postulated problem of high levels of anger (Davey, Day, & Howells, 2005).

Given what we see as these fundamental problems with the traditional models seeking to explain and understand the anger-aggression/violence relationship, and based upon recent developments in experimental psychopathology and emotion science, specifically with regard to processes of emotion regulation, we have previously provided an alternative theoretical model for understanding the relationship between anger and aggressive/violent behavior. This model, which we have termed the Anger Avoidance Model (AAM; Gardner & Moore, 2008), will be presented in detail in Chapter 2. By way of a brief introductory summary, the Anger Avoidance Model suggests that it is not specific cognitive attributions nor anger itself that leads to aggressive/violent behavior, but rather, it is broad deficits in emotion regulation (in particular with regard to the understanding, tolerance, and modulation of the experience of anger) that results in intense and sometimes extreme cognitive and behavioral efforts to avoid and/or escape from those experiences. Avoidance of the experience of anger may take the form of an effort to over-control the experience of anger, as represented by cognitive processes such as suppression or (hostile) rumination, and/or under-control of the experience of anger, as represented by escape behavior in the form of aggressive/violent acts (Gardner & Moore, 2008). The essential difference between the traditional models and the Anger Avoidance Model is the degree to which the subjective/physiological experience of anger *itself* is seen as a problem to be reduced or controlled vs the degree that anger is seen as a natural part of the human experience that need not be controlled or avoided, but rather, experienced, accepted, and responded to in an appropriate values-directed manner for optimal personal and interpersonal functioning (Gardner & Moore, 2008). The differences between the traditional models and the AAM are therefore substantial.

The next logical point of discussion, then, is the treatment efficacy of psychological interventions generated from the traditional models seeking to explain the anger–violence relationship.

History of Theory, Research, and Treatment of Clinical Anger

Empirically informed psychological treatments for dysfunctional anger can be described as having begun with the work of Novaco (1975, 1977). Novaco adapted Meichenbaum's stress inoculation training (SIT; Meichenbaum, 1977) under the name Anger Management Training (AMT), a term that has remained in the public lexicon ever since. AMT is a traditional cognitive behavioral intervention that follows a three-phase intervention approach. Phase 1, *psychoeducation*, provides clients with a conceptualization of their anger difficulties, centering on the connection between provocative events, specific self-statements/lack of coping skills, and anger experience and expression. Phase 2, *skill acquisition*, provides coping skills in the form of more rational/positive self-statements and assertive behavioral options. Phase 3, *application*, provides clients with the opportunity to practice and strengthen/shape their coping skills while exposed to anger-inducing situations.

Since the development of AMT, multiple cognitive behavioral treatment packages have been presented that offer similar combinations of cognitive and behavioral change techniques. These treatments have most typically included relaxation training, cognitive restructuring, social skills training, problem-solving training, assertiveness training, and variants of exposure procedures. These procedures have been implemented both by themselves and in various combinations. Interestingly, while these treatment approaches are generally related to traditional models for understanding anger and violence in the most basic of ways (i.e. the assumption that specific cognitions result in the heightened experience of anger, which in turn results in aggressive/violent behavior), they have generally not been connected in any meaningful way to the specific theoretical models presented earlier, with the possible exception of Beck's cognitive model. The cognitive behavioral intervention packages presented for the treatment of dysfunctional anger have essentially followed the form of standard cognitive behavioral approaches for other emotional disorders in their adoption of a basic treatment package, which:

- assumes a cognitive meditational model, in which it is postulated that specific negative/inaccurate cognitions or attributions must be altered to more positive/accurate ones as an essential mechanism of change for reducing anger, and in turn, aggressive/violent behavior
- assumes that providing alternative methods of coping (i.e. social skills, assertiveness skills, relaxation skills, problem-solving skills) is essential as a mechanism of change for reducing anger, and in turn, aggressive/violent behavior.

Of note, the assumptions inherent in cognitive behavioral treatment packages of anger have certainly not been exclusive to the treatment of anger and violence. In fact, they have been central to traditional cognitive behavioral treatments described and tested across a variety of clinical disorders over the past 30 or so years (Nathan & Gorman, 2002), and recently have been under critical empirical scrutiny with regard to their actual mechanisms of change (Gortner *et al.*, 1998; Longmore & Worrell, 2007). Moreover, while traditional cognitive behavioral treatments have been generally effective across a wide range of mental disorders (Nathan & Gorman, 2007), there is much room for considerable improvement, and of importance, the actual mechanisms by which these interventions may work have not yet been clearly explicated. For example, according to Jacobson *et al.* (1996), cognitive therapy of depression, which has been considered a standard first line treatment of depression over the past three decades, demonstrates no better outcomes in its full package (including both cognitive and behavioral components) than the behavioral component administered alone.

When evaluating the efficacy of these cognitive behavioral interventions for clinical anger more specifically, it would seem logical to begin with reasonable benchmarks by which to compare efficacy findings within the broad area of anger-related problems. In this regard, we should begin with an understanding that meta-analytic reviews of traditional cognitive behavioral treatments of anxiety have consistently demonstrated effect sizes of more than 1.0 across a large array of outcome measures and across a wide number of studies (Chambless & Gillis, 1993; Nathan & Gorman, 2007). Similarly, traditional cognitive behavioral treatments for depression have consistently reported effect sizes of more than 2.0 (Nathan & Gorman, 2007). With this benchmark in place, a review of the meta-analytic and qualitative reviews of anger treatments follows.

Since the inception of psychological treatments for anger-related problems, numerous efficacy studies have been published. Tafrate published the first meta-analytic review of anger treatment studies in 1995. This initial review of 17 studies indicated effect sizes ranging from .8 to 1.1 when using cognitive, relaxation, skills-training, and multi-component interventions, but methodological issues including reliance on undergraduate (non-clinical analogue) populations, few studies studying individual treatment, and short treatment lengths hampered the ability to draw broad and clinically meaningful conclusions. A second review (Edmondson & Conger, 1996) of studies utilizing similar treatment modalities found effect sizes ranging from .6 to .8. However, similar methodological issues resulted in the authors drawing similarly tempered conclusions. A third review, by Beck and Fernandez (1998), included only treatments that contained a combination of cognitive and behavioral components, and found a weighted mean effect size of .7. Once again, however, methodological problems inherent in the treatment studies included in their review limited the conclusions that could be reasonably drawn from them.

Unfortunately, problems prevent us from drawing meaningful conclusions from these three reviews. Namely, the significant methodological problems include: (a) a small number of studies included in the analyses; (b) a lack of specific criteria for anger in the studies sampled; (c) very diverse population types utilized (e.g. inmates, children, inpatients, child-abusing parents, undergraduates); (d) the utilization of only published studies (which inevitably inflates effect sizes); and (e) a wide variety of measures utilized, including some that are not necessarily directly related to anger and violence (e.g. hostility, assertiveness).

Several recent meta-analytic reviews have attempted to improve upon those previous reviews. A review by Del Vecchio and O'Leary (2004) included only studies in which subjects manifested clinically significant levels of anger, as defined by scores on standardized anger assessments. In addition, both published and unpublished studies utilizing adult populations were included, and moderator analyses were conducted to evaluate the efficacy of different treatments on different anger problems. The final sample included 23 articles, 15 of which were not included in prior reviews. Results suggested that cognitive behavioral treatments, cognitive therapy, relaxations training, and other various treatment types provided an effect size of .6 to .9, which despite the methodological improvements, remained consistent with the effect sizes found in earlier reviews. The authors concluded that the data offer some support for the efficacy of psychological treatments for anger, and added that cognitive behavioral therapy appears most effective for problems of anger expression while cognitive therapy appears most effective for problems involving anger suppression. However, despite these apparently positive findings, the authors suggested that their findings must be cautiously interpreted for a variety of reasons. First, effect sizes were in some cases derived from less than five studies. Additionally, a large number of studies were conducted by the same research team. Finally, and of greatest importance, 73% of the studies' samples were carried out on college students desiring treatment for some degree of anger-related problem, and not clinical samples. As clinical populations seeking or referred for anger treatment have often been described as resistant to treatment/lacking in treatment engagement, and are frequently unaware of and/or unwilling to acknowledge their anger-related difficulties (Howells & Day, 2003), comparisons between motivated college students and more typical, less motivated (externally mandated) clinical samples are problematic at best.

In a second meta-analysis seeking to overcome earlier problems, DiGiuseppe and Tafrate (2003) also utilized both peer-reviewed studies and unpublished doctoral dissertations, albeit with a wider range of selection criteria than the Del Vecchio and O'Leary review, and included a total of 50 between-group studies. This review aggregated effect sizes according to dependent measure categories (i.e. aggression, anger). In their meta-analysis, an overall effect size of .71 was found, which was once again consistent with the findings of previous reviews. The authors suggested that these results were cause for optimism, but also noted that the magnitude of this effect size for anger treatments was in fact less than those found in anxiety and depression treatment reviews (DiGiuseppe & Tafrate).

A related meta-analytic review by Babcock, Green, and Robie (2004) considered the efficacy of domestic violence treatments. In their review, 22 studies evaluating treatment efficacy for domestically violent males were included. These studies included controlled quasi-experimental and experimental studies evaluating the relative efficacy of Duluth model interventions (note: intervention goals of Duluth model interventions are the reduction of paternal power and control attitudes and behaviors, the reduction of an authoritarian control/dominance-oriented relationship style, and an increase in an egalitarian relationship style), cognitive behavioral therapy, and other types of interventions on subsequent violent recidivism. Overall, effects due to treatment were in the small range (< .40), suggesting minimal impact on reducing recidivism beyond the effect of simply being arrested. Further, no differences existed between Duluth model interventions, cognitive behavioral treatment, and other types of intervention.

Finally, most recently, a meta-analytic review was conducted to examine the effects of treating anger via a variety of psychological treatments (Saini, 2009). This analysis included 96 studies and 139 treatment effects. The nine types of psychological treatments, as defined by the author, included cognitive, cognitive-behavioral, exposure, psychodynamic, psychoeducational, relaxation-based, skills-based, stress inoculation, and multicomponent interventions. The overall weighted standardized mean difference across all treatments was 0.76 (95% confidence interval [CI],

0.67–0.85), suggesting a moderate effect of anger treatments. The results also suggested a considerable degree of variability in the effect sizes of specific treatments for anger, which was explained as being due to the number of treatment sessions offered to participants across treatments, the inconsistent use of manuals to guide delivery of the treatment, the use of fidelity checks, the setting of the research (i.e. university students vs community participants), and whether the study was published or unpublished.

It is evident that substantial problems exist in drawing firm conclusions from these various meta-analyses. Most directly, those listed below.

- There are limitations in meta-analytic procedures themselves, which, while providing relevant treatment information, are not sufficient for drawing clear conclusions regarding treatment efficacy (Moore, 2003). In addition, they are subject to significant change based on even the slightest modification of method (Dieckman, Malle, & Bodner, 2009), and as such, are prone to allegiance effects (findings in support of the stated beliefs or expectations of the authors; Barlow *et al.*, 2010).

- Even if the methodology of meta-analyses could be reliably agreed upon and followed, in the studies that have to date been included in meta-analyses of anger treatments, significant methodological problems including clinical relevance of population, measures used to measure efficacy, and treatment length and fidelity were consistently noted.

- Across all of these meta-analyses, there were huge variations in effect sizes for the specific psychological treatments described. For example, in DiGiuseppe and Tafrate's review (2003), cognitive restructuring effect sizes ranged from 0 to 1.26, and combined treatments effect sizes ranged from −1.08 to 1.94, a finding that was similarly noted in each and every meta-analysis described above. This, of course, leads to many questions regarding the veracity of the results and further calls into question the meaningfulness of average effect sizes.

- None of the meta-analytic reviews suggests efficacy reaching the aforementioned benchmarks for anxiety and depression, suggesting that at best, these treatments are lacking when compared to empirically supported procedures for other emotional disorders.

- As aptly pointed out by Olatunji and Lohr (2005), the demonstrated efficacy of psychological treatments for anger-related problems cannot be separated out from the impact of possible non-specific treatment factors (i.e. relationship, enhanced hope, beliefs about success). That is, as the four theoretical assumptions of cognitive behavioral treatment of anger-related problems noted earlier have never been directly studied, to date, no evidence exists that the assumed mechanisms of change of these treatments are correct. In essence, the data do not tell us why the minimal improvements that have been found have occurred, and the modest effect sizes found could just as easily be ascribed to non-specific factors as active components of treatment.

Given the aforementioned lack of a clear connection between cogent theory and treatment selection with regard to anger and aggression/violence, and given the weak empirical support for traditional treatments for anger and aggression/violence, it is reasonable to question the traditional cognitive behavioral approach to understanding and treating clinical anger. More specifically, the results of the treatment reviews noted above could certainly suggest that the basic premise that specific cognitive content results in heightened anger, which in turn results in aggressive/violent behavior, may be faulty. As such, we decided several years ago that the weak empirical data required a careful reconsideration of the theoretical foundation for understanding problems related to anger experience and expression. Additionally, we hoped that following the development of a more contemporary model of anger and violence, a more theory-driven and empirically informed psychological treatment for this serious personal and societal problem could be developed.

Based upon that personal mission, the next chapter describes the outcome of this endeavor: the Anger Avoidance Model (AAM). The AAM was developed as a theoretically derived and empirically informed model for understanding the development, experience, and expression of anger and aggression/violence, and is the driving force behind our treatment known as Contextual Anger Regulation Therapy (CART), which is the essence of this text.

2 The Anger Avoidance Model (AAM)

In recent years, as greater emphasis has been placed on the development of a more comprehensive understanding of the transdiagnostic processes noted across emotional disorders, rather than focusing on topographical features (i.e. signs and symptoms), findings in experimental psychopathology have highlighted the significant overlap/comorbidity between anxiety and mood disorders (Barlow, Allen, & Choate, 2004; Brown *et al.*, 2001; Mineka, Watson, & Clark, 1998). In fact, it has been suggested that emotional disorders share core psychosocial and biological diatheses, and the expression of slightly different signs and symptoms across anxiety and mood disorders may in fact be minor variations of a broader syndrome. This broader syndrome has been referred to as *negative affect syndrome* (NAS; Barlow, Allen, & Choate, 2004). Using structural equation modeling as a base methodological approach to studying the similarities and differences across emotional disorders, Barlow and colleagues (2004) developed a model for understanding anxiety and mood disorders (referred to as "emotional disorders") that confirms the description of a tripartite model of emotional disorders previously proposed by Clark and Watson (1991).

The tripartite model suggests that emotional disorders, including clinical anger, can be distinguished by varying combinations of negative affect, positive affect, and autonomic arousal. Thus, from the perspective of the tripartite model, commonalities across the varying *DSM*-defined emotional disorders are more significant than their variations, thus calling into question the construct validity of the various *DSM* categories. For instance, negative affect and autonomic (somatic) arousal are highly and positively correlated with panic disorder, which in turn is negatively correlated with low levels of positive affect. Conversely, both social anxiety and depression are highly and positively correlated with high levels of negative affect, and negatively correlated with low levels of positive affect, yet are minimally correlated with autonomic arousal.

Informed by the tripartite model for understanding emotional disorders, and given the myriad of empirical findings regarding the comorbidity of anger with a variety of current diagnostic classifications, we suggest that clinical anger may therefore best be viewed as a specific variation of NAS. In fact, consistent with this position, Mineka and colleagues (1998) previously suggested, "it now is obvious that this general Negative Affect dimension is not confined solely to mood and anxiety disorders, but is even more broadly related to psychopathology" (pp. 397–398). Recent empirical research supports this position and clearly suggests that anger is positively correlated with negative affect, is negatively correlated with positive affect, and is positively correlated with somatic arousal (Gardner *et al.*, 2009). As such, we assert that clinical anger may be best conceptualized as a mixed emotional disorder manifesting as heightened subjective distress (i.e. negative affect) typically seen in both anxiety and mood disorders, heightened autonomic arousal as noted in panic disorder and generalized anxiety disorder, and by an absence of positive affective experiences such as happiness and joy (i.e. anhedonia), which is typical of social anxiety disorder and depression. Using the tripartite model to help inform our understanding of clinical anger, a comparison between anxiety, depression, and anger is presented in Table 2.1.

We hope that the implication of this approach to studying anger will be readily observed across the chapters in this text. In essence, the tripartite model tells us several important things and poses additional questions to be answered. First, it certainly suggests, as noted in the previous chapter, that additional *DSM* diagnoses of anger-related disorders may be at best unnecessary, and at worst supportive of the somewhat dated notion that overt signs and symptoms are more important than underlying pathological processes in understanding problematic human behavior. We believe that this way of thinking about clinical anger has limited the development of efficacious psychological treatments for this problem area in the past. Second, it suggests to us that when looking for transdiagnostic processes that could help us better understand clinical anger, we may appropriately start by looking at those processes that have relevance to aspects of anxiety and depressive disorders. Third, viewing anger from this perspective leads us to important questions regarding the difference in etiology between other emotional disorders and clinical anger, as well as to questions regarding how recent research in the emotion sciences may aid us in better understanding the clinical presentation of anger-related difficulties.

Table 2.1 Anger and the Tripartite Model

Emotion	Positive Affect	Negative Affect	Physiological Arousal
Anxiety	High	Low	High
Depression	Low	High	Low
Anger	Low	High	High

What follows below is a detailed presentation of the Anger Avoidance Model (AAM). The AAM was initially published in 2008 (Gardner & Moore, 2008), and has since been slightly modified as new findings from empirical research have steadily been incorporated. This model will hopefully, among other things, begin to answer the questions posed above. As readers will see, the AAM incorporates recent advances in emotion science and experimental psychopathology to better understand the development of clinical anger, and in particular the relationship between the experience of anger and aggressive/violent behavior. A visual representation of the AAM can be seen in Figure 2.1.

As briefly described above (and as will be highlighted in depth below), we find it exceptionally useful to utilize the basic tenets of the triple vulnerabilities model (Barlow, 2002), which we incorporate into the AAM in order to aid in the understanding of clinical anger. According to the triple vulnerabilities model, three distinct diatheses have been suggested to interact in a synergistic manner to result in the ultimate development and clinical presentation of emotional disorders. These diatheses, or causal pathways, are labeled the *biological, general psychological*, and *specific psychological* diatheses. We describe these diatheses below, including how we personally conceptualize them to be related to clinical anger and its behavioral manifestations.

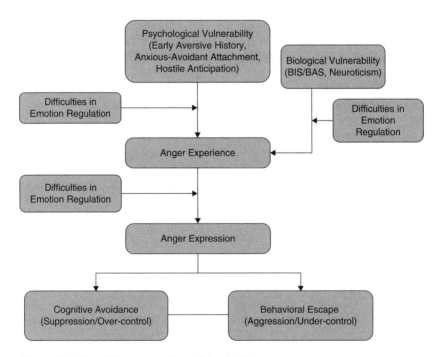

Figure 2.1 Visual Representation of the AAM

Biological Diathesis: Temperament

The first diathesis is *biological*, and reflects the empirical research demonstrating the biological and genetic contribution to basic temperament (Barlow, 2002). Specifically relevant to the understanding of clinical anger, Barlow (2002) has theorized that people with heightened levels of anger and those with panic disorder appear to be very similar in their biological vulnerabilities. In support of this proposition, recent research has found that those experiencing the emotions of anger and/or anxiety experience similar levels of physiological arousal (Wenzel & Lystad, 2005).

Further, over the last decade or so, the empirical literature has presented in some detail the importance of a biologically based motivational system that orients an individual to respond to punishment and reward, as well as a need for immediate action (Higgins, 1997; McNaughton & Gray, 2000). One motivation function reflects a behavioral inhibition system (BIS), which triggers preventative behavior aimed at the avoidance of threatening or potentially threatening or painful stimuli. Another motivation function reflects a behavioral activation system (BAS). BAS triggers promotion behavior, which is approach behavior when faced with rewarding or positive (goal-relevant) end-states. Research has demonstrated that the behavioral inhibition (threat prevention) system is highly related to neuroticism (Campbell-Sills, Liverant, & Brown, 2004), which in turn is highly associated with negative affect.

These systems are biologically based, function independently, and can be activated either alone or in unison. Recent studies suggest that individuals high in state and trait anger manifest threat sensitivity (i.e. high levels of the behavioral inhibition system; BIS) similar to individuals experiencing anxiety, yet also manifest high levels of the goal seeking behavior (i.e. high levels of the behavioral activation system; BAS) not typically noted in anxiety disorders (Donahue *et al.*, 2009; Smits & Kuppens, 2005). These findings are consistent with our previously presented conceptualization of anger as being an emotional disorder that has both similarities to and differences with other emotional disorders.

Of course, it is important to understand that although an individual's biological vulnerability serves as a natural risk factor for the later occurrence of an emotional disorder, it does not in and of itself predict the later development of a specific emotional disorder. Rather, a biological diathesis is in essence a biological hard wiring, which simply increases the *vulnerability* for the later development of an emotional disorder, such as clinical anger, panic disorder, or depression. In effect, it sets the stage for the ultimate manifestation of a disorder, acting as a propensity toward physiological over-reactivity when faced with stress and/or challenge. Consistent with the AAM, it has been noted that individuals referred for the treatment of anger-related problems consistently demonstrate high levels of autonomic arousal (DiGiuseppe & Tafrate, 2007; Moore &

Gardner, 2007). We therefore suggest that this biological vulnerability places an individual at risk for being more sensitive to threat, whether internal/somatic (often resulting in panic/anxiety-based clinical presentations), or external/interpersonal (often resulting in anger-based clinical presentations). The question, of course, is why do some individuals later end up with anxiety-like symptoms and yet others manifest anger-related problems?

General Psychological Diathesis: Etiology

The second diathesis of the triple vulnerabilities model is the *general psychological* diathesis, which reflects the impact that specific life experiences have on an individual. It has been postulated that life experiences contribute to the development of depression, anxiety, and associated emotional disorders by producing a general sense of uncontrollability (Barlow, 2002). Specifically regarding anger, Barlow (2002) has previously proposed that patients experiencing high levels of anger may differ from patients experiencing high levels of anxiety, in that rather than experiencing a sense of uncontrollability as is most typically seen in anxious patients, patients experiencing problems with anger may instead experience an exaggerated sense of mastery and control. Interestingly, our own clinical observations from working with patients experiencing clinical anger do not support Barlow's hypothesis that angry individuals experience an exaggerated sense of mastery and control. In fact, consistent with our clinical observations, a recent study from our research lab found that individuals experiencing high levels of anger also manifest high scores on measures of threat sensitivity (Dettore, Pabian, & Gardner, 2010) indicative of a heightened sense of vulnerability/uncontrollability. Therefore, in contrast to Barlow's assertion, we suggest that patients experiencing clinical anger actually exhibit as much of a sense of uncontrollability/vulnerability as anxious clients, but instead respond with fight-based (as opposed to flight-based) behavior due to both biological factors noted previously and specific early learning histories and modeling experiences that are very different from individuals experiencing anxiety. Our conceptualization is consistent with the idea of a natural defensive system, such that when withdrawal (e.g. behavioral inhibition) from severe threat is blocked or perceived as being unavailable, an individual will process information in a manner that promotes (e.g. BAS system) defensive escape in the form of aggression (Rothbart & Sheese, 2007). It would therefore seem that when examining etiological factors, we would expect that harsh and chronically aversive early environments, which often do not allow for withdrawal or escape from threat, would be an expected etiological factor in the development of anger difficulties.

Continuing from this perspective, we postulate that when withdrawal from threat is blocked or unavailable, the emotion associated with threat (i.e. anxiety) would over time become a discriminative stimulus for the threat itself, and a learned overuse of defensive escape in the form of anger and its behavioral action tendency (i.e. aggression) will occur. It is important to note that, unlike Barlow's hypothesis, in our Anger Avoidance Model, a sense of uncontrollability/vulnerability is as problematic for the clinical anger client as it is for the anxious client. However, since angry and anxious clientele typically experience very different early learning histories, they develop different affective and behavioral responses to their perceptions of uncontrollability. Consistent with our predictions that both anxiety and anger would share a sensitivity to threat, recent studies have found a strong relationship between social anxiety, trait anger, and low levels of positive affect (Erwin *et al.*, 2003; Hofmann, Heinrichs, & Moscovitch, 2004; Kashdan & Collins, 2010), and provide strong support for the notion that anger does not in fact reflect an exaggerated sense of mastery or control, but is instead reflective of an alternative affective, and with it behavioral, response that is often a result of an extreme sense of uncontrollability and vulnerability. In summary, we suggest that the early aversive life histories (described later in this chapter) that are typically found in angry individuals, in which withdrawal was not readily available, trigger intense feelings of uncontrollability, and in turn, the resultant vulnerability becomes a discriminative stimulus for the experience of anger. This is consistent with the clinical presentation of patients who manifest clinical anger, whereby any experience of vulnerability and/or anxiety results in an immediate (and often intense) angry reaction.

It has previously been determined that the biologically based temperaments of angry and anxious patients share some direct similarities (Wenzel & Lystad, 2005). Although some similarities have been shown to exist between anxious and angry clients, there do appear to be a number of important ways that the *learning histories* of anxious and angry clients differ, thereby resulting in very different general psychological diatheses. Specifically, clients with anxiety disorders typically describe significant caretakers as less supportive of independent action, less socially engaged, exerting heightened control over the decision making of their children, and generally more over-involved in the lives of their children (Barlow, 2002). However, this pattern of over-engaged parental behavior is not consistent with the typical report of patients experiencing clinical anger, which instead can be generally described as chronically, and often substantially aversive. Recent studies from our clinical research laboratory (Dettore, Pabian, & Gardner, 2010; Gardner, Moore, & Dettore, 2011; Moore & Gardner, 2007) have suggested that the early experiences of angry clients are actually more similar to the early experiences of chronically depressed clients (specifically those meeting criteria for persistent depressive disorder-dysthymia, as per *DSM-5* criteria) as described by McCullough (2000). This early environment has best been described as chronically aversive, and is characterized by: (a) a harsh, punitive, and inconsistent environment, often including a significant history of emotional and physical neglect or mistreatment; (b) being subjected to a hazardous and toxic familial and/or social environment where caregivers and/or other family members cannot protect or even harm their children as well as one another; and, (c) the experience of chronic emotional and/or physical pain and hardship. Data from our clinical research laboratory have confirmed the presence of this type of early environment. In fact, 100% of a sample of 88 individuals court mandated for the treatment of domestic and non-domestic violent offenses reported experiencing physical and/or emotional abuse and/or neglect as a child (Gardner, Moore, & Dettore, 2011). This early aversive history culminates in an intense emotional environment in which physical and psychological safety and survival become most salient. We postulate that individuals who have faced such early learning histories tend to experience intense emotion and a pervasive sense of powerlessness, as withdrawal/escape is frequently not possible. In turn, this culminates in a level of chronic anger/rage that is often perceived as overwhelming. Additional studies (Dettore, Pabian, & Gardner, 2010; Gardner *et al.*, 2010; Gardner, Moore, & Dettore, 2011; Moore & Gardner, 2007) have confirmed that in both clinical and non-clinical samples, an early aversive history characterized by physical and emotional neglect and abuse does in fact predict levels of trait anger, as measured by the State Trait Anger Expression Inventory-2 (STAXI-2; Spielberger, 1999), the Anger Disorders Scale (DiGiuseppe & Tafrate, 2004), and the Multidimensional Anger Inventory (Siegel, 1986), and is similarly related to aggressive/violent behavior. In addition, individuals exposed to a chronic early aversive history manifest significantly higher levels of anger reactivity (in terms of both the scope of triggering events and the intensity of response) than individuals who have not been exposed to such a harsh early history (Gardner, Moore, Wolanin, Alm *et al.*, 2006; Gardner, Moore, Wolanin, Deutsch, & Marks, 2006). Finally, a recent study evaluated the impact of various attachment styles, which can certainly be understood as a direct consequence of the early aversive experiences noted above, on the level of experienced anger. This study suggested that anxious adult attachment, theorized to be a direct result of the experience of early maltreatment, is directly predictive of high levels of trait anger in a non-clinical sample (Pess *et al.*, 2012), and is also related to both lack of anger control and excessive efforts to suppress anger. Avoidant attachment has been shown to be related to high levels of hostile attributions, lack of awareness of physiological signs of anger, and escape behavior (Mikulincer, 1998).

The fact that empirical findings confirm our assertion regarding the etiological similarities between patients experiencing clinical anger and those experiencing chronic depression (Gardner, Moore, Wolanin, Alm *et al.*, 2006; McCullough, 2000) does of course lead to another important question: As the early learning histories consistent with clinical anger and chronic depression are both generally characterized as neglectful, harsh, and aversive, what determines whether an individual ultimately develops chronic depression or clinical anger? Our answer to this question is found in and is consistent with the triple vulnerabilities model presented earlier. We suggest that individuals who are more biologically (i.e. temperamentally) prone to *heightened* levels of autonomic arousal (which, as noted previously, is essentially hard wiring for intense physiological reactivity) are likely to respond with clinical anger, whereas those with biologically based temperaments prone to *lower* levels of physiological arousal demonstrate overt and covert manifestations consistent with a chronic depressive disorder. Although this hypothesized explanation remains an open empirical question, it is consistent with both recent research and our conceptualization of anger as sharing tripartite model characteristics with both depression and anxiety. In addition, consistent with our transdiagnostic view of clinical anger, our clinical experience has suggested that patients referred for treatment due primarily to anger-related problems often manifest heightened levels of depressive affect. We envision that many readers will also be able to reflect upon numerous clients who fit this portrayal.

This then leads to the question of how other cognitive-emotional processes are impacted by the interaction between temperament and early learning. The interaction of biological/temperamental vulnerabilities and early learning histories noted above also results in a variety of specific cognitive schemas (also known as internal rule systems and cognitive [information processing] biases), which guide the appraisal and interpretation of external stimuli. As previously discussed, when withdrawal from threat is blocked, a defensive predisposition inherent in human beings results in information processing biases that serve to protect from further threat and mobilize the individual for safety seeking behavior. In the case of clinical anger, the interaction of an individual's biological temperament toward high physiological arousal and his or her early aversive social learning history in which personal safety and wellbeing are challenged, will often culminate in the development of cognitive (information processing) biases/schemas related to fear and anticipation of violation/vulnerability, and will lead the client to scan for and overly respond to such stimuli. Recent empirical research from our laboratory has confirmed the hypothesized relationship between early aversive histories; early maladaptive schemas related to emotional deprivation, emotional inhibition, and insufficient self-control/self-discipline; and anger (Smyth *et al.*, 2010). We postulate that in response to the highly negative early social-familial environments that are frequent for clients with clinical anger, a functional survival-based tendency evolves in which the client scans the external environment for early signs of potential personal (physical or psychological) violation/vulnerability. We previously coined the term *hostile anticipation* to represent the angry patient's ruminative hypervigilance for signs of hostile intent and personal violation (Gardner & Moore, 2008). We have suggested that the hypervigilance for evidence of external danger in angry patients as analogous to the hypervigilance for evidence of internal danger (in the form of somatic or social preoccupation) often noted in anxious patients. Further, while anxious patients often present with excessive self-focused (internal) attention to bodily processes, and in turn interpret physical sensations, social evaluation, and even thoughts seen as unacceptable as a sign of potential danger requiring avoidance or escape, the angry patient is likely to manifest an excessive and ruminative *external* focus of attention. Thus, among clinically angry individuals, external stimuli (i.e. people and events) are regularly (and ruminatively) scanned for early signs of possible physical or psychological threat, often taking the form of over-interpretation of personal slights, physical affronts, and a wide array of perceived threats and/or behaviors reflecting "disrespect" in some manner or form. An inordinate number of otherwise innocuous life events are therefore interpreted, and responded to, as in some way threatening or dangerous.

Consistent with this premise, a number of recent studies have demonstrated specific information processing biases in angry individuals. One particular study found that those individuals in a college student sample who scored high on trait anger did in fact make more global and external attributions than non-angry/anxious controls (Langton & Wenzel, 2004). Similarly, Aquino, Douglas, and Martinko (2004) found that hostile attributions of others' intentions mediated the relationship between external events and reported anger in an organizational setting. In another study, Cohen, Eckhardt, and Schagat (1998) determined that individuals high in trait anger demonstrated attentional biases toward anger-related cues following perceived insult. Wenzel and Lystad (2005) also found that angry individuals rated the likelihood of angry explanations for ambiguous events higher than anxious or non-anxious/non-angry control participants. Finally, a recent study demonstrating a significant relationship between social anxiety and high levels of trait anger (Kashdan & Collins, 2010) suggested that socially anxious individuals respond to social evaluation, and their own internal reactions to those evaluations, as personally threatening stimuli, and in turn respond with both anxiety and anger. When seen together, these studies strongly indicate that, as predicted by the AAM, specific information processing biases do exist among patients experiencing clinical levels of anger.

We suggest that these cognitive biases/schemas are verbal/linguistic representations of the early aversive learning histories experienced by individuals with clinical levels of anger, and these biases/schemas then become strongly intertwined with a very rigid affective-behavioral response style. In fact, years of research in applied behavior analysis have demonstrated that patterns of behavior formed under strong aversive control, such as the type of early aversive histories noted above, tend to be relatively narrow, inflexible, insensitive to consequences, and difficult to change, as logical analysis and even occasional contradictory experiences are not readily assimilated. Over time, the internal linguistic/verbalizations associated with early aversive histories become stimuli in and of themselves, and result in anger responses even in the absence of actual environmental threat. From this perspective, the cognitive biases manifesting as ruminative attention to and interpretation of threat, are not themselves the problem, but in effect are representations and consequences of actual experiences. These attentional biases in turn become discriminative stimuli for anger responses just as strong as actual external threat. In effect, *thinking about threat* becomes the equivalent to actual threat, and can evoke the same affective and behavioral responses.

With all of this considered, we suggest that even in the presence of the biological and early environmental vulnerabilities (i.e. diatheses) noted above, the third and final specific psychological diathesis ultimately determines the extent of one's difficulties with anger.

Specific Psychological Diathesis

The third synergistic vulnerability for emotional disorders has been labeled the *specific psychological* diathesis (Barlow, 2002), which follows from the integration of the individual's biological temperament and his or her early social learning history, which constituted the first two diatheses. The specific psychological diathesis relates to specific psychological processes that interact with the two previous diatheses, resulting in enhanced vulnerability to develop emotional disorders. In Chapter 1, we described the adaptive function of anger for survival and goal direction. From this perspective, emotions, including anger, can provide us with important information that helps us solve problems and/or achieve goals, by signaling the relevance of our basic motivations or values. For instance, fear can provide information that can mobilize us to withdraw from potential threat, sadness can provide information about a salient loss, joy can help us seek out experiences and people that enhance our lives, and anger can mobilize us toward personal safety and goal attainment. Of course, all of these examples assume that emotion is appropriately generated and effectively understood, utilized, and expressed. However, we certainly all know that while emotions can frequently be experienced and expressed effectively, the effective experience and utilization of emotion does not always occur, and can lead to a myriad of psychological and behavioral difficulties.

The Anger Avoidance Model suggests that the specific psychological diathesis most related to clinical manifestations of anger is *emotion dysregulation,* which is the inability to be aware of, tolerate, modulate when necessary, and appropriately express anger. But, in order to truly understand emotion *dysregulation,* one must first understand emotion *regulation*. Emotion regulation has been defined by numerous scholars, and includes definitions such as the capacity to tolerate and appropriately express an emotion (Rottenberg & Gross, 2003), and our own view that emotion regulation includes those processes related to understanding, tolerating, modulating, and responding to emotions, a definition that is somewhat similar to definitions proposed by others (Gratz & Roemer, 2004). Emotion dysregulation then naturally refers to difficulties with any or all of these processes. The adaptive use of emotion requires that a specific emotional experience be appropriately labeled and differentiated in order to gain meaning from the experience. In order for emotions to be fully experienced (i.e. processed and understood), they also need to be tolerated. That is, the individual must be able to accept the presence of the normal range of human emotions, not *excessively* interpret emotion as a signal of impending and *overwhelming* danger and/or pain, and not impulsively seek immediate relief/escape from the experience. After emotions are fully experienced and processed, they may need to be modulated in some way. That is, at times they may need to be somewhat enhanced or diminished based upon the specific situational context and personal goals. Finally, when emotions are well understood, tolerated, and modulated appropriately, they give rise to a variety of behavioral choices, which can be generally classified as either threat (withdrawal) or reward (approach) based, and can include such specific skill-based behaviors such as problem-solving, assertiveness, and conflict management.

Thus, an emotion, even when intensely experienced, can be a signal for an adaptive response. On the other hand, if the emotion is not tolerated, is poorly processed/understood, and/or is not appropriately modulated as needed, it is often responded to not as a relatively neutral signal triggering reflection and action, but rather as a negative stimulus triggering avoidance or escape from the experience itself. This process has often been described by the term *experiential avoidance* (Hayes *et al.*, 1996). Experiential avoidance, which is the unwillingness to remain in contact with uncomfortable internal experiences (cognitions, physical sensations, subjective feelings), has in turn been empirically associated with a broad array of psychopathology. In fact, emotional intolerance/avoidance has been described as a general risk factor for emotional disorders (Barlow *et al.*, 2010) and the development of psychopathology in general (Kashdan *et al.*, 2006); poor emotional understanding has been related to depression (Mennin *et al.*, 2007), bulimic behavior (Norman *et al.*, 2009a, 2009b), and anxiety disorders (Mennin *et al.*, 2005); and poor emotion modulation has been associated with personality disorders (Gratz & Roemer, 2004; Gratz & Gunderson, 2006), posttraumatic stress disorder (Tull *et al.*, 2007), and general emotional maladjustment (Berking, Orth *et al.*, 2008).

It should be pointed out that emotion dysregulation can occur immediately before, during, or immediately after an emotional experience, such as during a given single encounter with a triggering stimulus (see Figure 2.1). For example, in circumstances in which emotion, and in particular anger, is learned to be a toxic experience that takes on highly aversive stimulus qualities, emotion dysregulation may occur *before* the intense affective experience actually occurs, and the individual may therefore engage in efforts to minimize (i.e. inhibit) the anger experience. Of course, when one avoids the experience of anger, negative expectancies regarding anger are never contradicted, and the individual subsequently continues to view the world as physically and psychologically dangerous. Individuals who have developed this pattern of anger-inhibition tend to overuse emotion regulation strategies that focus on directly choosing to either be in or avoid anger-inducing situations, they make efforts to change situations to be less anger-creating, and they disengage from the anger by focusing attention on other past or future situations. Gross (1998) has referred to these strategies as situational selection, situation modification, and/or attention redeployment, respectively. While use of these antecedent-focused emotion regulation strategies (i.e. strategies utilized *before* the full experience of emotion) is not in any way abnormal, excessive or singular use of these strategies as a means of avoiding and/or reducing the experience of anger is likely to be pathological. A frequent consequence of these efforts at anger avoidance, especially in those cases in which these strategies are rigidly and/or near exclusively utilized as a means of controlling anger, is that there is a subset of those individuals with clinical anger difficulties that actually report that they do *not* experience anger. While this has sometimes been interpreted as motivation to deceive, or a reflection of a lack of motivation for change (DiGiuseppe & Tafrate, 2007), our experience is that these patient self-reports often reflect the above noted extreme efforts to avoid the experience of the emotion of anger. In essence, anger is such an aversive stimulus for these individuals that they place massive amounts of effort into arranging life so that this emotional response is minimized, and they do this to the point that ultimately, the emotion actually seems nearly completely absent. This type of anger-related problem has been described elsewhere as inhibited/unexpressed anger (Davey, Day, & Howells, 2005). Of course, the behavioral pattern employed by such individuals is by definition narrow and rigid, and thus, the goal of not experiencing the emotion of anger is more powerful than the life consequences and limitations inherent in this behavioral pattern. Maybe most importantly, avoidance and its associated affective-inhibition prevent the opportunity for new learning to occur in which the individual might come to see that external events and even anger itself are actually not necessarily a signal of impending danger and overwhelming affect.

We suggest that inhibited anger is very much a form of clinical anger. Yet rather than reflecting hyper-intense anger that is overtly and clearly manifested and most popularly assumed to be representative of problematic anger, it reflects an excessive avoidance/inhibition of the anger experience that is much more difficult to readily see. The desire to avoid or otherwise not experience anger is so powerful that efforts to control the environment can be excessive, and can even result in aggressive and/or violent behavior. So, for example, if an individual is having a disagreement in the context of a close relationship, the need to terminate the disagreement (i.e. situation modification) might be so strong in response to the first sign of angry feelings that excessive behavior might very well occur. This behavior may take the form of some effort to prematurely terminate the disagreement by removing oneself from the situation, such as leaving the home abruptly or hanging up the phone while someone else is speaking. Or, even worse, it could involve engaging in some form of: (a) verbal aggression, such as yelling or screaming; (b) indirect aggression, such as breaking objects; or (c) direct violent behavior, such as pushing or slapping. These behaviors should be seen as anger-induced, not by high *intensity* of anger, but rather by an *intolerance* of anger, including the subjective and physiological components of angry feelings.

As previously described, the avoidance or inhibition of the emotion of anger does not allow for the processing of the information that anger can adaptively provide, and in addition to not learning that anger and a variety of life situations are actually not necessarily dangerous, the individual also does not develop an appropriate range of behaviors required for optimal interpersonal functioning. That is, by engaging in a highly restrictive and avoidant pattern of behavior that allows for the minimal experience of anger (i.e. avoiding people and situations even if they are necessary to enhance life in some substantial way), the individual often does not develop appropriate and necessary social, conflict management, and problem-solving skills.

Of course, emotion dysregulation can also occur *during* or immediately *after* an experience of intense anger (often of long duration). Likewise, due in large part to the biological and learning history diatheses noted earlier, the intensity of the anger that is generated is often so great, and the ability to tolerate, understand, and/or modulate the emotional experience is either absent and/or not well enough developed, that significant difficulties can emerge. Results from our clinical research laboratory indicating that emotion regulation difficulties in fact mediate the relationship between early aversive histories and intensity of trait anger/anger reactivity (Dettore, Pabian, & Gardner, 2010; Gardner *et al.*, 2011; Moore, Gardner, & Wolanin, 2006) are consistent with this proposition.

We previously discussed how single or even several anger-inducing encounters, no matter how intense, should not in and of themselves be viewed as problematic. Quite simply, no one has ever been arrested or gotten in trouble of any kind for *being* angry. Rather, intense anger occurring across situations, with corresponding deficits in emotion regulation skills (i.e. tolerance/acceptance of emotion, understanding of emotion, modulation of emotion, expression of emotion), can result in increased and excessive avoidance of triggering situations, similar to what has been presented above in the discussion of inhibited anger, and chronic use of maladaptive response-focused strategies (i.e. emotion regulation efforts that occur *following* the experience of anger) in an effort to manage or escape from the heightened affect in some way. A fundamental premise of the AAM is that it is the use of these chronic and inflexible strategies to reduce, eliminate, or in some way control the experience of anger that is the most maladaptive aspect of clinical anger, and that is ultimately the cause of aggressive and/or violent behavior. So, what avoidant/escape behaviors are chronically, excessively, and inflexibly used that have such a toxic outcome? The answer to this question quite clearly appears to be the noxious avoidance/escape behaviors of: (a) aggression/violence, and (b) cognitive avoidance.

When emotion regulation skills have not been adequately developed, maladaptive response-focused strategies (after the emotion) are utilized to limit, reduce, or otherwise control the emotional experience deemed as unacceptable. These include extreme efforts to exert control over: (a) verbal reports of emotions, such as denying that one is experiencing intense anger; (b) emotional behavior, such as suppressing the urge to cry or yell; (c) somatic responses, such as trying to breathe slowly when angry; and/or (d) the stimuli that are perceived to be the cause of the emotion, such as walking away during an argument, and ruminating about previous slights or about how to deal with the same situation if it were to happen again. The problem is not these normal and often adaptive responses to emotion. Rather, as we have noted a number of times, the problem is the *rigid, inflexible use* of these strategies to *avoid* or *escape* from the experience of emotion (i.e. anger) instead of acting to achieve important life goals. One such strategy, which is certainly harmful to the self and others, is aggression/violence.

Aggression/Violence

The AAM posits that high levels of anger in the presence of difficulties in emotion regulation (including deficits in tolerance/acceptance, understanding, modulation, and expression) can frequently result in aggressive and/or violent behavior, which should be seen as a maladaptive means of avoiding or escaping from the "intolerable" experience of anger. In support of this view, recent studies have found that aggressive/violent behavior in general (Bushman, Baumeister, & Phillips, 2001) and interpersonal violence in particular (Jakupcak, Lisak, & Roemer, 2002) function as an escape-based emotion regulation strategy. Our own recent research findings offer further support for this proposition, as we have found that in both court-mandated non-interpersonal violent offenders and offenders mandated for interpersonal violence, emotion regulation deficits mediated the relationship between anger experience and under-controlled anger expression (i.e. violent behavior; Dettore, Pabian, & Gardner, 2010). Thus, according to the AAM, ineffectively processed anger becomes a cue for avoidant/escape behavior, which often takes the form of overt verbal or physical aggressive/violent behavior. Herein, aggressive/violent behavior is conceptualized as an overt avoidance or escape response and functions to reduce or in some way attenuate the full experience of anger and the associated uncontrollability/vulnerability that may have been the initial stimulus for the anger. As the distressing emotion is reduced or eliminated, this behavioral pattern is consequently negatively reinforced due to the immediate effect of emotion reduction.

Indeed, clinicians commonly note that patients with clinical anger often report "feeling nothing" both *during* and *immediately after* an aggressive outburst (DiGiuseppe, Fuller, & Fountain, 2006; Gardner, Moore, Ronkowski, & Wolanin, 2006). This makes sense, as the AAM suggests that overt aggressive/violent behavior functions as an escape from the stimulus that led to the anger response by either eliminating the stimulus itself (i.e. the person who "wronged" the angry client withdraws from the situation) or by altering the form of the stimulus (i.e. the person acts differently toward the angry client). So, when clients report a lack of "angry" feelings either during or following an aggressive outburst, this reflects the attenuation (avoidance/escape) of the emotional experience of anger, as opposed to simply reflecting a motivationally based reluctance to admit to experiencing anger or engaging in aggressive behavior.

Importantly, the theoretical viewpoint presented herein does not suggest that all acts of violence are borne out of an effort to avoid the experience of anger. Although the *form* of the behavior (e.g. violence) may be the same in both instrumental and reactive aggression groups, the *function* of the behavior differs in each case. In the avoidant/escape aggression group, the function of the behavior is the reduction or elimination of the experience of anger, whereas in the instrumental aggression group, the function of the behavior is appetitive and seeks to achieve a specific end product by way of control or manipulation. As such, we postulate that there are actually two subgroups within the population of individuals manifesting aggressive/violent behavior. The first subgroup includes those who use aggressive behavior in an instrumental fashion in order to achieve control over others or to make others feel, think, or act in a manner that achieves a clear and tangible goal. These individuals typically report no clear pattern of chronic early aversive history, demonstrate no significant difficulty in emotion regulation, and report experiencing little (if any) discernible anger. We use the term *instrumental* or *predatory aggressors* to describe this group. In contrast, the second subgroup includes individuals whose aggressive/violent behavior serves as a form of overt avoidance/escape from the experience of anger, as previously described. Individuals in this group are characterized by an early aversive history, and extensive deficits in acceptance/tolerance, understanding, and modulation of anger. It is this second subgroup, often referred to as reactive aggressors, which we now term *emotion dysregulated aggressors*. Emotion dysregulated aggressors appear to use aggressive/violent behavior as a form of avoidance or escape, as conceptualized by the AAM. Recent studies from our laboratory support this contention within a clinical population court mandated for treatment following violent offenses (Dettore, Pabian, & Gardner, 2010; Gardner, Ronkowski, Wolanin, & Moore, 2006).

Cognitive Avoidance

Of course, not all avoidance behavior takes the form of overt aggressive or violent acts. At other times, avoidance may take the form of subtle and less easily discernible cognitive processes. Here, we are talking about *cognitive avoidance*, which is defined as internal efforts to minimize or reduce the experience of anger. One way that some individuals engage in cognitive avoidance is through active efforts to suppress or in some way prevent angry feelings from being expressed. In such cases, individuals will hold anger "in," and go to great lengths to not demonstrate the feeling states they are actually experiencing. Another key form of cognitive avoidance is known as *hostile rumination* (Gardner & Moore, 2008). According to the AAM, while hostile rumination and hostile anticipation (introduced earlier in this chapter) both reflect ruminative processes, hostile rumination functions as a form of experiential avoidance by way of repetitive and recurrent thinking about perceived historical and/or possible future violations, with little if any focus on angry feelings themselves. On the other hand, hostile anticipation (which is the angry patient's ruminative hypervigilance for signs of hostile intent and personal violation) reflects a scanning for the presence of impending personal violation and/or maltreatment. Interestingly, the avoidant function of hostile rumination is hypothesized to follow the same pattern noted in worry (Borkovec, 1994), in which the negatively reinforced (i.e. avoidant) function of rumination has been shown to reduce emotional and physiological arousal and result in inadequate emotional processing (Clark & Collins, 1993; Pennebaker, 1997; Teasdale, 1999a). As such, hostile rumination appears to function in a manner similar to worry in patients with generalized anxiety disorder by attenuating the full experience of anger. This occurs because the construct of rumination is typically past or future oriented, and thus, the individual does not allow for a present moment experience of anger. In essence, ruminative processes can be seen as *avoidant concentration*, in which time is spent analyzing and replaying past events, or planning for and rehearsing for future events in an attempt to mitigate or completely avoid emotional distress. The emotion-attenuating function of ruminative processes is therefore negatively reinforced and results in an increase in the frequency of its use as an avoidance strategy (Borkovec, Ray, & Stober, 1998). Research findings support the proposition that rumination is a maladaptive effort to cope with affective experiences, and that it is associated with cognitive biases, sustained negative mood states, and impaired problem solving (Joorman, Dkane, & Gotlib, 2006). These outcomes are consistent with the numerous interpersonal difficulties frequently noted among patients experiencing anger difficulties, as well (Kassinove & Sukhodolsky, 1995). In addition, angry rumination can be a motivating operation, that is, a priming for later aggressive/violent behavior, when faced with situations that are to some degree similar to those that have been contemplated over and over again.

Finally, research has found that individuals self-referred or court mandated for anger-related difficulties tend to score high on psychometric scales measuring active efforts at anger suppression (Gardner, Moore, Wolanin, Alm et al., 2006), rumination (Dettore, Pabian, & Gardner, 2010; DiGiuseppe & Tafrate, 2007), and brooding (DiGiuseppe & Tafrate, 2007), all of which reflect forms of cognitive avoidance, as described in the AAM.

In attempting to come full circle and incorporate this information into a complete understanding of clinical anger, we return to the hypothesis regarding control and mastery in angry patients, as presented by Barlow (2002). Contrary to his hypotheses proposing that those experiencing high levels of anger posses an exaggerated sense of mastery and control, we offer that hostile rumination and/or aggressive/violent behaviors do not appear to be coping efforts indicative of an exaggerated sense of mastery and control, although at some level both might be desired. Instead, they seem to be ineffective efforts at reducing, eliminating, or totally blocking an emotion (such as anger) that has previously been associated with personal danger and vulnerability. We believe that individuals struggling with clinical anger have an exaggerated sensitivity to the experience of emotion. In fact, we have often referred to this sensitivity as somewhat of an emotional allergy that has become strongly associated with personal danger through chronic early aversive environments. Viewed in this manner, the angry client is often consumed with issues related to perceived interpersonal safety (both physical and psychological) in response to a world perceived as dangerous and uncontrollable. Thus, anger, even in small amounts, is a signal of the presence of that danger, similar to the presence of allergies in which the body misinterprets pathogens and responds by attacking what are otherwise harmless biological agents. This is also not unlike an individual suffering from panic disorder who interprets somatic arousal associated with anxiety as a signal of health-related personal danger (Barlow, 2002). Thus, the AAM posits that the problem in clinical anger is not the emotion of anger per se, even when anger is experienced intensely or for long duration. Rather, what is most problematic is the over-learned intolerance of anger (through the negative reinforcement of avoidance behavior), and the subsequent inflexible and over-generalized use of avoidance and escape strategies. The use of overt (behavioral) and covert (cognitive) behavioral responses are employed in a desperate effort to reduce, eliminate, or otherwise control the emotion of anger and maintain personal safety. For many patients, this pattern culminates with the long-term consequence of social-interpersonal problems and the absence of more functional processes such as problem solving, assertiveness, and conflict management.

So, in effect, the problem is not actually the *experience* of anger, even if that anger is incredibly intense. Rather, the real concern is the maladaptive need to inhibit the experience of anger, and/or maladaptive efforts to avoid/escape from the experience of anger. The chronic use of avoidance/escape behaviors in pursuit of these purposes, which begin and ultimately gain strength due to broad deficits in emotion regulation, typically results in ongoing functional impairments in health, occupational endeavors, relationships, and/or the legal system. The inhibition and avoidance/escape efforts, then, become the key clinical problems to address. We therefore suggest that traditional treatment efforts targeting the reduction of the experience of anger or targeting increased coping skills without addressing broad emotion regulation deficits, will inevitably achieve less than optimal results. As described in Chapter 1, this is consistent with the unsatisfactory treatment efficacy data found to date.

Clinical Implications of the Anger Avoidance Model

Although the construct of anger has historically not been explored to the same extent as other emotions such as depression and anxiety, anger remains a significant public health problem and challenging clinical phenomenon in need of greater attention and empirical exploration. Integrating recent findings in emotion science into an empirically driven theoretical model such as the Anger Avoidance Model can provide new targets for intervention with this challenging and as yet poorly understood form of emotional disorder. When we embarked upon the development of an empirically informed model for understanding clinical anger, we therefore hoped that it would advance the general study of clinical anger, provide a better understanding of the relationship between anger and its problematic behavioral manifestations, and lead to the development of newer and more effective treatments for anger and aggression/violence. The development of the AAM to understand anger and its relationship to aggressive/violent behavior has benefited from existing research on both emotion in general, and emotional disorders in particular, and has garnered a good deal of support in both laboratory and clinical settings. As will be described in the coming pages, rather than focusing on seemingly ineffective efforts at reducing anger by way of changing thinking patterns and promoting relaxation, and presumably in turn reducing the aggressive/violent behavior that is often associated with anger, psychological treatment based upon the AAM instead focuses on: (a) developing greater understanding, tolerance (acceptance), modulation, and expression of anger; (b) modifying rigid and overly used avoidance/escape behaviors that have developed; and, in turn, (c) developing greater use of emotion to guide and develop effective values-driven skill sets relating to interpersonal problem solving and conflict management. We now embark upon a discussion of clinical anger assessment and case conceptualization, and then present a comprehensive step-by-step treatment model known as Contextual Anger Regulation Therapy (CART). CART is an exciting nine-module intervention approach developed directly from the foundations of the Anger Avoidance Model, which focuses precisely on the critical goals noted above.

3 Assessment and Case Conceptualization of Clinical Anger

Psychological assessment can be most readily understood as a systematic approach to collecting clinical data that provide information relating to the distal and proximal antecedent conditions (both external and internal) that give rise to clinically relevant behavior and the short- and long-term consequences of that behavior. A key goal of clinical assessment is the determination of potentially modifiable processes associated with the development and maintenance of targeted problematic behavior. The clinical information collected in the assessment process is organized and utilized in a comprehensive conceptualization of the clinical issues presented by the patient. As such, assessment should directly inform case conceptualization, which in turn should directly inform treatment selection and implementation.

A comprehensive approach to assessment should be theoretically and empirically guided and should address both signs and symptoms (i.e. clinical topography) presented by the patient, and core psychological processes thought to be central to the development and maintenance of that topography. As discussed in Chapters 1 and 2, clinical anger is a complex problem often including a myriad of possible diagnostic classifications and complicating factors. In the present chapter, we provide clinicians with a detailed outline of strategies we find useful in the assessment and case conceptualization of clinical anger. We also discuss the use of interview strategies, the use of various specialized self-report measures, and an illustrative clinical anger case conceptualization that follows the AAM.

Core Features of Anger Assessment

Most fundamentally, the goal of psychological assessment should be to predict future behavior and/or aid in treatment planning. This chapter focuses primarily on treatment planning, although issues pertaining to prediction of behavior will be addressed at various times throughout this text. In order to effectively achieve the goal of treatment planning, clinicians should first and foremost understand that assessment should be idiographic, meaning *individual client focused*. While empirically informed clinicians understand that normative (i.e. group) data may guide our selection of assessment instruments as well as our understanding of the data collected, ultimately, effective assessment should focus on:

- clarification of the nature and course of the client's problems, and as such, clarification of behaviors to be targeted in treatment;
- an evaluation of the degree to which these problems impair the client's life functioning;
- the identification of pathological processes and reinforcing factors that led to and maintain the problem behavior(s);
- a formulation/case conceptualization of the client's problems, which in turn leads directly to the development of an appropriate intervention plan.

Each of these core features of assessment requires the clinician to utilize a clear theoretical model and the existing empirical literature in order to makes sense of the unique clinical presentation of each client. This idiographic approach to psychological assessment is more than basic diagnostic evaluation, in which the client's presenting problems are assigned to a category assumed to reflect a "disorder."

The psychiatric disorder model, characterized by the *DSM* classification system (American Psychiatric Association (APA), 2013), is defined by identifying specific signs and symptoms, most often represented by a variety of emotional experiences and behaviors. If a threshold number of these markers is displayed, a diagnostic category is assigned. Treatment choice is then defined by the diagnosis, and the focus of treatment is on the amelioration of the noted signs and symptoms. While we will address issues pertaining to diagnoses in the course of this chapter, since anger and aggressive/violent behavior are often noted across several existing *DSM* disorders (social anxiety disorder, posttraumatic stress disorder, depression, bipolar disorders, substance abuse disorders, personality disorders, etc.), the focus of our model of assessment is not simply or exclusively the determination of psychological markers such as overt signs and symptoms associated with specific diagnoses. Rather, as noted in Chapter 2 and consistent with recent approaches to transdiagnostic considerations in treatment planning (Barlow *et al.*, 2010), of great importance is the identification and understanding of the core processes that are at the foundation of the client's presenting anger-related problems. In essence, the approach to assessment endorsed herein focuses on both the identification of the overt signs and symptoms of clinical anger that bring the patient to treatment, as well as the identification of the empirically derived psychological processes related to clinical anger that are at the core of the Anger Avoidance Model. Table 3.1 presents the range of information required when engaging in psychological assessment for the purpose of providing a diagnostic classification, while Table 3.2 presents the range of information required when engaging in an assessment for the purpose of determining relevant psychological processes and contingencies related to anger as a presenting problem. Determining a psychiatric diagnosis requires the assessment of a range of emotional and behavioral signs and symptoms, whereas idiographic psychological assessment for the purpose of determining core elements of anger pathology requires the determination of a more subtle variety of psychological processes. It should be noted that there is nothing in these two approaches that is necessarily mutually exclusive. Certainly, clinicians can both determine diagnosis and at the same time develop an understanding of relevant psychological processes. However, clinicians should always remember that assessment that seeks out information for one of these purposes does not necessarily provide the information required for the other.

A perusal of Tables 3.1 and 3.2 illustrates that, while Table 3.1 offers an overview of those factors necessary for a traditional psychiatric diagnosis, and certainly provides a certain type of representative picture of the client's psychological state, use of the Anger Avoidance Model in understanding the client's presenting anger-related problems requires that the types of information noted in Table 3.2 be obtained. As effective assessment can contain elements of both of these basic models, clinicians working in settings requiring formal psychiatric diagnoses must insure that their approach to assessment is inclusive enough to collect all relevant information.

This chapter presents an approach to assessment of anger-related referrals that allows clinicians to assess both relevant diagnostic considerations as well as core psychological processes at the heart of clinical anger. By the time the anger assessment is complete, a clinician should be able to have:

- a comprehensive understanding of the client's anger-related problems, including questions related to (a) what the "angry behavior" looks like; (b) in which situations it manifests; (c) in response to which life events and which internal cognitive-affective conditions (over/under-controlled anger, hostile anticipation/rumination, emotion dysregulation, etc.) it is likely to emerge; (d) how it overtly manifests (e.g. aggression, violence); (e) for how long it lasts; and (f) what the maintaining (i.e. reinforcing) contingencies involved are; essentially, answering these questions provides a clear description of the problem behaviors and an understanding of the contextual factors involved in those problem behaviors; this aspect of the interview is often referred to as a functional analysis of behavior (Hayes *et al.*, 1996)
- a complete personal history that allows for an understanding of both the etiology and developmental pathogenesis of the problem behaviors; namely, in response to what early learning and what environmental/family circumstances did the problem behaviors develop?

Table 3.1 Information to Be Collected for the Assessment of Signs and Symptoms

Personal and Clinical History	Negative Affect (Distress)	Positive Affect	Anger	Aggression/Violence	Alcohol/Substance Abuse/Other Problematic Behavior	Functional Impairment
Psychiatric history	Anxiety-arousal	Anhedonia	Intensity, duration, scope	Impulsive	Type	Family, friends, social
Presenting and associated problems	Depression	Mania	Over-controlled	Planned	Frequency	Work, education
	Alexithymia	Mixture	Under-controlled	Frequency		Legal, societal

Table 3.2 Information to Be Collected for the Assessment of Psychological Processes

Early Environment	Temperament	Emotion Regulation Skills	Experiential Avoidance	Behavioral Skills	Personal Values/Goals
Physical and emotional abuse	Physiological arousal	Emotion acceptance/tolerance	*Cognitive avoidance:* suppression, rumination	Conflict management	Family, friends, and social
Physical and emotional neglect	Threat sensitivity	Emotion understanding	*Behavioral avoidance:* aggression/violence, interpersonal withdrawal	Problem solving	Work and education
Chronicity	Reward sensitivity	Emotion modulation		Assertiveness	Legal and societal

- a differential diagnosis, especially in light of the broad diagnostic array in which clinical anger is often seen; as previously noted, clinical anger can be seen in social anxiety disorder, posttraumatic stress disorder, depression, bipolar disorder, substance abuse disorders, the new *DSM-5* (2013) category known as disruptive mood dysregulation disorder, a variety of personality disorders, and so on
- a determination of the client's orientation to behavioral change efforts; specifically, are the life problems often resulting from clinical anger seen by the client as requiring change, or does the client simply view his or her reason for attending sessions as due to external (societal) demands such as court order or other mandates?
- a determination of the available behavioral repertoires and skills available for dealing the interpersonal realities in the client's life; what is the availability of skill sets related to effective interpersonal problem solving, conflict management, social skills, and communication/assertiveness skills?
- the establishment of the beginnings of a client–therapist relationship. While the clinician is in fact collecting information necessary to conceptualize the client's presenting problems and develop a treatment plan, the client most often does not differentiate assessment from treatment, and as such, the early establishment of a therapeutic contract/professional relationship is of critical importance in the assessment phase of professional care.

AAM as a General Guide for the Assessment Process

In our experience with anger assessment, the goals listed above are likely to be fulfilled when clinical information is collected using the Anger Avoidance Model as a basic template by which to guide the clinical data collection process. Table 3.3 provides such a template, including all of the necessary components of the AAM that need to be assessed, which in turn

Table 3.3 Clinical Data Collection Template

Please ensure that each topic below can be fully described through data from the clinical interview and/or self-report measures:

1. **Distal Variables of Importance:** Early Environmental History, Temperament, Internal Rules, Hostile Anticipation
2. **Proximal Variables of Importance:** Triggering Event(s)/Antecedent Conditions
3. **Emotion Regulation Skills/Deficits:** Awareness, Tolerance, Modulation
4. **Emotional Experience:** Anger Intensity, Duration, and Direction
5. **Problem Behavior:** Direct Expression or Avoidance of Anger
6. **Short-Term Consequences:** Positive or Negative Reinforcement
7. **Long-Term Consequences:** Impact of Life Circumstance and Overall Quality of Life

increases the likelihood that all relevant data are collected and organized, and that subsequent case conceptualization and treatment planning can occur. As we move through the assessment process, strategies for assessment will also be suggested, via both clinical interview and the use of self-report questionnaires, to help the clinician collect relevant information.

Importantly, the collection of clinical information recommended by the AAM case conceptualization method does not have to follow a neat and linear format. For example, we have personally found it most beneficial to begin with examining and defining the problem behavior, followed by gaining an understanding of the triggering events related to that behavior, before moving on to other relevant aspects of the problem, such as early learning history. As a clinician, you too will form your own preferences in this regard, and we encourage you to remain flexible in doing so.

Presenting Problem

When clients referred for anger treatment initially present the reasons for which they are seeking services, we encourage clinicians to listen to the client without interruption for a reasonable period of time, preferably at least 10 minutes. Allowing this time provides clients with an opportunity to present their "story," and conveys a true interest on the part of the clinician. It also allows clinicians the opportunity to assess how clients relate; organize their thought processes; and relay events, actions, and outcomes. Of course, it is critical that clinicians clearly understand the problematic behaviors that are the foundation of clients' complaints and/or referral issue. Frequently, clients will begin with vague or incomplete presentations of their problems, either due to embarrassment, distrust of the clinician, or a true lack of understanding of why they have ended up in treatment. With regard to anger-related problems, clients will often think that the experience of anger is the only issue to be discussed (e.g. "I was referred for 'anger management'"), and may not initially understand the relevance of a range of behaviors that may be associated with their inhibited or under-controlled expressions of anger. As discussed in Chapter 2, the AAM posits that the problematic behavior is most often related to the manner in which clients respond to being angry, and not the emotion of anger itself. Overt aggressive or violent behavior is most often understood by clients as constituting a large part of the reason for referral (although often these behaviors are explained away as though they were appropriate, necessary, and/or non-problematic). Likewise, while other anger-related behaviors such as interpersonal withdrawal, physical posturing, verbal aggression, and passive aggressive behaviors are often present, clients often fail to see them as part of an "anger" problem. Table 3.4 provides a list of possible interview questions to help clinicians convert clients' anger-related referral issues into clearly identified problem behaviors.

Table 3.4 Sample Interview Questions for Identifying Problem Behaviors

- "How would you (or others) describe the reason for you seeking help?"
- "What is the problem/issue, as you see it?"
- "Give me two or three examples of what you or others would see as the primary issue."
- "When was the first time that this type of problem occurred? Please describe the situation."
- "What do you think, or what have others suggested to you, are the things you need to change?"
- "How has this issue affected your family life? Your work? Your relationships? Your problems with the law (if applicable)?"
- "Has anything changed in your life since this problem/issue has occurred?"

Once the problematic behavior is clearly identified, clinicians should next seek to understand the antecedent conditions (also known as triggers) related to the problematic behavior(s) in question.

Assessing Antecedent (Triggering) Conditions

Antecedent conditions refer to those specific stimuli that are likely to be a triggering signal for the occurrence of the problematic behavior. For example, being spoken to harshly by someone in a position of authority and being criticized by a spouse in front of others would be examples of environmental antecedent conditions for problematic behavior associated with clinical anger. These external events are often described in the behavioral literature as *discriminative stimuli*, as they signal the likelihood of reinforcement or punishment. Discriminative stimuli are essentially those antecedent conditions that are the likely proximal triggers of the problem behavior. Another type of antecedent that sets the stage for certain behaviors is known as *motivating operations*, which refers to the influence that events have on the behavior in question by changing the reinforcing or punishing properties of those events. For instance, let's conceptualize a client who has spent the day engaging in hostile rumination. This individual is therefore primed to respond to the words or behaviors of others perceived as negative, threatening, or disrespectful in some way. If this individual returns home from work and perceives that he or she is being even mildly criticized for doing or not doing a chore at home, the individual may be more likely to engage in aggressive or violent behavior in order to stop the actions of those who are seen as creating their anger. Just as hunger can be a motivating operation for the reduction of hunger through food seeking behavior (negative reinforcement), the emotion of anger *or* angry rumination may be motivating operations for aggressive/violent behavior via the priming influence of the rumination, and/or the negative reinforcing properties of its ultimate reduction of the anger.

Table 3.5 provides a list of possible interview questions to help the clinician identify antecedents of problem behaviors. Once antecedent conditions of an angry response are fully assessed, clinicians can then turn their attention back to the problem behavior and begin to assess the relationship between the triggering (antecedent) events, anger, and the problem behavior.

Assessing Early Environment and Temperament

While the clinician is most apt to assess for the presence of an early aversive environment by way of a standard clinical interview, we have found that the use of a targeted self-report measure for this purpose is also highly useful. This is in part because the information is quickly and easily obtained through a self-report measure, thus saving time for the clinician to assess other areas (i.e. specific target behaviors and antecedents) that are somewhat more difficult to access via self-report, and also due to the fact that for some clients, talking to a clinician (who is essentially a stranger) about childhood maltreatment and victimization in a first interview can be quite difficult. In these cases, more complete information can be gathered by use of appropriate self-report measures. We have found that the Childhood Trauma Questionnaire (CTQ; Bernstein & Fink, 1998) is our personal instrument of choice. The CTQ is a 28-item self-report inventory that provides a brief, psychometrically sound screening for histories of abuse and neglect. It assesses five types of maltreatment that are consistent with the AAM's description of an early aversive history: emotional, physical, and sexual abuse; and emotional and physical neglect. It also includes a three-item minimization/denial scale for detecting false-negative trauma reports, which is certainly a useful component. Our recent research has found that emotional and physical abuse, as well as emotional and physical neglect, are directly predictive of clinical anger in perpetrators of both domestic violence and non-relational violence

Table 3.5 Sample Interview Questions for Identifying Antecedents of Problem Behaviors

- "Give me some details about the situations that you just told me about."
- "When, or in what specific situations, does the problem occur? Who, or what kind of person, tends to be involved? What do they say or do?"
- "Tell me what is happening just before the problem occurs."
- "Just before the problem occurs, tell me what you are experiencing? What do you feel? What are you thinking about? What are/were you thinking might happen? What do you do when you start thinking those things?"
- "What do you think this kind of behavior of others mean to you? Mean about you?"
- "What emotions do you feel when these things happen (use a specific example, if available)?"
- "When you start feeling the things you just described, what do you do? What do you think those feelings mean to you? Mean about you?"

(Dettore, Pabian, & Gardner, 2010). Administration of the CTQ takes approximately 5 minutes, and the instrument is normed for ages 12 and older.

In addition to early aversive history, which constitutes the general psychological diathesis, the clinician should examine the client's temperament, which constitutes the biological diathesis. The simplest and quickest way that we have found to assess this dimension is through the use of the Behavioral Inhibition System/Behavioral Activation System Scales (BIS/BAS; Carver & White, 1994). As described in Chapter 2, Gray (1981, 1982) has suggested that two general motivational systems, reflective of temperament, underlie behavior and affect. The behavioral inhibition system (BIS) and the behavioral activation system (BAS) represent these two motivational systems. The BIS/BAS Scale is a 24-item self-report instrument designed to assess dispositional BIS and BAS sensitivities. The scale is quick and easy to administer, and has demonstrated adequate psychometric properties.

We have noted that the intersection of temperament and early aversive history results in a verbal/linguistic representation of our early learning. In addition to emotional states serving as frequent motivating operations for violent and aggressive behaviors, another motivating operation can be the personal "rules" (usually in the form of "if–then" internal verbalizations) that the client forms, and the "fusion," or belief that thoughts about events and the events themselves are essentially the same. These internal rules, which are also known as cognitive schemas, often directly and rigidly guide behavior, a process frequently referred to as *rule-governed behavior* (Malott, Malott, & Trojan, 2000). For example, an anger client recently possessed the rule, "If I let him disrespect me and get away with talking to me like this, I will look like an idiot and he and other people will keep treating me this way." This rule, which was triggered by a myriad of interpersonal situations, was a discriminative stimulus in and of itself for highly aggressive and at times violent behavior. Accessing and assessing these internal rules is actually quite easy within the context of a clinical interview. More specifically, we have found that when clients present external situations that they describe as the proximal "cause" of their anger or behavior, simply asking what those situations mean *to* the client, as well as their meaning *about* the client, is often sufficient to access the internal rules that are operating. While we do not personally use self-report questionnaires to gain information related to these rule systems (as they are quite long), other practitioners have found it helpful to use such instruments as the Young Schema Questionnaire (YSQ; Young, Klosko, & Weishaar, 2003) as a means of assessing schema-related constructs. The YSQ measures internal rules via what Young and colleagues have described as early maladaptive schemas, which are defined as broad and pervasive rules regarding oneself and relationships with others. There are both long (205 questions) and short

(75 questions) forms of the instrument, and both forms have demonstrated adequate psychometric properties (Oei & Baranoff, 2007). The YSQ provides a comprehensive assessment of a wide variety of possible early maladaptive schemas.

Assessing Anger

The greatest difficulty in assessing anger in clients referred for anger-related problems is determining the degree to which the emotion of anger is actually fully experienced and understood, and conversely, the degree to which the emotion of anger is inhibited and thus not fully experienced. Clients will often deny feeling angry in an initial interview, either because they go to such great lengths to avoid/inhibit the experience of anger that they rarely actually reach the point of an angry experience, or because they do not understand what they are feeling and instead describe the anger experience as "stress," "tension," or some other vague presentation. In our experience, interview questions seeking to access the emotion of anger must be very specific, and should assess many of the physiological signs of arousal as well as directly addressing the subjective experience of emotion. Table 3.6 provides a list of possible interview questions to help clinicians access clients' experiences of anger.

As you can see by the interview questions in Table 3.6, a range of information is capable of being obtained. As we view anger (and in fact any emotion) as having separate components of cognition, subjective feelings/physiology, and behavior, questions relating to intensity, duration, frequency, cognitive content, and physiological experience are all addressed. Of course, it is not uncommon for clients referred for anger-related problems to answer these questions in ways having nothing to do

Table 3.6 Interview Questions to Access the Experience of Anger

- "Tell me how you felt, that is, what emotion you experienced when . . ."
- "Tell me where you felt that emotion. In your chest, in your stomach, in your head, etc.?"
- "Describe the feeling, the physical sensation."
- "On a scale of 1 (lowest) and 10 (highest), how intense was this feeling? And, is that typical when you feel this way, or lower/higher?"
- "When you feel this way, how long does it last? Several minutes, much/all of the day, etc.?"
- "Tell me another time and another situation where you felt that way."
- "Give me some examples of other situations where you feel a similar way."
- "For how long have situations like this led to you feeling this way?"
- "When you feel this way, are you focusing on your own feelings, or on the situation occurring or other person involved?"
- "What do you typically do when experiencing these feelings?"
- "What do you do to make these feelings stop or lessen?"
- "Have you ever gotten into trouble due to these feelings?"

with the question being asked, and yes, this can be an added challenge. As an example, a question related to one's feelings often results in answers related to thoughts or situations. A rule of thumb that we have long used is this: If an answer to a question about feelings/emotions includes the word "that," a thought or situation is likely being described. For instance, "I felt *that* he should not have said that to me" does not reflect an emotional experience at all, but rather, reflects a thought ("I believe that he should not have said that to me"). On the other hand, a sentence such as, "I felt angry and hurt," in fact reflects an emotional experience. When a mismatch occurs, the clinician should gently guide the client back to the question in order to collect the necessary information.

While a clinical interview that involves asking clients to talk about their experiences with anger, particularly with regard to the problem behavior that has led to the treatment request, will often provide a good deal of necessary information, we do believe that the use of anger-specific self-report measures is often invaluable and can provides a range of pertinent information useful for both case conceptualization and the assessment of treatment efficacy. Before describing these measures, however, we offer a word of caution: Just as clients may deny and/or underreport emotion and related processes in a clinical interview, especially those who are either motivated to appear "healthy" or those whose emotion is highly inhibited and thus not truly experienced, the same may be seen in self-reports given at the onset of treatment (especially prior to the establishment of a strong therapeutic alliance). As such, clinicians must not deify the scores on self-reports and should recognize that they are useful as an aid, but not a replacement for sound structured interviewing procedures.

Probably the most common self-report measure of anger experience and expression is the State Trait Anger Expression Inventory-2 (STAXI-2) developed by Spielberger (1999). The STAXI-2 is a 57-item self-report inventory that measures the intensity of anger as an emotional state (state anger) and the cross-situational tendency to experience angry feelings as a personality trait (trait anger). The instrument consists of six subscales: (1) trait anger (dispositional anger); (2) anger expression-out (the outward display of anger); (3) anger expression-in (the inward display/ruminative experience of anger); (4) anger control-out (the effort to control the form and frequency of one's overt angry behavior); (5) anger control-in (the effort to not display overt angry behavior); and (6) state anger (the intensity of anger as an emotional experience). The STAXI-2 also includes an Anger Expression Index, which is a composite of the anger expression and control scales. An added benefit is that the measure can be administered in approximately 10 minutes to individuals with at least a 6th-grade reading level. Scoring is also brief, taking only about 5 minutes.

While there exists a wide array of additional self-report measures for anger and aggression, we suggest the use of three additional self-report measures. The first is the Anger and Violence Impairment Scale (AVIS).

The AVIS is not intended to be a psychometric devise, it is simply a short measure that we adapted to assess, on a week-to-week basis, the degree to which anger and violent behavior are negatively impacting the client's life (see Appendix 3.1). The second and third recommended self-report measures are highly useful in developing a comprehensive case conceptualization and treatment plan, and engaging in ongoing evaluation of treatment effectiveness. They are the Anger Disorders Scale (ADS; DiGiuseppe & Tafrate, 2004), and the Novaco Anger Scale and Provocation Inventory (NAS-PI; Novaco, 2003).

The ADS is a 74-item self-report inventory that requires a 6th-grade reading level and takes approximately 20 minutes to complete. Hand and computerized scoring options are available. The psychometric properties of the ADS have been shown to be adequate, and it has been standardized on both non-angry and clinically angry adult populations. The ADS provides an Anger Reactivity/Expression factor, which includes scope and duration of anger, physiological arousal, rumination, impulsivity, coercion, and verbal expression subscales; an Anger-In factor, which includes hurt/social rejection, episode length, suspiciousness, resentment, brooding, and tension reduction subscales; a Vengeance factor, which includes revenge, physical aggression, relational aggression, passive aggression, and indirect aggression subscales; and a Total Anger score, which is essentially a composite of the factors. In addition, an Impression Management subtest is also included to assess efforts to present oneself in an overly positive/non-pathological manner. We have used the ADS extensively in both research and clinical work, and have found it to be a useful measure to help form a comprehensive understanding of a client's anger pathology and help determine specific components of anger pathology as a target for treatment. We have also found that results from the ADS are sensitive to therapeutic intervention, and as such, it is a useful measure for treatment planning and evaluation. We do, however, offer one caution with regard to the Impression Management (IM) subtest. We have found that clients who truly have no anger pathology will often score as though they are engaging in impression management. A perusal of the IM items suggests that people who have never had difficulties with anger or associated behaviors will often answer the questions on this scale in a very similar way to clients who are clearly making an effort to deceive the clinician. Thus, we have found that this particular subtest should be used cautiously, and encourage clinicians to view the IM results as simply a hypothesis to be tested in other ways.

Finally, the Novaco Anger Scale and Provocation Inventory (NAS-PI; Novaco, 2003) is a self-report instrument that assesses anger experience, anger control, and anger triggers. The NAS-PI comprises two main components: Part I is the Novaco Anger Scale (NAS), which measures the general tendency to experience anger reactions. The NAS comprises 48 items that are divided equally into four subscales. These four subscales are then divided into four additional components. The Cognitive subscale measures hostile attitude, rumination, anger justification, and suspiciousness; the Arousal subscale assesses irritability, somatic tension, anger intensity, and duration; the Behavior subscale assesses verbal aggression, indirect expression, impulsive reaction, and physical confrontation; and finally, the Anger Regulation subscale considers the individual's ability to promote self-calm, regulate anger-triggering cognitions, and take part in constructive behavior when provoked. Part II is the Provocation Inventory (PI), which consists of 25 items that describe situations that bring about anger in particular individuals. The 25 items are grouped into five subscales that characterize the nature or type of the provocation. These include unfairness, annoying traits of others, disrespectful treatment, irritations, and frustration. The questionnaire can be completed in approximately 25 minutes and requires a 4th-grade reading level. The NAS-PI can be administered as a whole or in two parts, can be hand or computer scored, and provides normative data for individuals aged 9 and above. In this regard, separate norms are provided for preadolescents through adolescents (9 to 18), and adults (19 and older). While we have personally not used the NAS-PI as extensively as other measures, it does serve a function similar to the ADS, in that it provides a much more complete understanding of the breadth of anger pathology within a client than is typically obtained in a single interview.

Unfortunately, there are no data that directly compare the ADS and the NAS-PI, and we therefore suggest that clinicians try both instruments and determine which is more useful for their own professional work. Certainly, one advantage of the NAS-PI is the childhood/adolescent norms, which allow for a greater array of population use. In either case, we have found that both the ADS and the NAS-PI provide much greater depth and breadth of information than the STAXI-2, and have found that the ADS data, in particular, are more meaningfully integrated into treatment planning and evaluation. Later in this chapter, we provide a sample case conceptualization that utilizes the ADS, in order to demonstrate how to integrate specific components of the scale into the AAM. A simple review of the scales and subscales of both the ADS and the NAS-PI allows the reader to readily see how a great deal of information (related to multiple components of the AAM) can be gleaned from their use in the anger assessment process.

Assessing Other Emotional States

In keeping with the transdiagnostic model we have readily adopted to aid in our understanding of clinical anger, in addition to assessing for anger pathology, it is critical that the clinician assess for a variety of other affective states that frequently co-occur with anger, such as anxiety and depression. This is especially important when the clinician desires or is required to determine the client's *DSM* diagnosis. We personally utilize the Beck Scales, which include the Beck Depression Inventory-2 (BDI-2; Beck, Steer, & Brown, 1996), the Beck Anxiety Inventory (BAI; Beck, Epstein, Brown, & Steer, 1988), the Beck Hopelessness Scale (BHS; Beck & Steer, 1988), and the Beck Scale for Suicide Ideation (BSS; Beck & Steer, 1991). These scales assess severity of affective states related to depression and anxiety, as well as cognitive domains of hopelessness and suicidal ideation, which have been strongly associated with suicide risk. These scales all demonstrate adequate psychometric properties, are relatively short (20 or 21 items each), are quick and easy to administer and score (i.e. the total administration time for all four scales is approximately 20 minutes), and are normed on adolescents as well as adults. In addition, we utilize the Positive and Negative Affect Schedule (PANAS; Watson, Clark, & Tellegen, 1988) as a measure of general distress, physiological arousal, and positive affective experiences. Use of these scales in combination with a clinical interview allows the clinician to gain an overview of possible comorbid affective and/or anxiety disorders. We also utilize our own semi-structured interview that gleans enough information associated with each relevant *DSM* condition (i.e. initial criteria for each relevant condition), and follow up as needed to determine a *DSM* diagnosis (when required).

Additionally, two self-report measures are utilized to assess psychological distress and quality of life, and both are excellent means of evaluating treatment effectiveness/outcome. The two measures are the Quality of Life Inventory (QOLI; Frisch, 1994) and the Outcome Questionnaire-45 (OQ-45; Hansen & Lambert, 1996). The QOLI is 32-item self-report measure that assesses an individual's overall satisfaction with various domains of life. The total score comprises items that include areas of life that have been found to be associated with overall life satisfaction, such as health, friends, learning, and work (Frisch *et al.*, 1992). The OQ-45 is a 45-item self-report inventory that measures subjective discomfort or symptoms, difficulties in interpersonal relationships, and problems in social role performance (Ellsworth, Lambert, & Johnson, 2006). Scores can range from 0 to 180, where a score of 64 or greater indicates symptoms of clinical significance. Both instruments are relatively easy to administer, have sound psychometric properties, and can be completed in approximately 20 minutes. In addition, both measures provide a good general assessment of life functioning and are extremely sensitive to change during psychological intervention.

We encourage clinicians to also carefully assess for: (a) the presence of current substance abuse and substance abuse history, which are frequently seen in clients presenting with anger pathology, and (b) medical/psychiatric history. In our experience, both of these important elements are best assessed during the natural course of a comprehensive clinical interview, typically during the personal history portion of the interview. Direct questions on these topics, and appropriate follow-up, tend to be quite effective in this regard.

Assessing Psychological Processes: Experiential Avoidance and Emotion Regulation

As described in Chapter 2, the AAM posits that experiential avoidance and the emotion regulation skills/deficits that emanate from it will impact the degree to which the emotion of anger is a motivating operation for aggressive and/or violent behavior. Thus, developing a full understanding of their presence or absence is central to case conceptualization and treatment planning. While there are many instruments to choose from, we have found that three self-report measures of relevant psychological processes are particularly useful in both research and practice with clinical anger clients. They include the Difficulties in Emotion Regulation Scale (DERS; Gratz & Roemer, 2004), the Acceptance and Action Questionnaire-2 (AAQ-2; Bond *et al.*, 2011), and the Toronto Alexithymia Scale (TAS-20; Bagby, Parker, & Taylor, 1994).

As emotion regulation is a central psychological process and is therefore a major focus of attention in the AAM, it is critical that this area be thoroughly assessed. We typically utilize the Difficulties in Emotion Regulation Scale (Gratz & Roemer, 2004), which is a comprehensive measure of emotion regulation, as a primary assessment tool. The DERS is a 36-item self-report measure that takes approximately 15 minutes to complete and demonstrates sound psychometric properties. It provides a total score, as well as six individual subscale scores measuring difficulties with various aspects of emotion regulation. The DERS is a core component of our assessment battery, as we have found both the total score and the individual subtests to be quite useful in both research and practice. The six subscales include: awareness of emotions; clarity of emotions; acceptance of emotions; ability to engage in goal-directed behavior when distressed; impulse control; and access to strategies for emotion regulation. The measure's results can be easily incorporated into a thorough assessment of anger pathology. For example, clients who are referred for violent behavior who manifest anger inhibition, and in turn engage in violent behavior in order to avoid the experience of anger, will typically score very high on DERS subscales of deficits in awareness, clarity, and acceptance of emotions. Conversely, clients referred for violent behavior that generate a great deal of anger and subsequently engage in violent behavior as a means of escaping that experience, often score high on deficits in emotional acceptance; impulse control; ability to engage in goal-directed strategies; and access to emotion regulation strategies.

It should be noted that deficits in acceptance of emotions are found in anger pathology that involves either inhibited anger or excessive anger, and as such, while emotional acceptance is measured on the DERS, we have found it useful to include the AAQ-2 (Bond *et al.*, 2011) in our assessment battery as an additional measure of emotional acceptance/ non-acceptance. Consistently demonstrated to be reliably and validly associated with a wide range of psychopathology (Bond *et al.*, 2011), the AAQ-2 is the most common measure of experiential avoidance/acceptance and the psychological inflexibility/flexibility that is associated with it. Since it is a self-report measure of experiential avoidance/acceptance, it provides solid information regarding one's unwillingness/willingness to remain in contact (i.e. experience) with particular emotions and cognitions, as well as an unwillingness/willingness to act in an intentional goal-directed manner while experiencing internal distress. There are actually several versions of the AAQ available. Nine-item, sixteen-item, and newer ten-item versions of the AAQ are available for use in research and practice settings. The ten-item version, known as the AAQ-2, appears to hold the most promise, as its questions are written more clearly and it has been reported to have better psychometric properties (Roemer & Orsillo, 2009). To date, the AAQ is considered to be the gold standard for the assessment of experiential avoidance, and psychological inflexibility/experiential avoidance has been found to be highly related to and/or serve as a mediator of an extremely wide variety of clinical syndromes and problem behaviors (Bond *et al.*, 2011; Kring & Sloan, 2009), including clinical anger (Gardner *et al.*, 2010; Gardner, Moore, Wolanin, Alm *et al.*, 2006). We have found that the AAQ is also very sensitive to therapeutic efforts, and as such is a valuable measure of change across time in therapy.

Given the importance that the AAM places on identifying and describing emotions in order to understand clinical anger, we often include the Toronto Alexithymia Scale (Bagby, Parker, & Taylor, 1994) in our assessment package. The 20-item TAS-20 is a self-report measure that assesses for the tendency to minimize affective experiences. It provides a total score and three subtest scores, including difficulty describing feelings, difficulty identifying feelings, and externally oriented thinking. This instrument is easy and quick to administer (5–10 minutes), demonstrates adequate psychometric properties, and has been normed on adult populations.

In addition to these three scales, the clinician may choose to utilize a variety of self-report measures that assess the construct of "mindfulness," which has been defined as consisting of attention to and non-judging awareness of one's internal experience, the capacity to engage in activities without distraction, and non-reactivity to inner experiences (Baer *et al.*, 2006). Mindfulness measures that we have found useful are the Mindful Attention and Awareness Scale (MAAS; Brown & Ryan, 2003) and the Five-Facet Mindfulness Questionnaire (FFMQ; Baer *et al.*, 2006). The MAAS is a brief 15-item scale that provides a good overall measurement of the mindfulness construct. The MAAS focuses more on the attention and awareness aspects of mindfulness and less so on the observation and non-judging aspects of the construct. The FFMQ is a 39-item measure that assesses the various components of the mindfulness construct.

Many of the above scales assess overlapping constructs, and so individual clinicians will need to determine the combination of scales with which they are most comfortable, and which measures specifically fit their setting and evaluation time frames. In the sample case presented later in this chapter, we demonstrate the utility of the use of a specific subset of the measures described above.

Short- and Long-Term Consequences

Once the problem behaviors have been defined, the antecedent conditions are established, and an understanding is gained with regard to the client's affective experience and emotion regulation skills/deficits, the clinician will assess (often deductively) the short- and long-term consequences of the client's problematic behavior. As postulated by the AAM, the short-term consequence of aggressive or violent behavior is very likely to be the negatively reinforcing outcome of the emotion of anger being reduced, eliminated, or otherwise controlled. The long-term consequences are typically the most noxious, and include such outcomes as failed and/or problematic interpersonal relationships, legal difficulties, work/school-related difficulties, and significant deficits in necessary interpersonal and conflict management skills, each of which often do not develop due to premature avoidance/escape from challenging situations. As such, essential skills for coping with life's realities frequently fail to develop, and instead, an increasing reliance on avoidance and escape occurs. The assessment of consequences is most readily obtained from logical deductions based upon the range of information already collected. For example, a client referred for domestic violence who is highly avoidant, has difficulty tolerating the experience of anger, uses aggressive behavior to "make the other person stop" what they are doing that angers the client, and has had a pattern of this behavior throughout adulthood, can readily be seen to have negatively reinforcing short-term consequences of emotional escape, and long-term consequences of problematic relationships, legal difficulties, and an absence of functional conflict management skills. In such cases, it may be additionally helpful to administer the Revised Conflict Tactics Scale (Straus *et al.*, 1996), which is a 39-item psychometrically sound self-report measure that assesses both the manner in which and extent to which partners who are living together, dating, or married engage in psychological and/or physical attacks on one another. It also assesses individuals' use of reasoning and/or negotiation to deal with relationship conflict.

Now that we have collected information that allows us to identify the target problem behavior; develop hypotheses about likely antecedents for this behavior; assess early environment and temperament; and gain an understanding of the client's anger experience and expression, emotion regulation skills and deficits, and the short- and long-term consequences of the client's tendencies to use avoidance or escape as a means of coping with internal experiences, we can turn our attention to obstacles to assessing anger and violence.

Obstacles to Assessing Anger and Violence: Context, Motivation, and Anger Pathology

The obstacles to conducting an anger assessment are for the most part related to context. That is, most clients referred for psychological services due to anger-related difficulties are "mandated" by others, be it school, work, family, lawyer, or courts/correctional systems. As such, the reality is that being "mandated" is the same as being required/coerced into evaluation and/or treatment, and this is inevitably going to impact the manner in which clients perceive themselves and the assessment process. We cannot stress enough that clinicians need to fully discuss with their clients issues such as confidentiality, the relative independence or interdependence of the clinician/facility with the referring agency, the uses of the assessment material (treatment planning vs sentencing/probation decisions), and/or similar considerations before engaging in any assessment or treatment efforts. It is only when these contextual factors are fully discussed and understood, and complete and appropriate informed consent is obtained, that the assessment process should truly begin. We also add that in circumstances in which the client has been referred for "anger management," it is important to make an effort to explain that: (a) some of the measures utilized in the assessment can distinguish efforts at being less than truthful, and thus, it is best to simply answer openly and honestly; and (b) scores on the administered measures and answers to questions asked will not determine when the mandated treatment is adequately completed. Rather, overall open cooperative work with the clinician will culminate in successful treatment. The assessment process and any self-report measures that are utilized should be described as the equivalent of a physician taking a history and ordering lab tests before providing any medical treatment. While this may seem obvious to clinicians, it is our experience that a thorough and open presentation and discussion of these realities will result in an easier and more accurate assessment and ultimately will allow for a sound beginning of the treatment process. One should not assume that the client understands what the clinician is assessing for and how the information will be used. Remember that since very few clients coming to our offices for anger-related problems have gotten there without being prodded, coerced, or even forced (i.e. mandated) by courts, attorneys, family members, or employers, we therefore begin with, at best, a less than intrinsically motivated client, and at worst, a hostile and suspicious client.

Along this line, clinicians may find it useful to consider a client's "readiness" for anger treatment. The most cited work in regard to what is known as *readiness for change* is the transtheoretical model of change developed by Prochaska, DiClemente, and Norcross (1992). This is essentially a model of motivation for change, which suggests that individuals pass through five identifiable stages of change as they move to resolve an identified problem. The first stage is the precontemplation stage, which refers to a stage in which individuals do not recognize that a problem exists and/or do not wish to change their behavior. The second stage is the contemplation stage, a stage in which individuals are accepting that a problem exists, and are genuinely considering engaging in behavior change efforts. The third stage is the preparation stage, a stage in which people have previously (and unsuccessfully) attempted to change behavior and are ready to once again engage in behavior change efforts. The fourth stage is the action stage, the stage in which individuals actively modify their behavioral repertoire in an effort to overcome their difficulties. It is within this particular stage that the most concerted and overt behavioral changes tend to occur, and this stage understandably requires a considerable commitment of both time and energy. The fifth and final stage is the maintenance stage, which is when individuals work diligently to prevent relapse and consolidate the gains they attained during the previous action stage. It has been hypothesized that clients will move across these discreet stages in the course of addressing behavioral issues. We have, in the past, used a brief self-report measure known as the University of Rhode Island Change Assessment Scale (URICA; McConnaughy, Prochaska, & Velicer, 1983) to assess these stages of change.

Yet while this model has gained a large amount of professional interest, we have serious concerns about this construct for a variety of reasons. First and foremost is its inherent circularity. For instance, in response to the question, "How do you know the client's stage of change?," the answer would inevitably be some variation of, ". . . by his/her behavioral choices." But, the obvious follow-up question, "Why does he/she behave the way he/she does?," would likely in turn be answered with, ". . . because of the stage of change he/she is in." In our opinion, this presents a problematic circularity. And, in response to the question, "Why does the client not commit to treatment?," the answer typically provided is, ". . . because he/she is in the precontemplation stage of change." The problem with this circularity is hopefully clear. When used as a *behavioral description*, we see some value in measuring characteristics of a client's "stage of change," as it reflects specific behaviors relating to treatment engagement. However, when used to *explain* a client's behavior, we see little conceptual value. Second, there is a lack of empirical data to suggest that these various characteristics of "readiness" actually follow any clear movement through stages.

Rather, we suggest that clients' "readiness" for change, or put differently, their willingness to actively commit to behavior change efforts, is better understood as an *orientation to change*, which can be conceptualized as a continuum between extrinsic and intrinsic motivation. Clients coming to the clinician for treatment will fall across varying points of that continuum. In the most difficult of cases, such as those in which a client comes to treatment due exclusively to external social sanctions such as a court mandate, the clinician hopes to help the client move from these external demands for treatment in which treatment success is defined simply as the act of being there for whatever length of prescribed time (i.e. oriented external demands and consequences), to a more internally motivated orientation from which striving for enhanced behavioral functioning allows for personal goals and values to be actively pursued. We see the process of moving the externally oriented client toward a more internal orientation as a critical aspect of the successful psychological treatment of clinical anger, and specific strategies toward this goal are fully incorporated into Contextual Anger Regulation Therapy described in detail later in this text. In this regard, measures such as the URICA (McConnaughy, Prochaska, & Velicer, 1983) can be used as a way of assessing client behaviors that can reflect her or his level of intrinsic/extrinsic motivation, rather than reflect a "stage" category membership.

Complicating the understanding of readiness for change is, as noted in Chapter 2, the fact that the core pathology of clinical anger often involves significant inhibition of anger, including its awareness and understanding. Thus, clients will often deny experiencing anger, or minimize the relationship between anger and more overt behaviors, and thus not understand the purpose of or need for treatment. This is not necessarily due to a lack of readiness or an external orientation to change, but rather, can be a consequence of an actual dysfunctional psychological process, such as inhibited anger. Clinicians should therefore gauge motivation to change by carefully considering one's external/internal motivation *and* the emotion regulation deficits that result in inhibited affect.

One thing that becomes clear when working with a clinical anger population, when adding the obstacle of client motivation for treatment to the difficult features of the core pathology of clinical anger, is that clients will frequently question the need for psychological treatment. It thus becomes quite obvious that the clinician needs to view the early development of an open and honest relationship, including ample discussion of all facets of the assessment process, as a critical first step in working with this population.

Putting It All Together

Ultimately, the purpose of psychological assessment is to develop a comprehensive understanding of the client for the purpose of treatment planning. In order to develop an appropriate treatment plan, the clinician must organize and conceptualize client data in a meaningful way that integrates an understanding of the client's overt difficulties with the psychological processes that underlie those difficulties. This also allows the clinician to explain to the client how he or she has gotten to treatment, how the past and present are connected, and how treatment can have a positive impact on the client's life. Our approach to case conceptualization/formulation of clinical anger involves taking acquired data from both interview and self-report measures, and organizing it around the components of the AAM.

Up to this point, we have discussed the assessment of components and processes central to the entire AAM model via clinical interview and a wide variety of self-report measures. Clinicians should now have enough information to organize the clinical data into a relevant case conceptualization. Following the AAM framework, the case conceptualization model that we utilize is presented below as we walk through a sanitized clinical anger case example. As a way of integrating the case conceptualization and assessment process, we highlight the methods that were used to collect the information presented.

Anger Conceptualization Using the AAM: The Case of Joann

Referral and Problem Definition

Joann is a divorced 43-year-old Caucasian woman with five children. The two oldest children have the same deceased father. Four of the five children remained in Joann's care during the majority of their lives, but were all placed with other family members as a result of the incident that led to her current court-mandated treatment resulting from an aggravated assault charge. She is currently allowed court-supervised visits with her children. Joann was court mandated for treatment as part of an alternative sentencing arrangement following the aggravated assault. The incident involved Joann's 18-year-old niece, and led to the client spending three days in jail.

Joann reported experiencing long-standing interpersonal difficulties with family members and close friends, which were described as being related to feeling rejected and disrespected. For example, Joann described the incident with her 18-year-old niece that occurred one year prior, which was the reason for her court-mandated treatment. She reported confronting her niece about using marijuana. In the course of the argument that ensued, Joann reported that she felt mistreated and described feeling hurt and "disrespected." In turn, this led to the violent behavior, which was described as gripping her niece's neck and choking her. A neighbor heard the commotion and called the police, resulting in Joann's arrested. Joann stated that she remembered becoming "tense," "heated," and "stressed," but denied experiencing the emotion of anger.

Joann currently has a job that provides a substandard income, which is supplemented by government support. She uses Medicaid for health insurance, and lives in a very poor neighborhood, which she describes as dangerous. Joann stated that she needs to remain "tough" when dealing with other people, as "they will take advantage of you if you don't." She describes this attitude as the "rule of the streets."

Antecedent (Triggering) Conditions

A number of similar experiences with other family members, intimate partners, and neighbors had reportedly occurred in the past when Joann believed that she was being disrespected. According to Joann, "disrespected" is associated with either the manner to which she is spoken, or the manner in which people act toward her. This perception/interpretation of "disrespect" has always been a proximal trigger for her aggressive and/or violent behavior. During the clinical interview, it was also determined that a similar incident involved a prior friend. Reportedly, the friend "disrespected" her by way of critical words regarding Joann's parenting abilities, which led Joann to feel hurt. She described this experience as unbearable. This culminated in verbal aggression and physical violence toward the friend, which ultimately ended their relationship.

Another example involved a prior boyfriend. She reported joking with the boyfriend, but reported that he then began calling her derogatory names and began "play hitting" her on the leg. Joann recalled feeling hurt by his "disrespect," which led to an unsuccessful attempt to hit her boyfriend with a baseball bat. An additional example involved an incident with Joann's current work supervisor. Joann perceived critical performance feedback as "disrespectful," which led to feeling "stressed" and "flushed." Joann reported raising her fist to hit the woman, but a co-worker who was present stopped the situation from escalating further. A final example involved Joann getting into a verbal altercation on a bus when another passenger gave her "a dirty look and turned her back," which was seen as an overt sign of disrespect. Clearly, overt acts and internal verbal rules (i.e. schemas related to maltreatment/disrespect), and associated subjective feelings of hurt and physiological arousal consistently function as discriminative stimuli for aggressive/violent behavior. This is further reinforced by self-reported sociocultural norms associated with basic survival in her community, which suggest that disrespect cannot be tolerated.

Temperament and Early History

In her interview, Joanne reported a distant and negative relationship with her mother. She reported always trying to get close to her mother, but that the mother "pushed me away . . . I'm not sure why." She also remembered her mother telling her on multiple occasions throughout her life that she wished Joann had never been born. Joann's father was minimally involved with the family during her childhood, and tended to be "cold" in his interactions. When angered, her father was described as being "hurtful and nasty" in the way he would "look or talk" to his children or wife. Joann described the household atmosphere as stressful and unpredictable. She lived with both of her parents until the age of 20, at which time her father moved out and Joann shifted homes for several years between both parents. Joann indicated that at the time of interview, she had a close relationship with her younger brother who still lives with her mother, a distant relationship with her older brother, and essentially no relationship with either parent. Consistent with interview material, Joann's scores on the Childhood Trauma Questionnaire (CTQ) indicated significant emotional abuse and neglect.

Joann described her mother as highly "nervous" and easily stressed. Her father was described as easily angered and "explosive." Both wanted the children to be quiet and "not cause problems," which was interpreted by Joann as "don't get them pissed off." On the Anger Disorders Scale's physiological arousal subscale, Joann's score suggested clinically significant levels of physiological arousal (95th percentile). Further, her responses on the Behavioral Inhibition and Behavioral Activation Scales (BIS/BAS) indicated a clinically significant sensitivity to aversive stimuli (high BIS) and minimal sensitivity (30th percentile) to anticipated or acquired rewards (low BAS). Joann denied previous psychological or psychiatric treatment and did not believe that any family members had previously received mental health services.

In response to this early environment and temperament, Joann developed an extreme level of hostile anticipation, which is an attentional bias to believe that others are, or are about to mistreat her. This manifests as frequent interpretations of the actions, words, and perceived non-verbal posturing/behavior of others as reflecting imminent personal or psychological danger. Joann frequently referred to this as "disrespect." Indeed, Joann appears to scan the environment for early detection of signs that external danger (i.e. disrespect) is present.

Anger and Associated Emotional States

Clinical interview and STAXI-2 scores suggested that Joann actually reports experiencing below average levels of (trait) anger. However, when we take a closer look at high scores on the ADS physiological arousal subscale, interview descriptions of becoming "heated" and "stressed," ADS and STAXI-2 scores assessing anger-in, as well as the PANAS arousal score, data suggest that Joann is experiencing the physiological components of anger. Yet, she has learned to exert a great deal of effort to minimize or inhibit the subjective experience/interpretation of anger, while at the same time acknowledging the experience of a high level of general negative affect (PANAS negative affect score). In addition, Joann's scores on the Positive and Negative Affect Schedule (PANAS) suggest that she is also experiencing low levels of positive affect and high levels of arousal, which are also consistent with interview and anger self-report data.

In terms of other negative emotional states, Joann's score on the Beck Depression Inventory-2 (BDI-2) is indicative of a moderate level of depressive symptomatology (BDI = 17), such as sadness, self-dislike and self-criticalness, and feelings of worthlessness. This finding is neither unexpected nor unusual given her social, familial, and legal difficulties. However, sad mood, as well as many items endorsed on the BDI-2, were denied as occurring consistently or for an extended period of time, and as such, a primary diagnosis of depression would not be appropriate for consideration. Joann also endorsed clinically significant distress on the Beck Anxiety Inventory (BAI), which measures physiological symptomatology of anxiety, not dissimilar to the physiological arousal experienced as part of the emotion of anger (BAI = 15). Additionally, Joann did not report feelings of hopelessness or suicidality as assessed by the Beck Hopelessness Scale (BHS) and Beck Scale for Suicide Ideation (BSS). Finally, Joann denied use of substances and reported minimal amounts of social drinking.

As a result of her behavioral difficulties (i.e. verbal, indirect, and direct physical anger expression), which were described as "frequent," Joann described herself as being alienated from family members and having few if any friendships outside of her family. Consequently, both interview and Joann's scores on the Outcome Questionnaire-45 (OQ-45) indicated that she is experiencing moderate overall psychological distress, yet significant difficulties with regard to interpersonal relationships; more specifically, loneliness, conflicts with others, and family problems. Similarly, on the Quality of Life Inventory (QOLI), Joann reported a low level of satisfaction with the quality of her life, particularly in the areas of social and family life.

Experiential Acceptance/Avoidance, Emotion Regulation/ Dysregulation, and Consequences of Problem Behaviors

Given all of the above, the question as to the mechanism by which Joann engages in violent behavior, and how her violent behavior relates to anger, remained unanswered. Joann appears to have learned from an early age that minimizing or inhibiting the experience of distress, particularly anger, results in a more peaceful environment and results in less possibility of being hurt (i.e. is negatively reinforced). Expressing her feelings was not encouraged or even tolerated, and constant emotional abuse/neglect left her feeling vulnerable and from which there was no ready escape. As such, she learned that the experience and expression of negative emotions, particularly anger, was ineffective and even threatening. In addition, she learned that criticism and most forms of negative verbal interactions were psychologically and physically dangerous. This hurt was likely associated with a great deal of anger, both of which were uncontrollable for much of her life. This vulnerability, without the possibility of withdrawal, resulted in a "defensive escape" style of behavior as a primary approach to dealing with external threat and associated emotions such as anger, which itself became a signal of impending personal danger. In essence, she did not develop the capacity to experience/accept emotions as a normal aspect of life; did not develop an awareness, understanding, and/or utilization of emotions for effective problem solving; and did not develop the capacity to modulate her emotions in the service of personal values and goals.

A variety of psychometric measures provide support for this process. Joann's score on the Difficulties in Emotion Regulation Scale (DERS) suggests broad and clinically significant deficits in overall emotion regulation, specifically with regard to acceptance of emotions, understanding of emotions, strategies for regulating (modulating) emotions, and non-impulsive behavior in response to emotions, the latter of which is also indicated by elevated scores on the ADS Impulsivity subscale (90th percentile). Further, Joann's score on the AAQ suggests that substantial avoidance of negative internal experiences is her normative response. These scores are also consistent with the previously noted elevated anger-in and anger expression-in scores on the ADS and STAXI-2, respectively (>75th percentile). When viewed together, these scores suggest a pattern in which Joann scans for possible external threat in order to control her environment, all in an effort to seemingly protect herself from experiencing hurt, rejection, and ultimately, the personal distress associated with the emotion of anger. This pattern of avoidance behavior includes not only efforts at situational control, such as avoiding people and situations that might trigger her hurt/anger, but also cognitive efforts of concentrated attention such as rumination and brooding, in which she focuses on past mistreatment or potential future mistreatment (i.e. disrespect). The future-oriented control efforts are implemented in order to: (a) minimize the likelihood of the occurrence of mistreatment, and (b) attenuate the full experience of anger, by virtue of the excessive cognitive activity. This can be seen in extremely elevated scores (99th percentile) on ADS subscales of Rumination, Brooding, and Resentment. When this effort at situational control and/or cognitive avoidance proves ineffective at controlling and/or inhibiting the experience of hurt/anger, Joann engages in verbal aggression and/or overt violent behavior in order to quickly escape from the experience of anger, which she can neither tolerate nor accept. This escape behavior is ultimately negatively reinforced in the short-term, as it effectively prevents Joann from experiencing the distressing emotion for more than a brief moment. Interestingly, it also provides some measure of positive (self) reinforcement, as Joann believes that she is protecting herself from the disrespectful actions of others. Yet unfortunately, the long-term consequences are quite significant, resulting in legal, social, and familial difficulties as well as sadness and general life dissatisfaction. In addition to these obvious long-term negative consequences, one could argue that the most pernicious long-term negative consequences of Joann's emotion regulation difficulties and over-use of avoidance and escape behaviors has been the near total absence of skill development with respect to interpersonal problem solving and conflict management. These skills were never developed, as she continuously avoided precisely those situations that would naturally support such skill development. In fact, without these essential skills, significant interpersonal difficulties are likely to remain. Most importantly, until Joann develops an increased capacity to tolerate/accept, utilize, and modulate her emotions, it is unlikely that she will be able to develop these skills. Figure 3.1 presents the diagrammatic representation of the AAM case conceptualization for Joann's case.

Diagnostic Considerations

Certainly, when the clinician looks at the entire assessment package, some clear diagnostic categories stand out for consideration. It has been our experience that *DSM-IV-TR/DSM-5* disorders such as posttraumatic stress disorder, general anxiety disorder, panic disorder, dysthymia, substance abuse disorders, and personality disorders (most often antisocial, borderline, and personality disorder not otherwise specified) are the most frequent diagnoses, either alone or in some combination, given to those referred for the treatment of clinical anger. However, as noted in Chapter 1, the new *DSM-5* diagnosis of disruptive mood dysregulation disorder (DMDD) appears as if it would capture a much higher percentage of cases seen in our clinical setting if allowable as a diagnosis for adults (Dettore, Kempel, & Gardner, 2010).

Yet while the *DSM* system focuses on signs and symptoms and not pathological processes, research has suggested that emotion dysregulation and resultant behavioral instability (particularly interpersonal behavior) is a core pathological process for each of these disorders (Kring & Sloan, 2009). The one exception to this would be antisocial personality disorder, which actually represents a non-reactive predatory form of a violence-related disorder. Within the context of antisocial personality disorder, anger is rarely involved in aggressive or violent behavior, but rather, the desire to get one's desires met by any and all behaviors available is the primary motive. From our perspective, the specific *DSM* disorder is not as relevant as a comprehensive understanding of the core pathological processes, as these processes are ultimately targeted in treatment, with enhanced personal functioning as the intended result.

That said, *DSM* diagnoses are often required of those working in the mental health field. In this case example, Joann did not reach criteria for a diagnosis of a mood or anxiety disorder, and similarly did not meet criteria for any singular personality disorder, although presenting with some

Aversive History and Biological Vulnerability
- Emotional abuse and neglect (CTQ emotional abuse and neglect scores)
  - Mother rejecting, unavailable, easily angered/"stressed" (interview)
    - Father distant, easily angered (interview)
- Unpredictable early environment where behaviors designed to maintain calm were negatively reinforced (interview)
- Highly sensitive to aversive stimuli (threat)/Minimally sensitive to reward (goals) (high BIS/low BAS scores)

⇩

Hostile Anticipation
- Hypervigilant to actual or interpreted signs that others may mistreat her (attentional bias)
  - Excessive interpretation of vulnerability or "disrespect" (personal violation/external focus of attention) (interview and elevated score on ADS Suspiciousness Scale)

⇩

Antecedent (Triggering) Events
- Criticism, negative words from others, hostile words or facial expressions (interview, high scores on ADS Scope of Anger Provocations and Hurt and Social Rejection Scales)

⇩

Experience of Anger
- High levels of physiological arousal (interview, high scores on ADS Physiological Arousal, PANAS Arousal Scales, and BAI)
  - Body temperature rises/"stressed and heated" (interview)
  - Denies the experience of anger (interview, low-moderate scores on STAXI-2: S-Anger/T-Anger)

⇩

Experiential Avoidance/Emotion Dysregulation
- Unable to allow self to "feel angry" (fully process/experience affect) in response to triggering events
- Significant effort at controlling/inhibiting anger (high scores on ADS Anger-In, STAXI-2: AX-I)
- Difficulties with accepting/tolerating, being aware of/utilizing, modulating emotions (clinically significant scores on the DERS and AAQ-2)

⇩   ⇩

Internalized Avoidance	**Externalized Avoidance**
• Ruminates about the past (high score on ADS Rumination Scale), such as other times people have mistreated her, previous coworkers who have disrespected her.	• Physical and verbal aggression toward others to escape angry feelings by modifying external situation(s) (i.e. overuse of situational control emotion regulation strategies as a form of avoidance) (High scores on reactivity/expression subscale of ADS and STAXI-2: Anger Expression Index).

Short-Term Consequences: Violence and aggression lead to reduction of negative experiences such as anger (negatively reinforced) and result in her believing that she is defending her reputation/garnering respect.

Long-Term Consequences: Physical and verbal aggression lead to increased instability in family and social relationships and work environment and difficulty with the law. Prevents her from living a life in line with her values.

Figure 3.1 AAM Case Conceptualization for Joann

signs of most Cluster B personality disorders. She was therefore given the *DSM-IV-TR* diagnosis of personality disorder NOS (APA, 2000; the *DSM-5* had not yet been released). This diagnostic conundrum is common among clients referred for clinical anger, and typifies why, from our perspective, *DSM* diagnostic categorization is not particularly necessary or useful for effective treatment planning.

Summary and Conclusions

The focus of this chapter was to provide guidance to the clinician for an effective and comprehensive assessment of the critical psychological processes related to anger and/or aggressive or violent behavior, and to provide an organization and structure for the careful conceptualization of the client's presenting problem, thereby leading to an appropriate treatment plan.

With assessment and conceptualization of anger problems through the use of the AAM now complete, the remainder of this text focuses on the treatment of clinical anger through the systematic use of Contextual Anger Regulation Therapy (CART).

Appendix 3.1

AVIS

Name: Date: Gender:

The following questions ask about your experience with anger and aggressive or violent behavior over the past week. For each question, please circle the answer that best describes your experience of anger and aggression/violence *over the past week only.*

1. **During the past week, how often have you felt angry?**

    a. No anger this past week
    b. Became angry only once or twice this past week
    c. Became angry occasionally (several times) this past week
    d. Became angry frequently (daily) this past week
    e. Became angry constantly (several times every day) this past week

2. **During this past week, when you felt angry, how intense was the anger?**

    a. Very low intensity. My anger was barely noticeable
    b. Mild intensity. My anger was not too uncomfortable

    c. Moderate intensity. My anger was uncomfortable. At times it affected my ability to relax and/or concentrate

    d. Severe intensity. My anger was very uncomfortable. It made concentrating on anything else very difficult

    e. Extreme intensity. My anger was overwhelming. It was nearly impossible to focus on anything else

3. **During the past week, how often did you avoid situations or people because of feeling angry or concern about becoming angry?**

    a. Not at all. I did not avoid anything because of anger or concern about becoming angry

    b. Infrequently. I avoided people or situations once or twice, but usually confronted difficult situations

    c. Occasionally. I avoided people or situations a few times due to anger or concern about becoming angry

    d. Frequently. I often avoided people or situations due to anger or concern about becoming angry

    e. Almost all of the time. I avoided people or situations due to anger or concern about becoming angry constantly

4. **During the past week, how often did you engage in aggressive or violent behavior (screaming, cursing, threatening, throwing objects, or physical acts/fights)?**

    a. Not at all. I did not engage in aggressive or violent behavior

    b. Infrequently. I engaged in aggressive or violent behavior once or twice

    c. Occasionally. I engaged in aggressive or violent behavior a few times

    d. Frequently. I often engaged in aggressive or violent behavior

    e. Almost all of the time. I engaged in aggressive or violent behavior constantly

5. **During the past week, how much did your anger, concern about becoming angry, or aggressive/violent behavior, interfere with your ability to do the things necessary for work, school, or home life?**

    a. None. My anger, concern about becoming angry, or behavior did not interfere with my life

    b. Mild. My anger, concern about becoming angry, or behavior led to some interference with work, school, or home life, but most necessary things still got taken care of. My life has generally not been affected

c. Moderate. My anger, concern about becoming angry, or behavior definitely interfered with work, school, or home life. Most things still got taken care of, but not everything, and some things were handled less well. My life has been affected somewhat

d. Severe. My anger, concern about becoming angry, or behavior has strongly affected work, school, or home life this week. Many things didn't get handled like they should. My life has definitely been affected

e. Extreme. My anger, concern about becoming angry, or behavior has become overwhelming. I have been unable to function consistently or adequately at work, school, or home. I have experienced or appear about to experience clear consequences such as loss or threat of loss of job, school status, or family life.

4 Contextual Anger Regulation Therapy
Treatment Overview

The psychological treatment outlined in this chapter and presented in detail throughout the remainder of this text is known as Contextual Anger Regulation Therapy (CART; originally named Anger Regulation Therapy, ART). We developed CART a number of years ago to be an intervention package that at its core is a mindfulness and acceptance-based behavioral therapy, which combine to represent a contemporary iteration of cognitive behavioral therapy (CBT). Yet, as CART also includes essential components of interpersonal and emotion-focused treatment strategies, we are very comfortable viewing it as a truly integrative psychological treatment designed specifically to address the emotion dysregulatory processes identified by the AAM as central to the development and maintenance of clinical anger and its behavioral manifestations. Our goal is not theoretical orthodoxy or treatment of signs and symptoms, but rather, to provide a psychological treatment designed specifically to address the core pathological processes inherent in clinical anger. This chapter therefore presents the foundations of CART, discusses the core pathological processes targeted by CART, and provides an overview of the nine-module CART treatment protocol, which will be elaborated upon in detail throughout the remainder of the text.

Traditionally CBT has long focused on the reduction of emotional distress by explicitly targeting a change in the content of one's thoughts (i.e. beliefs). The assumption is that necessary behavior change would inevitably follow from a reduction in distress, which would in turn follow from a modification of "negative" cognitions. However, recent research has questioned the relative necessity of such direct efforts at cognitive change (Jacobson et al., 1996; Longmore & Worrell, 2007), and other researchers have reduced the time spent on, and the goals of, cognitive change within contemporary versions of CBT (Barlow et al., 2010). In addition, researchers have recently begun questioning whether emotions should be seen as a dependent variable in treatment, namely whether a reduction of experienced emotion should be necessarily targeted as a treatment outcome. It can be argued that emotions may be better viewed as an independent variable—that is, a component of treatment to be manipulated/

utilized in the service of enhanced functional behavior and quality of life as the ultimate treatment outcome.

Acceptance-based behavioral therapies (ABBTs) reflect a class of psychological treatments that represents newer developments within CBT, which seek to promote a somewhat different approach to psychological care. ABBTs emphasize reducing clients' avoidance of internal experiences such as cognitions and emotions (including the emotion-driven behaviors that follow from such avoidance), and weakening the power and rigidity of rule-governed behavior, as central mechanisms of therapeutic change. The ultimate goal is the promotion of values-driven behavior change in the service of enhanced quality of life (Hayes, Strosahl, & Wilson, 1999; Roemer & Orsillo, 2009).

Foundational to the development of CART has been the notion that the treatment of clinical anger should directly target those empirically derived psychological mechanisms that the AAM's theoretical model and research have identified as being central to the development and maintenance of clinical anger, which are emotion dysregulatory processes. From this perspective, efficacious treatment would necessitate utilizing intervention strategies that directly target those specific processes that underlie the development and maintenance of the identified problematic behavior. This is precisely what we have done in the development of CART, as treatment strategies are utilized that directly target the empirically demonstrated pathological processes of clinical anger, as established by the AAM.

On a strategic level, CART draws heavily on the work of both Hayes, Strosahl, and Wilson (1999), and Barlow and colleagues (Barlow *et al.*, 2010), which suggests that when an individual experiences an emotional response to external stimuli—such as when one reacts with intense fear and anger in response to maltreatment as a child—he or she is likely to experience a comparable emotional reaction to both similar stimuli and thoughts about the those stimuli, even in the physical absence of such stimuli. This, in turn, leads to excessive efforts to control one's internal experience (cognitions and emotions), as well as overt efforts to avoid stimuli that might evoke these internal reactions. In essence, although cognitions and emotions are transient passing states that inevitably come and go as a natural and unavoidable part of the human experience, and are often triggered by stimuli that only have a marginal similarity to those from where they were originally learned, individuals often respond to their cognitions and emotions as though they are dangerous realities that must be judged as good or bad, and acceptable or unacceptable; and in turn, behavioral choices are typically determined based on these assumptions and judgments. To continue with the previous example, the individual who became fearful and angry in response to childhood maltreatment may now experience similarly intense emotions and anticipation of maltreatment when faced with a spouse who manifests non-verbal displays of unhappiness/frustration in the course of a disagreement (i.e.

stimulus generalization). These cognitions and emotions are subsequently experienced as unacceptable, and as such, serve as a trigger for aggressive or violent behavior in order to reduce or eliminate this uncomfortable internal experience. These emotion-driven behaviors neither solve any existing problems nor promote long-term healthy relationships. Likewise, the behavioral choice (i.e. emotion-driven behavior) in the example given above is not likely to be in any way congruent with long-term goals or values of the client, but instead serve a sole function of immediate avoidance and/or escape from internal experiences. As described in Chapter 2, this process is directed by *experiential avoidance* (Hayes, Strosahl, & Wilson, 1999), which is a core pathological process that acceptance-based behavioral therapies such as CART seek to modify.

Expanding the example provided above, thoughts such as, "no one is going to disrespect me this way," or "I'm not going to take this crap from anybody," reflect the use of internal processes to explain or direct behavioral choices. In turn, the behaviors that result from these rules, such as aggressive or violent behavior, are intended to reduce internal experiences deemed unacceptable, such as vulnerability, frustration, and/or anger. The affect-reducing function of these behaviors is in stark contrast to the more adaptive function of behaviors intended to promote goals and values, such as engaging in conversation (regardless of which emotions are experienced) to solve a relational or life issue needing attention. However, these more life enhancing, values-driven behavioral choices will not occur if the primary goal of the "rules" being employed is avoidance of, or escape from, discomfort. The distinction between "rule-governed" or "emotion-driven" vs "values-directed" behavior is critically important when we consider the reality that optimal functioning requires regular and consistent management of behavior in the service of distal goals, often at the expense of immediate gratification. As such, as treatment evolves, the development of tolerance and acceptance of internal experiences, such as thoughts or emotions, are necessary for disrupting and ultimately changing the pernicious (avoidance-based) intra and interpersonal behavior patterns that our clients bring into the therapy room.

So, rather than being seen as something that is unacceptable and requires avoidance, culminating in rigid and often extreme maladaptive behavior, acceptance of the experience of emotions such as anger (including all aspects, such as thoughts, subjective feelings, and physiological arousal), allows for more flexible behavioral responses based upon contextual (i.e. situational) demands and provides information that can be used as part of adaptive problem solving in the pursuit of valued life goals.

CART Treatment Goals

Given the basic pathological processes outlined in the AAM presented in Chapter 2, CART is a form of ABBT in which an emotion regulatory framework is adopted as a central unifying theme. This emotion regulatory framework is the underlying foundation of CART, and helps define the central treatment goals of:

- Developing a greater capacity to accept/tolerate and understand anger as a normal and necessary emotional experience.
- Developing a greater capacity to effectively reflect upon and utilize the information provided by emotions (anger in particular), as well as modulate anger when necessary, to solve problems and manage interpersonal conflict.
- Developing greater flexibility in available behavioral responses (including enhanced skills) to anger eliciting situations that are in accordance with personal values, culminating in enhanced interpersonal effectiveness and quality of life.

While historically, cognitive behavioral therapy utilized for the treatment of anger has emphasized cognitive restructuring and relaxation exercises as a means of *reducing* anger, and hopefully the aggressive/violent behavior that is often associated with it, CART focuses on helping clients develop a *different relationship* with anger-related cognitions and the subjective and physiological experience of anger itself. Driven by the AAM theoretical model and associated empirical findings which suggest that the avoidance of anger is more pathological than the emotion itself, CART promotes a greater level acceptance and tolerance of the full emotional experience of anger, through a reduction of experiential avoidance. This, in turn, is expected to result in reduced avoidance/escape-based aggressive or violent behavior.

It should be noted that CART is not the only contemporary psychological treatment that has incorporated an emotion regulatory framework in its development. Targeting emotion regulation as a central component of treatment has been suggested previously for the amelioration of generalized anxiety disorder (Mennin, 2004), depression (Hayes & Feldman, 2004), posttraumatic stress disorder (Cloitre *et al.*, 2002), the entire spectrum of emotional disorders (Barlow *et al.*, 2004, 2010), borderline personality disorder (Linehan, 1993), and for inpatient clientele receiving psychotherapy (Berking, Wupperman *et al.*, 2008). However, CART does reflect the first psychological treatment model to utilize an emotion regulatory framework specifically for the treatment of clinical anger. The following therapeutic strategies and techniques are utilized within CART to directly target those processes that give rise to problematic clinical anger and its behavioral manifestations:

- psychoeducation
- values identification and motivation enhancement
- self-monitoring

- mindfulness exercises
- cognitive defusion/decentering
- emotion-focused/exposure activities
- behavioral activation and commitment
- interpersonal problem solving and conflict management training
- use of the therapeutic relationship to modify toxic interpersonal behaviors.

These intervention strategies and techniques are provided within a flexible modular approach, outlined below.

CART Treatment Modules (1–9)

The modular approach utilized by CART allows for therapist flexibility while at the same time maintaining treatment fidelity. Rather that presenting CART as a 9-, 18-, or 27-session treatment protocol, we recognize that clinical settings often have different session length constraints, and individual clients bring into treatment differing motivations, levels of anger pathology, comorbidities, and external treatment demands that warrant consideration. Thus, each treatment module is organized around a *theme*, or mini-treatment goal. A module is deemed complete when the accompanying mini-treatment goal has been effectively satisfied, at which time the therapist would move sequentially to the next treatment module, and so on. Modules are sequenced so that the knowledge and skills developed within each module are necessary for each subsequent module. We therefore strongly encourage clinicians to resist the temptation to skip or reorganize modules, as each CART module sets the stage for the successful completion of future CART modules. CART has been tested over a number of years, and the nine sequenced modules have stood the test of time in our clinical setting. When we have attempted to reorganize or skip modules, we have hit treatment roadblocks. We therefore encourage readers to follow the sequenced CART protocol, as presented herein.

While we generally think that a minimum of 12 sessions is optimal, the CART protocol can be as short as six sessions (to be described later) or as long as is necessary for all treatment components to be complete. Importantly, CART has been intentionally developed with the needs of clinical settings and clinician flexibility in mind. In essence, achieving the treatment goals established for each CART module should be the viewed as the core treatment strategy, while the specific techniques utilized within each module to achieve those goals can be seen as the tactics used to accomplish the core strategic goals of treatment. As we progress through a description of the treatment modules, the reader should remember that no single number of sessions would be required for completion of any module. Clinical realities, such as client motivation, specific court-mandated treatment lengths, and therapist training and experience, may impact the delivery of CART in such a way that each module would need to be approached as multiple sessions, a single session, or less than one session. Herein, we present the treatment modules based on what theory and research have suggested are most essential for positive therapeutic outcomes.

What follows in this chapter is a brief overview of the intent/goals of each treatment module, with a focus on the specific processes to target. Additionally, brief reference will be made to the specific techniques to be utilized in each module. Subsequent chapters will provide a detailed examination of all modules, their goals, and their techniques, including illustrative case examples.

Module 1: Psychoeducation, Values Identification, and Motivation Enhancement

Goals of Module 1

The specific goals of Module 1 are to:

- Discuss the purpose of treatment within the context of the reason for referral.
- Establish an open, honest, and collaborative therapeutic relationship.
- Present the Anger Avoidance Model with a clear connection to the client's current life circumstance.
- Validate the historical development of the client's current behavioral patterns, while noting its negative impact on valued life goals.
- Determine the client's valued life goals and engage in a decisional balance to promote client motivation.
- Define the goals and expectations inherent in CART.

As with all psychological treatments, particularly those developed out of the cognitive behavioral tradition, the first module of CART begins with psychoeducation. Psychotherapy outcome research has led us to understand that psychological interventions work best when three basic conditions are established at the beginning of treatment. The first is the establishment of an effective working alliance between the client and therapist. The second condition is that the client develops a way of reconceptualizing his or her problems through use of a better explanatory system. Finally, the third component is that the client gains an enhanced sense of hope (Castonguay & Beutler, 2006). If Module 1 is successfully completed, our clinical experience is that these three basic conditions of effective psychological treatment are in fact more than likely to be realized.

The core of Module 1 is to help clients understand: (a) the AAM model; (b) how the issues and behaviors that culminated in clients finding themselves in therapists' offices can be explained by the AAM; (c) the historical roots of their problems; (d) the benefits (short-term) and costs (long-term) of their current behavioral patterns; (e) what they truly desire out of life (i.e. values), along with the costs and benefits of current behavioral patterns; (f) what psychological treatment is, and what responsibilities it entails from therapists and clients; and (g) how (if relevant) treatment fits into their personal (court/family) mandates.

If each of these specific points is addressed, clients should be left with an enhanced sense of hope, a means of thinking differently about their current problems and future possibilities, and the foundation of a sound and effective working alliance with their therapist (the three characteristics identified earlier that are related to positive therapeutic outcomes). Likewise, the stage is now set to begin the process of real therapeutic change.

Module 2: Using the Therapeutic Relationship to Recognize and Modify Clinically Relevant Behavior

Goals of Module 2

The specific goals of Module 2 are:

- The therapist consistently identifies in-session behavior(s) that is directly relevant to the identified out-of-session client problem behavior(s).
- The therapist consistently and appropriately responds to clinically relevant behavior in a manner that provides information to the client and the opportunity to learn new and more appropriate interpersonal behaviors.

As previously described, CART utilizes a strong and ever-present interpersonal component in its treatment package. The interpersonal focus in CART is modeled after Kohlenberg and Tsai's functional analytic psychotherapy (2007), and follows a behavioral-interpersonal model. Fundamental to this approach is an understanding that the client's interpersonal behavioral difficulties will manifest themselves in some form or another within treatment sessions, particularly with respect to the therapist as a discriminative stimulus for negative affect, anticipatory cognitions, and problematic interpersonal behavior. As such, opportunities regularly arise to help modify these behavioral patterns in-vivo.

This module is a natural continuation of Module 1, and in reality continues as a core component throughout the entire CART treatment process. The therapist should always be open to recognizing and responding to clinically relevant interpersonal behaviors, which are those behaviors seen within sessions that correspond either directly or in more subtle ways to problematic behaviors described/known to occur outside of sessions. Despite the fact that we view the recognition and response to these interpersonal clinically relevant behaviors as a core aspect of the entire CART process, our clinical experiences have suggested to us that early focus on this aspect of treatment without the encumbrances of additional goals, is particularly important. This is especially true since in-session client reactions/behaviors with regard to session time/scheduling, cancellations of sessions, payment, therapist questions, style, gender, race, etc., typically arise early in treatment and offer a perfect opportunity to note clinically relevant behavior and begin the process of addressing them in a structured and systematic manner. If these clinically relevant in-session behaviors are not appropriately noted and addressed, it is unlikely that treatment will be successful, as it therefore becomes likely that treatment (and in particular interactions with the therapist) will follow the same unhealthy course that the client's life has taken. In contrast, when these behaviors are noticed, pointed out, and responded to appropriately, especially in light of the AAM and in the context of previous values identification, a collaborative treatment process will be underway and the motivation and framework for significant change will be in place.

Module 3: Developing Mindful Emotion Awareness

Goals of Module 3

The specific goals of Module 3 are to:

- Increase non-judging, present moment awareness of emotional experiences including cognitions, subjective feelings, bodily responses/ sensations, and related behavioral action tendencies associated with those experiences.
- Increase non-judging, present moment attention to both internal experiences and external stimuli (both appetitive and aversive).
- Increase the client's understanding that internal experiences such as cognitions, feelings, and bodily sensations are transient events that are both informative and passing.

The core feature of this module is a process in which the client becomes more comfortable with having, observing, and remaining in increasingly longer contact (without avoidance or escape) with his or her internal experiences. This in turn sets the stage for the enhancement of proactive values-driven behavior, rather than the reactive emotion-driven (avoidance) behavior that often typifies anger problems. The process begins with education about emotion and its adaptive value and occasional maladaptive outcomes. This is followed by education about emotion awareness/ mindfulness, what it is, what it is not, how it relates to the issues that have brought the client to treatment, and how its development may be helpful for the client in the future; and then progressively moves through a series of mindfulness enhancing exercises. These exercises are intended to help clients: (a) learn to slow themselves down and disengage from their automatic behavior; (b) learn to non-judgmentally observe and enhance awareness of external stimuli and ultimately their internal experiences; (c) increasingly develop the capacity to remain in contact with previously uncomfortable internal experiences; and (d) learn to focus attention to relevant tasks and redirect attention when distracted by one's internal state.

Central to the CART program, mindfulness promotes the full experiencing of anger and related cognitive, affective, and physiological processes; disrupts the avoidance/escape process; and thus, directly targets the core pathological process of clinical anger. The development of enhanced mindfulness requires both in- and out-of-session practice, and clinicians must be diligent in communicating to clients the importance of engaging in out-of-session mindfulness training assignments so that in-session work can be most productive.

Module 4: Cognitive Defusion and the Reduction of Problematic Rule-Governed Behavior

Goals of Module 4

The specific goals of Module 4 are:

- The client gains an understanding of the concept of cognitive fusion and its relationship to problematic behavioral patterns.
- Enhanced client awareness of relevant internal rules (schemas) and their associated automatic (fused) behaviors.
- The client begins to defuse those rules and behaviors through the process of decentering from anger-related cognitions.

In this module, therapists continue the process of helping clients develop an increasingly decentered perspective with regard to their internal experiences. Cognitive *fusion* is defined as the process by which an individual responds to his or her cognitions as though they are absolute truths/realities that require an immediate (and usually a rigid and narrow) range of behavioral responses. As we discussed in Chapter 2, clients typically come to treatment with very specific internal rules (i.e. schemas) that when triggered result in rapid and automatic behavioral responses. Many of these internal rules are self-destructive, and at times they are neither fully known nor completely understood. In turn, cognitive *defusion* is the process by which clients develop the capacity to decenter from their own thought process, thus learning to view their thought process as simply what their minds are telling them at that particular moment, and not an absolute truth/reality to which they must responded. This process is what many theorists believe is the mechanism by which traditional cognitive restructuring and reappraisal may actually work (Segal, Williams, & Teasdale, 2012).

Cognitive defusion begins with, and is enhanced by, the development of mindfulness (in Module 3), and increasingly allows clients to slow down, recognize their internal dialogue, make informed personal behavioral choices, and not be automatically rule-driven in their behavioral repertoire. The process of cognitive defusion begins with enhanced awareness of the problematic thought processes, their roots, and their triggers; and is followed by a series of in- and between-session exercises to develop a decentered (i.e. defused) perspective from these thoughts. It should be stressed that these thoughts/rules are not confronted by logical analysis or Socratic dialogue with the goal of changing or eliminating them. Rather, as previously stated, the ultimate goal is to develop the capacity to view thoughts as something that our minds tell us, which certainly does not represent what is *true* or what we *are*; something we learned previously that has stayed with us; something that comes and goes; and something that can be observed and allowed to pass without necessitating action.

Module 5: Understanding Anger and Anger-Avoidance

Goals of Module 5

The specific goals of Module 5 are:

- The client gains an understanding that the emotion of anger is a normal and unavoidable aspect of life, learns about its function, and learns the problems associated with seeing anger as something to be feared and avoided.
- The client gains an understanding of the common misconceptions about anger, which are that anger inevitably leads to aggression if not controlled, that venting is both healthy and necessary, that other people are the cause of anger, and that being angry and displaying anger are helpful.
- The client gains an understanding of the costs of his or her efforts to avoid the experience of anger, including costs in interpersonal, career/financial, health, and energy domains.
- The client develops an enhanced capacity to (increasingly) tolerate anger, and thus come to experience and understand anger better.

In this module, clients use the skills and knowledge acquired through previous modules and begin the task of relating differently to their anger. Rather than continuing to see their anger as an inherent problem that needs to be controlled or eliminated, clients come to understand the normal human reality of becoming angry, learn its place in their personal history, and develop the capacity to differentiate the costs of experiencing anger vs the costs of extreme automatic efforts to avoid or escape the experience of anger. In this module, the therapist systematically discusses the nature of anger and how the emotion of anger can be used effectively as a vehicle for action. In addition, common misconceptions about anger (often reinforced in various cultures) such as its lack of utility, its natural association with aggression, and its need to be vented, are discussed in detail. This module begins the process of normalizing the experience of anger and thus creates a treatment environment that supports and tolerates the full healthy experience and expression of this powerful emotion. In addition, clients develop an increased capacity to experience and tolerate anger without the need to avoid, escape, or otherwise reduce the feeling state.

Module 6: Acceptance and Anger Regulation

Goals of Module 6

The specific goals of Module 6 are:

- The client will increasingly develop the capacity to tolerate/accept the presence of anger (and the hurt/rejection with which it is often associated).
- The client will develop the capacity to distinguish between anger-driven behavior and values-driven behavior.
- The client will develop the capacity to modulate (i.e. down-regulate) anger when necessary—not to *feel* better, but to allow for behavior in the service of personal values.

In this powerful module, clients further develop the capacity to experience anger without needing to resort to historically over-learned avoidance or escape behaviors. Herein, patients and therapists explore the workability (i.e. effectiveness) of the variety of strategies previously used to avoid or escape from feelings of anger and hurt. In this context, therapists reinforce the idea that the lack of success in controlling anger and hurt has not been due to any personal failure or absence of adequate strategy, but rather, has been due to the impossibility of that goal. Namely, the reality is that: (a) people get angry and feel hurt, and nothing or no one can eliminate that possibility; and (b) the pursuit of that goal has led to more negative consequences than the experience of anger ever would.

Encouraging acceptance of emotional experiences and developing a willingness to remain in contact with these experiences also increases the ability to utilize information conveyed by emotions such as anger; for example, the detection of cues or signals that can guide decision making and motivate appropriate values-driven behavior. As such, during this module, clients develop an even greater understanding of the various cognitions, emotions, and physical sensations associated with anger and hurt, and begin the process of modifying the stimulus functions of anger and hurt so as to no longer require extreme and rigid avoidance/escape behaviors. Rather, clients learn to carefully consider available, functional behavioral choices. Enhanced acceptance/tolerance of anger promotes a greater distinction between emotion (anger/hurt)-driven behavior that has been the source of many of the clients' life difficulties, and values-driven behavior, which can promote an enhanced quality of life.

As there are some circumstances in which overly intense episodes of anger may interfere with optimal behavioral responding, therapists must at times help clients develop appropriate values-driven self-soothing skills. In such cases, values-driven behavioral approaches to down-regulating anger, such as the use of "opposite-action" as a coping response (discussed in detail later in this text), are presented. It is important that these self-soothing techniques be carefully considered prior to use, as therapists do not want to promote alternative means of avoidance. Rather, therapists promote emotion modulation skills in the service of mindful awareness of the emotional experience, rather than in the service of avoiding or escaping from the emotional state. It is also critical that these efforts be introduced *after* anger distress tolerance has already been enhanced. The development of anger acceptance and the associated differentiation between emotion-driven and values-driven behavior sets the stage for the next module, in which increasing commitment to consistent values-driven behavior is the overarching goal.

Module 7: Commitment to Values-Based Behavior

Goals of Module 7

The specific goals of Module 7 are:

- The client develops a clear connection between previously identified values and specific behaviors to be increased.
- The client continues to develop the understanding that experiencing intense anger can (and often must) occur at the same time as the need for effective values-driven behaviors (through the use of values-driven experiential exposure).
- The client develops a behavioral activation plan to record and monitor specific values-driven behaviors.
- The client learns to identify skill deficits needing correction, to further enhance values-driven behavioral choices.

As clients become increasingly comfortable with tolerating the anger experience, in Module 7, therapists work to enhance clients' ongoing commitment to pursuing meaningful personal values through the structured identification and activation of specific values-directed behaviors. In this critical module, therapists help the client continue to carefully distinguish between goals and values, asserting that goals have a clear end point (e.g. reaching a sales quota), whereas values is a concept that requires ongoing effort (e.g. being a good parent).

This module is intended to help clients develop a consistent approach to engaging in those behaviors that optimize what really matters to them and help them become the types of people they hope to be and live the lives they would like to have. While once again noting the distinction between emotion-driven and values-driven behavior, clients are encouraged to increase their willingness to act in accordance with their stated values *while* being angry or hurt. Of course, it should be noted that this cannot be accomplished without the skill development from previous modules. Such previous skill development helps clients understand, tolerate, and utilize their emotions such as anger more effectively. In this module, clients are encouraged to systematically confront, with new behavioral options, those previously avoided situations that are associated with the personal values that were previously identified. In so doing, new emotional meanings are developed in response to previously avoided situations, and clients increasingly gain a sense of personal effectiveness. A critical aspect of this module is the utilization of a behavioral activation plan to systematically identify and increase client behaviors that are consistent with identified personal values, often occurring *while experiencing* angry feelings. Finally, as chronic emotion dysregulation has most likely taken the form of behavioral avoidance and has typically resulted in deficits in necessary interpersonal skills, during this module, therapists will inevitably notice specific skill deficits that are likely to interfere with desired positive interpersonal outcomes. Thus, in the process of developing a consistent values-driven behavioral activation plan, clinicians catalogue communication, conflict management, and/or problem-solving skill deficits in need of development for optimal interpersonal effectiveness. This in turn sets the stage for the next module, which directly targets the development of these skills.

Module 8: Developing Effective Interpersonal Problem-Solving Skills

Goals of Module 8

The specific goals of Module 8 are to:

- Enhance interpersonal problem-solving skills.
- Enhance communication and assertiveness skills.
- Enhance conflict management skills.

In Module 8, the primary therapeutic task is the development of those interpersonal skills necessary for the ongoing pursuit of identified personal values. As noted earlier, it can be expected that a number of interpersonal skill deficits will have been previously noted, as clients have historically utilized over-learned avoidance and escape behaviors rather than proactive skill-based behaviors to respond to a wide array of social situations. As such, clients will often need to develop specific skills relating to problem solving, communication, and/or conflict management. These skills are taught and practiced within therapy sessions and are ultimately utilized between sessions, with concomitant feedback and further practice. In this regard, these skills are systematically shaped in order to promote the continued (effective) use of values-driven behaviors in the clients' lives. These skills can be effectively developed at this particular time in the treatment process, as clients have at this point developed the emotional tolerance needed to function adaptively, without the need to utilize emotion-driven behaviors as a means of avoidance or escape.

The importance of skill development in this module cannot be stressed too strongly, as the presence of more effective "positive" interpersonal behaviors increase the likelihood that clients will be personally reinforced by their environment, and will thus continue to remain values-directed in their behavioral choices while remaining willing to experience the emotional discomfort that comes with those pursuits.

Module 9: Integration, Relapse Prevention, and Treatment Termination

Goals of Module 9

The specific goals of Module 9 are:

- The identification of anger-inducing triggers and a discussion of possible lapses.
- The in-vivo practice of potential anger-inducing triggers.
- The development of ongoing action plans for continued use of CART principles and strategies.
- Proactive treatment termination.

The overarching purpose of Module 9 is to prepare clients for the completion of CART by stressing the lifelong nature of the skills and exercises to which they have been exposed. Essential is the development of a specific plan for the continued use of CART principles, including ongoing self-monitoring as a vehicle of self-reflection and self-correction. As part of this process, therapists work with clients to: (a) identify (and practice appropriate responses to) future anger-inducing situations that have not been attended to in the course of CART; (b) discuss the likelihood of occasional lapses and develop specific action plans to utilize in order to insure that these inevitable lapses do not become more extreme relapses of old behavioral patterns; (c) reaffirm that values are never fully attained but are instead aspirations that can and should guide behavior on a day-to-day basis; and (d) engage in an open discussion about a number of termination-related factors. Such factors include terminating therapy, the availability of future sessions if needed, encouragement of clients' readiness to work the program on their own, and reinforcement of the idea that as with medical illnesses (such as diabetes), the difficulties that brought them into treatment can be effectively managed with ongoing attention and care.

Of course, many, if not most, clients presenting with clinical anger have come from early environments that were emotionally abusive and/or neglectful. As such, termination as a natural and healthy process as opposed to an invalidating and hurtful one must be attended to directly. Certainly, the intention is to allow treatment termination to be a healthy, new-learning interpersonal experience.

Conclusion

As can be seen from this brief overview, the overall goal of CART treatment is the development of basic emotion regulation skills of acceptance/tolerance, understanding, and when necessary, modulation of anger as a vehicle to promote enhanced quality of life. The techniques utilized, such as mindfulness, cognitive defusion, behavioral activation, etc., are all used with the ultimate goal of helping clients find a better path through life via the vehicle of enhanced emotion regulation. We do not seek to help them become less angry (although often, they paradoxically do), nor do we seek to help them figure out a way to convince people to treat them better or to respond to them more effectively (although, often, this too occurs). CART ultimately seeks to empower clients to strive for something better, and not simply feel better in some immediate and transient way. In a very real sense, this is not *anger* management, but rather, *life* management.

Finally, we conclude this overview of the CART protocol by noting that clinicians' attitudes and behaviors are critical components of the ultimate efficacy of CART or any other empirically derived psychological treatment. While CART has a series of well designed and structured tactics and strategies, we have witnessed over and over again how therapists who do not value their clients, or who do not/cannot demonstrate an appropriate balance between demonstrating caring and establishing boundaries (which thus interferes with learning new and adaptive interpersonal experiences), will not be successful in working with this complex set of client problems. Ultimately, delivering effective evidence-based psychological treatments requires attention to both treatment procedures and our delivery system for these procedures, the professional therapist.

We now embark upon the most exciting portion of the text, which is a detailed, step-by-step presentation of each module of Contextual Anger Regulation Therapy, followed by a discussion of special considerations and a full and informative case example.

5   Contextual Anger Regulation Therapy
Step-by-Step Treatment Description

The present chapter is, to us, the most exciting, as it accompanies the reader through each of the nine CART modules in a detailed, step-by-step manner. For each module, we describe essential treatment goals, materials utilized for that particular module, expected number of sessions for completion of the module, and key concepts to be covered. We encourage readers to remember, however, that each module is intended to naturally evolve into the next module, and as such, treatment should seamlessly move from one module to another. An additional feature of note is that CART makes regular use of assessment measures, which are typically utilized in appropriate modules and regularly required for the purpose of monitoring and charting client progress throughout the course of treatment. We therefore discuss these in their respective places. Finally, all clinicians know that problems inevitably surface within the treatment context, and so we have included a discussion at the end of each module regarding the most common problems and/or obstacles that CART therapists have encountered during clinical practice with that module. We also regularly include case vignette material throughout the modules in order to accentuate the concepts being presented. After the entire nine-module CART program has been presented, future chapters will offer special considerations to consider when using CART, and will provide a full case example to illustrate the comprehensive CART protocol.

Module 1: Psychoeducation, Values Identification, and Motivation Enhancement

Estimated Number of Sessions to Completion: 1–2

Goals of Module 1

- Discuss the purpose of treatment within the context of the reason for referral.
- Establish an open, honest, and collaborative therapeutic relationship.

- Present the Anger Avoidance Model with a clear connection to the client's current life circumstance.
- Validate the historical development of the client's current behavioral patterns, while noting its negative impact on valued life goals.
- Determine the client's valued life goals and engage in a decisional balance to promote client motivation.
- Define the goals and expectations inherent in CART.

Materials Needed for Module 1

- Acceptance and Action Questionnaire-2 (AAQ-2)
- Anger and Violence Impairment Scale (AVIS)
- Decisional Balance Form
- Valued Living Questionnaire

The treatment goals of this first treatment module can essentially be separated into two segments. The first segment of Module 1 relates to what would best be described as developing the foundation of an open and honest collaborative therapeutic relationship. It is quite common (and in fact it can be argued that it's most often the case) that clients who come for psychological treatment of clinical anger are mandated in some way. These mandates can be through the judicial system (e.g. court, attorney), family members (e.g. parents, intimate partners), or employment (e.g. human resource, employee assistance program, union requirements). Each of these mandates present different issues for practitioners to confront. Issues such as specifics of external (i.e. court) mandates; confidentiality and its limits; treatment length expectations; and/or family expectations/involvements, all need to be directly, openly, and honestly discussed. For example, it is not uncommon for court-mandated clients to view clinicians as a continuation of the judicial system, which whether accurate or not, brings with it certain concerns, suspicions, expectations, and negative beliefs. In any event, clinicians must carefully and completely discuss their relationship with, and independence (or lack thereof) from the judicial system or employment setting, including all relevant concerns about confidentiality and treatment impact upon sentencing, probation, parole, job status, etc. We cannot state strongly enough that this critical discussion must occur before any treatment components are to begin, as these issues have a clear and direct impact on client openness and motivation for treatment engagement. Our own research has indicated that client suspiciousness is the best predictor of treatment non-completion, and as such, reducing suspiciousness through direct and honest discussion about the issues noted above can enhance the likelihood that treatment will not be prematurely terminated due to a lack of trust. A clear and easy-to-understand informed consent should be created and carefully read by and discussed with clients. Only when this conversation is fully complete and all related issues are discussed in depth should this particular segment of Module 1 be considered complete. Clinicians are then ready to move on to the second segment of Module 1.

Following the satisfactory completion of the discussion of mandates, confidentiality, and related issues, we encourage therapists to administer the AAQ-2 (Bond *et al.*, 2011) and the Anger and Violence Impairment Scale (AVIS). As noted in Chapter 3, the AAQ-2 is a measure of experiential avoidance, a significant process to be targeted for change in CART. Likewise, the AVIS (see Appendix 3.1) is a measure that we adapted from the Overall Anxiety Severity and Impairment Scale (Norman *et al.*, 2006) and the Overall Depression Severity and Impairment Scale (Barlow *et al.*, 2010) to assess the life impairment caused by clients' clinical anger on a week-to-week basis. These measures allow for an ongoing evaluation of both process and outcome of CART. Although these instruments should typically be administered at the beginning of each session throughout the CART protocol, this is not the case for Module 1. Instead, during Module 1, the AAQ-2 and AVIS measures should be administered either at the end of the first session of Module 1, or before the beginning of the second session of Module 1. Therapists may also want to administer brief measures such as the Beck Anxiety Inventory (BAI) and Beck Depression Inventory-II (BDI-II; described in Chapter 3; Beck & Steer, 1993; Beck, Steer, & Brown, 1996) on a regular basis if co-occurring depression and/or anxiety have been identified and warrant clinical attention.

In the second segment of Module 1, the therapeutic goal is essentially to connect clients' reasons for referral and the AAM. This psychoeducational goal of Module 1 requires that therapists fully understand the AAM and are thus able to help clients gain a new understanding of their current and, in most cases, previous difficulties. It has been our experience that most clients come in to treatment for clinical anger with expectations that therapists will make some effort to reduce the frequency or intensity of their experience of anger. When discussing clients' anger-related difficulties from the perspective of the AAM, therapists must take care to validate clients' current behavioral functioning as a natural consequence of their history. This is analogous to the validation/change dialectic inherent in Linehan's dialectical behavior therapy (1993), in which therapists seek to help clients see that their behavioral difficulties are fully understandable, and even predictable, given their personal histories. At the same time, therapists begin a process of helping clients recognize the unworkability (i.e. impossibility of success) of their current pattern of behavior; that is, the behavior is historically understandable but at the same time is not functional. We have found that presenting the AAM within the context of clients' difficulties easily allows therapists to both make this important point and begin the process of identifying alternative targets for effective treatment. Typically, clients readily understand and connect with the concept of difficulties in emotion regulation, and can understand and accept that treatment will target tolerance of anger, learning to better understand anger, and the development of strategies to modulate anger when necessary.

The following is a brief example of this process with a client court mandated for psychological treatment following a physical altercation with someone at his place of work (C = Client; T = Therapist).

C: It's like I just snapped. We were arguing about something stupid, no big deal really, and he turned in my direction. He started coming toward me, and I just hit him.

T: Do you remember what was going on in your mind or what you were feeling?

C: Not really. I usually don't let people get away with making any threats to me . . . and I don't think I was feeling much, but I do remember straightening up, you know, getting tense.

T: You know, this is really understandable considering how you were physically abused pretty regularly as a child. You are highly sensitive to being threatened from those experiences, so you quickly go into survival mode. This fits the Anger Avoidance Model we talked about earlier, you know, how your history has taught you that the world is a threatening place, and the tension you felt has also been learned to be a sign of danger. To you, being vulnerable is a trigger for intense feelings and extreme behavior. So, it's all perfectly understandable. But, like we talked about, while your history makes this understandable, the consequences for you now are pretty severe. Right now you are facing the possible loss of a job you like, possible incarceration, and serious family problems.

C: Yea, but like you said, if this is the way I am, what can I do?

T: Well, you're right about this being the way you have learned to behave, but you can learn to react differently and experience your own emotions a bit differently, as well. For example, like we talked about in the model, the emotion of anger includes thoughts about possible threat, physical changes . . . you know, your tension, which you don't like and typically don't even allow yourself to feel. Instead, you go into attack mode. Over time, we can work on helping you learn to distance yourself from your thoughts a bit so you don't have to instantly act, and learn to tolerate your tension and angry feelings so you have some choices. Now, I know this may not sound like an easy thing to do, but are the things you keep dealing with easy?

C: No, I guess not.

In this example, the client is helped to see the historical roots of his behavioral difficulties, as described in the AAM. However, while his current patterns of behavior are validated, they are also pointed out as being consistently associated with negative outcomes, and as such, this sets the stage for change efforts focusing on developing a different relationship with his thoughts and feelings. We have often found it useful to utilize a Decisional Balance Form, similar to those used in motivational interviewing interventions. The Decisional Balance Form that we use is presented in Appendix 5.1, and a sample of a Decisional Balance Form completed with the client from the previous example is located in Table 5.1.

At this point in Module 1, with clients considering the possibility of change in a fundamentally different way than they were likely to have considered before entering the consultation room, and in concert with an understanding of the historical roots of their current and past issues, therapists now present the concept of *values* and *values-driven behavior*. This discussion will begin to focus clients on what really matters in their lives, provides some clarity with regard to what therapeutic change might look like, and allows for an anchor point from which to compare behavioral choices going forward (i.e. "How does that behavioral choice you made promote the values that you said you wanted your life to be about?"). In this regard, we find it helpful to utilize the Valued Living Questionnaire-2 (VLQ-2; Wilson & Dufrene, 2008). This brief instrument asks clients to indicate (during the previous week) the level of importance of ten domains of life, and how consistently they have lived in accord with those ten domains. Using a rating scale of 1–10, the domains are: (1) Family, (2) Marriage/couples/intimate relations, (3) Parenting, (4) Friendship, (5) Work, (6) Education, (7) Recreation, (8) Spirituality, (9) Citizenship, and (10) Physical self-care. The VLQ can yield a total score in which behavior in the service of values is subtracted from the stated importance of values, thus providing a total commitment to values measurement (i.e. the lower the score, the greater congruence between stated values and committed behavior toward those values). We ask clients to complete this instrument weekly, as a way of monitoring, and maintaining a constant focus on, what is ultimately the most central goal of CART, which is enhanced values-driven behavior.

Understanding the concept of values-driven behavior first requires a careful consideration of the idea of personal values. It is important that therapists patiently discuss those values that are personally meaningful to

Table 5.1 Decisional Balance Form (Case Example)

Specific Problem Behavior	"Getting into fights when angry or challenged"
Benefit(s) of Current Behavior	"Self-protection. Won't let other people mistreat me"
Cost(s) of Current Behavior	"Trouble with holding a job, getting arrested, family arguments"
Benefit(s) of Changing Behavior	"I would have an easier, less stressful, happier life. Improved personal relationships would be likely"
Cost(s) of Changing Behavior	"Possible that at times I might actually be taken advantage of"

the individual client. Distinct from goals, which reflect what people want to achieve, values reflect how people might want to be remembered after their death, or what is truly meaningful to them on a day-to-day basis. For example, getting a job is a goal . . . you set out to do it, you achieve it, and it's done. On the other hand, being a good parent is a value . . . it is something that never has a final achievement point, but it is something that can drive one's behavior on a regular and daily basis. Discussing this distinction and developing a set of values (based upon the domains on the VLQ-2) is an important early step in CART, as this will ultimately become an important anchor for use throughout the CART program. Of course, the determination of personal values is not always easy to do with this clinical population, as often it is a concept that has not been given much previous thought. But, with patient persistence required of therapists throughout the entire CART program, these values can (and need to) be discerned and written down for future reference.

At this point, therapists might also discuss with clients the different ways in which they have tried to change their problematic behavior in the past, and may also discuss the assumptions that clients have held regarding the reasons for their difficulties. For example, it is common for clients to assume that the reason for their life difficulties is excessive anger, and thus, what they will describe are numerous efforts to control, limit, or in some way inhibit their anger. Some of these efforts would be described as response-focused emotion regulation strategies (i.e. counting to ten when feeling angry, walking out of a room) and some as antecedent-focused strategies (i.e. avoiding people or situations that may trigger anger). In addition to validating the historical roots of their difficulties while presenting the reality of negative life outcomes, therapists take the opportunity to present the AAM model of avoidance or escape from anger as more problematic than the subjective experience of anger. This discussion also reinforces the idea that clients' previous lack of success in changing their behavior is not necessarily the result of some inherent personal deficiency, but rather, is due to the impossibility of their efforts, namely trying to eliminate the normal emotion of anger. It is also presented that life and society may teach us that anger is bad, dangerous, or wrong, but in fact, anger is normal, and treatment will help clients become more comfortable with being angry, even if that currently appears impossible. This also leads to a discussion of the difference between values-driven behavior and emotion-driven behavior. An example of this discussion is as follows.

T: Tell me how you have tried to not become violent in the past.
C: [Laughs] Well, I try to stay away from the people that piss me off.
T: How has that worked out?
C: Not easy, especially when its my wife and kids. Sometimes, I'll stay out very late after work if we're going through a bad time just so I don't come home and get angry.

T: Sounds like you're trying to avoid getting angry at all costs, like you're afraid of it . . . but there does seem to be a cost. Time with your family, which you said was important to you a little earlier when we completed the Valued Living Questionnaire. It also sounds like you're telling me that you think the only way to avoid becoming violent is not becoming angry, is that right?

C: Yes. Whenever I get angry, it seems that I can't control myself from getting out of hand.

T: That must make getting angry pretty frightening. But, what if I told you that the reason it hasn't worked well for you is that it's impossible? Anger is normal and everyone feels it, and maybe the problem is, like we discussed a bit earlier today, that you've come to believe that anger in intolerable. Maybe another approach would be to learn, a little at a time, that anger *can* be tolerated, and then you can learn a different automatic behavior when feeling anger. That way, your choices in life can be based upon your values, and not your emotions.

C: It's OK to feel angry? [Laughs] Well, that's different. Seems like my whole life people told me my problem was anger. Not sure that it would work, but then again, nothing else has.

T: OK, let's hold onto that idea and go back to it as we continue on. You don't have to buy it now, but let's at least consider it.

C: Sounds good.

This type of discussion should then lead to an open an honest presentation about the goals, and mutual expectations of clients/therapists in the CART program. The difference between this treatment and more typical "anger management" programs should be clearly presented, including treatment outcome goals, the focus of treatment, and the length of time to complete the program. Of particular importance is the initial presentation of the central role that deficits in emotion regulation play in the development and maintenance of client problems. When presented in plain, simple, and easy-to-understand terms, this discussion sets the stage for later modules and allows clients to make sense of the sequence and structure of the program. Finally, it is important that this early discussion include the regular use and importance of between-session exercises.

Between-session exercises are very important in the CART program, as they are in cognitive behavioral treatments in general, and these exercises require careful attention on the part of therapists. We often use physical therapy as a comparison when discussing between-session exercises with our clients. Most of our clients have either experienced physical therapy or have known someone close to them who has undergone such treatment. In addition, it is a generally accepted intervention with few negative connotations or beliefs attached to it. In physical therapy, the reduction of pain is not typically the primary goal, although it often occurs over time. Rather, the goal is muscular strength and overall range of motion, so that patients can improve their functionality and live life to its fullest. We point out that physical pain is analogous to intense emotions such as anger, and minimization of the physical pain can occur if the patients are willing to move around less and accept a reduction in range of motion, with all of its consequences. We also point out that sometimes physical therapy can actually *increase* discomfort or even pain for a period of time, as patients gain strength and push themselves to increase their range of motion. Finally, we point out that physical therapy involves between-session exercises, as does CART, which allows patients to continuously work on important topics and increase their psychological strength and behavioral flexibility (i.e. range of motion in the physical therapy analogy). We have found this analogy to be easily understood, and think it helps promote clear expectations of treatment and the importance of between-session exercises. One additional important distinction is that we purposely use the term *between-session exercises* and not *homework*. "Exercises" suggests a proactive effort to practice and use session content and has little negative connotation, whereas "homework" is often learned from an early age to represent an aversive and undesirable activity, especially among those who were not academically advanced or motivated.

Obstacles Often Encountered in Module 1

The most significant obstacles commonly seen in Module 1 fall into two broad themes. The first is external to CART itself, and is when clients cannot or will not move from an extrinsic motivation for treatment to a more intrinsic one. Despite all of our best efforts, there are some clients for whom psychological treatment for their difficulties is unwanted and undervalued. These individuals often come to treatment to fulfill a requirement (i.e. anger management class), and upon learning that they have to do more than attend a three-hour class and get a certificate of completion, they opt out. Similarly, despite the best efforts of therapists, for some clients, the suspiciousness and distrust related to the judicial system make it nearly impossible for them to open up in any honest way and work toward their own best interest. In some cases, clients refuse to acknowledge anything about themselves that even remotely suggests the presence of a problem. For others, attendance in treatment is nothing more than a requirement for family members who have insisted that they "give it a try." And, after one or two sessions, they do not return. As previously suggested, therapists can often mitigate these external factors by engaging in the type of direct and open discussion of relevant factors in the early stages of Module 1. While it is difficult to accurately predict which clients will respond in a certain manner, we have found that clients who score above the 90th percentile on the Suspiciousness Subscale of the Anger Disorders Scale are substantially more likely to terminate treatment prematurely, and thus may require a more careful and lengthy consideration of the issues previously discussed.

The second obstacle is internal to CART, and is when therapists do not adequately understand the AAM when conceptualizing clients' reasons for referral. The AAM is not exceptionally complicated, but it is different than traditional cognitive behavioral and other theoretical formulations of clinical anger. If CART is to be used effectively, therapists must make sure that they have a sound grounding in acceptance-based behavioral therapies generally, and the AAM model specifically, before beginning treatment. In training settings, we have seen confused and inconsistent presentations to clients, therefore resulting in poor therapeutic outcomes (often premature termination of treatment) when the theoretical foundation of the AAM is not fully understood by the therapist.

Finally, the delineation of specific personal values can at times be challenging for this clinical population. As noted previously, many clients have never considered this concept, and for those coming from economically deprived environments in which economic and physical survival are daily challenges, the concept of personal values can seem very foreign. Therapists must, however, work slowly and patiently to help clients get in touch with those basic personal values that can ultimately replace moment-to-moment emotions as the primary driving force for behavioral choices.

Module 2: Using the Therapeutic Relationship to Recognize and Modify Clinically Relevant Behavior

Estimated Number of Sessions to Completion: Continuous Attention Throughout Treatment

Goals of Module 2

- The therapist consistently identifies in-session behavior(s) that is directly relevant to the identified out-of-session client problem behavior(s).
- The therapist consistently and appropriately responds to clinically relevant behavior in a manner that provides information to the client and the opportunity to learn new and more appropriate interpersonal behaviors.

Materials Needed for Module 2

- Acceptance and Action Questionnaire-2 (AAQ-2)
- Anger and Violence Impairment Scale (AVIS)
- Valued Living Questionnaire-2 (VLQ-2)

Module 2 should begin with the completion of the AAQ-2, AVIS, and VLQ-2. These measures assess key processes and outcomes inherent in

CART and should be administered before every session and graphed/ tracked consistently throughout the course of treatment.

In a very real sense, Module 2 is a continuation of Module 1, and the goals in Module 2 will continue as important therapeutic foci throughout the subsequent modules of the CART program. Therapists utilizing CART should always be mindful of, and respond to, clients' clinically relevant interpersonal behavior (CRB). As in functional analytic psychotherapy (FAP; Kohlenberg & Tsai, 2007), we define clinically relevant interpersonal behaviors as those in-session behaviors that are similar in content or in function to those behaviors that have been problematic for clients in their general lives. These behaviors may be almost exactly like those described in clients' lives or may be more subtle, having functional similarities while appearing quite different. For instance, a client who has been referred for treatment due to physically aggressive behavior may respond to the therapist with anger, a raised voice, dismissive body language, or sarcasm. Each of these behaviors represents a similar class of behavior and would thus be viewed as clinically relevant. Although not physical, and thus not identical in form to the problem behaviors that are noted in the client's life, these behaviors nevertheless are clinically relevant in that they are still aggressive in class and serve the same function as those behaviors that brought the client to treatment. In essence, these behaviors serve as an effort to get the therapist to stop doing whatever it is that he or she was doing.

A sound, behaviorally oriented interpersonal therapeutic strategy requires the awareness and recognition of these clinically relevant behaviors (even when subtle), the willingness to point out these (noxious) interpersonal behaviors in a direct and immediate manner, and the capacity to recognize and comment on changes in these behaviors to more appropriate positive behaviors later in treatment. This point cannot be stressed more strongly. While we, as clinicians, become competent at noting and responding to problematic behavior, in this interpersonally focused portion of CART, it is important that positive, particularly improved interpersonal behaviors be noted and commented on as well. In FAP, problematic clinically relevant behaviors are called *CRB1s*, and modified, more appropriate interpersonal behaviors are called *CRB2s*. The ability to respond to both CRB1s and CRB2s form the basis of an effective behavioral interpersonal strategy that we have found to be a core component of the effective use of CART.

While we view the recognition and appropriate response to these clinically relevant interpersonal behaviors as a core component of the entire CART process, early focus on this aspect of treatment without the encumbrances of additional goals is particularly important, as in-session client reactions/behaviors regarding issues such as session time/scheduling, cancellations of sessions/session lateness, payment, therapist questions, style, gender, race, etc., typically present themselves very early in treatment and offer the perfect opportunity to respond to clinically relevant behavior manifested by the client. In turn, responding early in treatment to these issues highlights the negative interpersonal outcomes associated with these behaviors, offers the therapist an opportunity to experience what others do in the client's world, and provides an opportunity to begin the process of modifying these behaviors in a structured and systematic manner. An example of one such interaction occurring in the third session of CART is as follows.

T:　[Client arrives 20 minutes late for his session] Bob, since you're 20 minutes late, maybe we should take a moment to review the rules we discussed last week about session times.

C:　[Client raises his voice] Oh jeez, please don't give me a hard time about that . . . shit happens, ya know?

T:　I'm not sure why you are raising your voice. You *are* 20 minutes late, and it seems reasonable to make sure you understand . . .

C:　[Voice raised loudly] I said, get off my back. I don't need this shit today.

T:　Bob, I want us to work together well, I really do, but I have to point out to you that I'm not at all pleased about being yelled at or interrupted. Now look, clearly you have had a rough day, and we can talk about that if you want to, but you need to see that this is nearly exactly the kind of behavior that got you here. You came home, you were late, your wife confronted you about it, you began screaming at her, and when she didn't stop you pushed her and left the house. Now, I know you didn't push me, but here is your difficulty, front and center. And, I need to point it out to you even if it's uncomfortable for both of us.

C:　All right already . . . I get it.

T:　Bob, I'm not trying to be difficult with you, but I have to say that it seems as though you are trying every way you can to make me stop saying things that lead to you being uncomfortable. Now, remember, when we talked about the Anger Avoidance Model, we discussed learning to tolerate the emotion of anger and developing a different pattern of behavior when angry? Well, here it is . . . right in front of us. Let's try a different way to handle stuff.

C:　[Sighs deeply] OK, I'm sorry, I really am. I see your point. Let's try to do this.

In this example, the therapist recognizes in-session behavior that relates directly to the issues that brought the client into treatment, is persistent about pointing them out, and includes comments about her own personal discomfort in having to be so direct. In addition, the therapist points out the function of the client's behavior (escape from angry feelings) in the context or reminding the client of the presentation of the AAM. These types of overt displays of clinically relevant interpersonal behavior can, and will, occur (and should be responded to) anywhere within CART. Yet, it is very common for the first behavioral themes to emerge very early in treatment, and thus, the therapist needs to pay particular attention to such opportunities at the outset of treatment. Of course, this is not always easy for therapists to do. None of us particularly likes confrontation, and none of us likes the discomfort and/or possibly even the anxiety that comes with confronting angry (possibly violent) clients about their behavior. However, ultimately, effective psychological treatment with this population requires therapists to engage in these therapeutic behaviors even if they are uncomfortable. After all, this is what we are trying to get our clients to do more effectively.

We have included this as a CART module not because we believe that behaviorally oriented interpersonal treatment strategies should be isolated in a discreet session or two, but rather, as a means of conveying their overall importance to effective treatment of this population, which in many ways is typified by its sometimes extreme noxious interpersonal behaviors. These behaviors often occur more frequently in the beginning stages of therapy, in which the interpersonal aspects of the therapeutic process are novel. Many stimuli may trigger these behaviors, as noted above, and it is inevitable that therapists will recognize them if they remain mindfully attentive to both client behavior and their own feelings.

It is not uncommon for clients experiencing clinical anger to occasionally engage in noxious behaviors that result in therapists becoming uncomfortable, angry themselves, or even scared. During these instances, therapists must be able to both note their own feeling states, but also connect them appropriately to their clients' behaviors. Additionally, clinicians should be able to express their observations and even personal reactions. What follows is another example in which a therapist makes use of a client's clinically relevant interpersonal behavior.

T: Tell me about the bar fight that led to your arrest.

C: Not much to say, these things happen.

T: Could you tell me what was going through your mind or what you were feeling before the fight happened?

C: Let me ask you something . . . why do you ask me such stupid questions?

T: You know Jen, I don't understand, why would you want to say something that you know will either make me angry or uncomfortable? Why do you think you would want that?

C: What are you talking about?

T: Well, it seems to me that you may think that if you say something that will make me uncomfortable or get me angry, then maybe I'll stop asking you stuff that you don't want to deal with. Which, by the way sounds exactly like what you told me your husband says to you. Remember? You told me that he said that when you don't want to deal with something important, you pick an argument.

C: Gotta hand it to ya doc, you got me I guess. I don't set out to do that, but I have been told that over and over again.

T: Think about it a minute, what does it get you?

C: You're right, I don't deal with stuff that makes me angry.

T: So in order to not feel angry, you act in these ways that lead you to get aggressive with people . . . In these moments, the things that matter to you, like your family and your freedom, are less important than not feeling bad for a while.

Once again, in this example, the therapist had to deal with an awkward moment, be completely direct and honest about how she felt, and connect the client's behavior in the session to out-of-session problems and patterns in the client's life. What may often be neglected is behavior that is markedly different than either previous in-session behavior, or behavior previously noted as part of the client's problematic behavior. For example, what follows is an interaction later in treatment with the same female client from the previous example.

T: Jen, tell me how you were feeling just before you walked out of the restaurant, leaving your husband sitting at the table alone.

C: I was hoping we wouldn't have to stay on that. OK, well, I'm angry even thinking about it, and I was furious at him for choosing that moment to tell me about his problems at work. He knew the day I was having and just did it anyway. I was pissed!

T: Let me just stop you for a minute. You know, I'm really impressed. Just a few weeks ago, you did everything you could to get me to not have you talk about your anger, and today, you are just talking about it. You look really miserable [laughs], but you aren't running away or trying to drive me away from having you talk about it. That's great.

C: [Long pause] Thanks. I'm not sure what to say. I hate feeling this way, but I guess it is better, huh? And, very different for me.

T: Yes, it is better, and different. Now let's work on extending that to situations at home.

This example accentuates the need for the therapist to not only recognize and respond to problematic clinically relevant interpersonal behaviors (CRB1s), but also the more adaptive positive clinically relevant behaviors (CRB2s).

At this point, the therapist is ready to begin the modules of CART that focus specifically on those psychological processes that are central to the AAM.

Obstacles Often Encountered in Module 2

The most frequent obstacle encountered by therapists in Module 2 is related to their own lack of mindful awareness. An interpersonal focus of treatment requires that therapists be adept at recognizing client behavior as it is happening, and have the clinical skill to recognize the similarities between in-session behaviors and problematic behaviors in life. In addition, it requires that therapists have the personal capacity to be aware of their own reactions and in turn be able to differentiate between reactions that are appropriate as a response to client behavior, and reactions that are not objectively related to client behavior. Therapists must remain vigilant to not engage in behaviors that are a function of their own personal history and interpersonal relationships. While this is true for any therapist working with any type of client, clients referred for anger treatment pose some very specific challenges, in that their interpersonal patterns of behavior are often aggressive, oppositional, and generally noxious. Therapists must be willing to regularly check their own personal reactions to assure that they: (a) are reacting to behavior that the majority of people would react to in a similar manner, and not simply responding to stimulus functions of clients that elicit personal and possibly idiosyncratic responses; and (b) can appropriately use their own reactions in a positive therapeutic manner. In this regard, therapists need to represent a model for appropriate experience and expression of emotion, including anger, and serve as a vehicle for new interpersonal client learning to occur.

Module 3: Developing Mindful Emotion Awareness

Estimated Number of Sessions to Completion: 4

Goals of Module 3

- Increase non-judging, present moment awareness of emotional experiences including cognitions, subjective feelings, bodily responses/ sensations, and related behavioral action tendencies associated with those experiences.
- Increase non-judging, present moment attention to both internal experiences and external stimuli (both appetitive and aversive).
- Increase the client's understanding that internal experiences such as cognitions, feelings, and bodily sensations are transient events that are both informative and passing.

Materials Needed for Module 3

- Acceptance and Action Questionnaire-2 (AAQ-2)
- Anger and Violence Impairment Scale (AVIS)

- Valued Living Questionnaire-2 (VLQ-2)
- Mindful Attention and Awareness Scale (MAAS)
- Between-Session Emotion Monitoring Form

The core feature of this essential module is the beginning of a process, which will continue for the rest of the CART program and beyond, in which clients become more comfortable with having, observing non-judgmentally, and remaining in contact, with their internal emotional experience (particularly anger) including thoughts, sensations, and subjective feelings, without efforts at avoidance or escape. This in turn sets the stage for the later enhancement of proactive values-driven behavior in place of reactive emotion-driven (avoidance) behavior, an outcome that is central to the positive clinical outcomes found in CART. In addition to being directly connected to the theoretical foundations of the AAM, the development of greater mindful emotion awareness has been associated with reductions in ruminative thoughts (Chambers, Gullone, & Allen, 2009) as well as reductions in intense emotional experiences and related impulsive behavior (Linehan, 1993).

Following the administration of the AAQ-2, AVIS, VLQ-2, and the MAAS (a brief measure of mindful awareness previously described in Chapter 3, which is now added to the weekly assessment packet) for the purpose of ongoing assessment of targeted psychological processes, Module 3 begins with education about emotion, including its features (thoughts, physical sensations/subjective feelings, and behavioral action tendencies), its adaptive value (providing information and readying us for effective action), and its occasional maladaptive outcomes, noted earlier. It has been our experience that most clients referred for problems associated with clinical anger have never considered emotions, particularly anger, to have any positive value. In fact, they have often been told (and often reinforced by society and mandating entities) that anger is bad and needs to be minimized and/or controlled in some way. As such, this conversation is of vast importance. Yet, it is also frequently challenging. What follows is an example of a session segment in which a therapist presents and discusses the adaptive aspects of anger with a client.

T: We are all taught that anger is somehow a bad emotion and that it is responsible for all the arguments and fights we get in trouble for. But, the reality is that anger, just like fear, is a normal response to possible danger. Anger is a natural response to potential danger such as maltreatment or victimization, as well. Everyone gets angry . . . it's not possible to avoid this or any other emotion.

C: Normal? My anger is anything but normal.

T: You're referring to the things you *do* when angry, or how bad it feels to you, but before we talk about the different components of anger, let's make sure we understand the value of anger.

C: I can't even imagine that there is any value to it.

T: I understand that given your history and what you've been taught, but let's take a look for a minute. The healthy or normal part of anger is that it does signal the need to prepare to defend ourselves from threat. Now, just like fear can become anxiety when the expectation of danger is exaggerated or misinterpreted, anger can become excessive when we exaggerate the possibility of maltreatment. And, like we discussed a few sessions ago, your history makes it understandable that you would scan the world for signs of maltreatment.

C: It sure has.

T: Exactly, but we can't and really even shouldn't make it go away. Remember when you told me about the huge mistake in the phone bill you got in the mail, and the anger you felt?

C: Yea, I thought I was going to lose my mind.

T: Yes, your reaction was intense, but putting that aside for a moment, the anger really had a positive value. It signaled to you that you were wronged and needed to do something about it. The problem is, rather than viewing anger as a helpful although uncomfortable emotion, you have learned that anger *itself* is dangerous and threatening, so whenever you feel it, you immediately go into self-protect mode and try to immediately do something . . . anything, to make it go away. Actually, because of that, you can't even get the benefits of the emotion, and end up causing secondary problems due to the behavior that is part of your experience of anger.

C: Wow . . . I have to think about that. I can't say that your wrong, but it is a completely different way of looking at things. Jeez. You're telling me anger can be helpful . . . [Laughs], I'm not sure what to say.

T: You don't have to say anything. Just think about it and we'll come back to this idea frequently.

Completing the Between-Session Emotion Monitoring Form (in-session) with the client at this point in the module is particularly useful (see Appendix 5.2). Completing this form with the client, using the most recent situation in the client's life that evoked anger, is a good way to accelerate emotion understanding and primes the client to successfully complete the form on his or her own between treatment sessions. On the Between-Session Emotion Monitoring Form, the client is simply asked to record the person, place, or event that served as the trigger for anger, and then record the Cognitive ("what I'm thinking"), Physical/Subjective ("what I'm feeling/how my body is reacting"), and Behavioral ("what I'm doing before, during, or after I get angry") components of the anger experience, consistent with the previous education about the three components of emotion. What follows is an example of the use of this form as a means of promoting education about emotion in general, and anger in particular, with the same client used in the previous example. The completed form can be seen in Table 5.2.

Table 5.2 Between-Session Emotion Monitoring Form (Case Example)

Triggering Situation (Person, Place, Event):
"Received incorrect phone bill"

What I was thinking?
"What are they trying to pull? Do they think I'm stupid? Do they think I'll just pay for this?"

What I was feeling?
"Angry," "furious," "enraged"

How was my body reacting?
"Face became red, fists tightened, breathing changed"

What did I do when I was experiencing this emotion?
"Crumpled and threw the bill, yelled out loud, walked out of the house, then called the company and screamed at the person who answered"

T: So let's complete this form I have here to organize your understanding of anger. We call it the Between-Session Emotion Monitoring Form, and let's use the situation we talked about earlier to show you how to use it.

C: You mean the phone bill situation? Sure.

T: OK, so the top line here asks you to write down the situation that was the trigger for your anger.

C: Well . . . I opened my phone bill and saw a $5,500 bill, when my bill is almost always around $70. I just flipped. I became furious.

T: Let's look at that in detail . . . can you tell me what was going through your mind? And let's put that in the next line, where it says, "What I was thinking."

C: Yea, I can remember thinking, "What are they trying to pull? Do they think I'm stupid? That I'll just pay it?"

T: All right, now, let's write that onto the "thinking" line. OK, now can you tell me what you were feeling? Both what you felt and where you felt it?

C: Yea, I felt flushed and I'm sure my face got red. I was so mad that I crumpled the bill and threw it across the room.

T: Let's hold off on what you did for a minute. So you felt flushed and you said that you were mad, can you describe that to me?

C: My breathing changes I think, I know I clench my fists, and I know I feel this rage inside me that makes me feel like I'm going to explode.

T: So, you are saying that you can feel it physically; body temperature, breathing, muscle tension in your hands, and you have this intense feeling of anger, which you call being mad, being furious, is that right?

C: Yup, that's exactly it, and I can feel a little of that now just thinking about it.

T: I can see you're moving around in your chair a lot. It's obvious that this emotion is distressing for you. Let's fill out the next line, the "feelings" line on your form while you are feeling these things right now. Just write down what you just told me.

C: [Client fills in appropriate line] I see the next line on the form is about what I do. Well, in this case, like I said before, I crumpled the bill and threw it, and I think I yelled out loud while I did it.

T: OK, write that in there, and tell me what you did after that.

C: [Laughs] Actually, I walked out of the house, I wanted to just get away, but before I reached my car, I decided to walk back in and call the company.

T: Then what?

C: Unfortunately, I called the phone company and screamed at some woman who answered the phone.

T: Write that down as well. So, how did the yelling thing work out?

C: She hung up on me [laughs]. My wife had to call the next day to straighten it out, and it was just a simple mistake that took 5 minutes to correct.

T: Is there anything else I should know about what you did?

C: That's about it. Pretty embarrassing and it got me nowhere. That's when my wife insisted that I get some help for this. It's typical of me.

T: Like we've talked about before, anger can have some positive value, but in this case, it sounds like you reacted pretty intensely and automatically. Let's take a look at what you wrote down. As you can see, your anger had three very clear components. First, you thought about the bill in a very specific way, like it was purposeful and personal; you experienced physical arousal, flushing, muscle tension, breathing changes, and subjective feelings of intense anger; and the automatic action associated with your anger, we call that an action tendency, was indirect aggression, throwing an object, and verbal aggression, yelling at someone you didn't even know over the phone. Each of those three parts is part of your experience of anger. Now, like we discussed, this treatment will help you separate these three components of anger, respond to your thoughts and feelings differently, and ultimately change your action tendency, you know your behavior, to something more consistent with your goals and values in life.

Following its introduction to the client, a review of the Between-Session Emotion Monitoring Form should occur at the beginning of each session of this module and is used as a means of connecting sessions together and also as a means of detecting the presence or absence of relevant skill development. In fact, this form is included throughout the CART program, as it provides an ongoing vehicle for client self-monitoring and information that both the client and therapist can use to evaluate skill development. In this regard, it is important that therapists begin sessions with a review of this form or a discussion of why the form was not completed, and not with standard introductory lines such as, "How was your week?" While this question may in and of itself be interesting, it tends to allow the client to utilize each session as a week-to-week problem-solving enterprise, and to avoid the more difficult skills building work inherent in CART.

Module 3 then moves on to providing education about the importance of being mindful (i.e. aware) of our emotional experiences. This education includes what emotion awareness/mindfulness is, how it relates to the problems that have brought the client to treatment (i.e. how it fits into to the AAM presented earlier), and how developing greater mindful emotion awareness may be helpful to the client in the future. In this discussion, the therapist should contrast mindful emotional experience with mindless emotional experience, in which emotions, and all the related components including overt behavior, occur in an automatic and seemingly unconscious manner. It's hopefully clear how this conversation would easily and naturally follow from the example provided above, as noted in the following therapist–client segment.

C: How do I do this? Honestly it seems kind of hopeless. I've been this way for as long as I can remember.

T: It will take some time, but it can be done. Let's talk about the next step. Like I pointed out, the whole process was very automatic for you, and the first thing we need to do is slow it down and help you become mindful of what you are thinking and feeling so that you have some choices in your actions.

C: I can see that. But how do I do that?

T: We need to help you to develop a greater awareness of what you are thinking and feeling *while* it's happening. We might describe that as "being present," in a way that your mind and your body are in the same place at the same time, as opposed to your body being in one place and your head being somewhere different. Now, you can tell me about your experiences *after the fact*, but *in the moment*, probably not so much.

C: [Laughs] That's very true. Sometimes I wouldn't be able to tell you afterward, everything seems like a blur.

T: OK, so that's where we start. We have some exercises that we can practice together, and then you can practice at home, that if you commit to practicing them daily, will help you develop this skill. Research tells us it works, but it will take time. These exercises are called mindfulness exercises, and they are a form of meditation. Not to help you relax, but to help you become more aware of thoughts, feelings, and sensations as you're experiencing them.

As can be deduced from this interchange, emotion awareness training evolves naturally to an introduction to mindfulness enhancing exercises, followed by the completion of a series of such exercises. It begins with simple exercises focusing first on external stimuli, then moves on to simple breathing, and ultimately moves on to more elaborate mindfulness exercises such as the "mindfulness of the breath" exercise. Our own personal iterations of these exercises are provided in Appendices 5.3, 5.4, 5.5, and 5.6. We suggest introducing the "washing a dish" exercise first (see Appendix 5.3), in the next session introducing the "centering" exercise (see Appendix 5.4), and in the next session introducing the longer and somewhat more complex "mindfulness of the breath" exercise (see Appendix 5.5). Self-compassion meditation (see Appendix 5.6) should be introduced as the final mindfulness exercise. These exercises are intended to achieve a variety of objectives: (a) clients first develop the capacity to notice events, thoughts, and emotions in-the-moment (as they occur); (b) clients increasingly develop the capacity to slow themselves down, which over time helps them disengage from previous automatic emotion-driven behavior; (c) clients learn to non-judgmentally observe and increasingly enhance awareness of their emotional experiences; (d) clients develop the capacity to remain in contact with previously uncomfortable internal experiences (thoughts, physical sensations, subjective feelings); and (e) clients learn to focus attention onto moment-to-moment relevant tasks and objectives rather than ruminative cognitive processes.

A critical outcome of this module is this decentered stance with regard to experienced emotion, including the non-judgment and tolerance of emotions, and anger in particular. Importantly, clients referred for clinical anger frequently not only view anger as "bad," but view themselves as "bad" and/or deficient for even experiencing anger and other intense emotion. This can even include intense positive emotions such as joy and love. As such, non-judging mindful self-awareness, and ultimately mindful self-compassion, is critical in order to develop the capacity to reduce negative judgments about emotion; develop a greater capacity to experience emotions without the need to escape in some way; and develop a greater overall understanding of the normal and unavoidable place that the experience of emotion has in the lives of human beings.

Following the introduction of the externally based mindfulness exercise, which could include a piece of fruit in-session, and the "washing a dish" exercise between sessions, it is helpful to briefly discuss the client's experience of the exercise, and by doing so, reinforce effort, normalize the difficulties often experienced by clients trying to begin this process, and correct any misconceptions that may arise. An example of such a discussion following a first time, in-session practice of the "mindfulness of the breath" exercise is presented below.

T: So, tell me about your experience with that exercise.

C: I'm not sure. I was able to do it for the most part, but my mind constantly wandered, so it felt like I was constantly screwing up. I felt kind of stupid doing it.

T: That is a completely normal reaction. That was how I felt and just about everyone else felt whom I've ever worked with. Actually, that is the way the human brain works . . . we tend to think about many things at the same time, and we often aren't comfortable with something new. You're likely never going to stop having a variety of thoughts pop in and out of your mind. Remember, it's a new skill you are learning. That's exactly why we do this, to help you develop the ability to notice when your mind drifts, not get angry or frustrated with yourself, but see the struggle as a normal and natural thing. Notice where your mind is drifting to, and then gently bring your attention back to the task at hand. Sometimes it will seem easy and sometimes it will be a struggle. But over time you will get better and better at it, and this will help you become more mindful of the thoughts and emotions that you are having at any given moment without having to do anything about them. Just notice them and move on.

C: I don't know if I could ever do that.

T: I think you just might be able to. Let's give it a try and see.

Clients often have difficulty beginning mindfulness training with exercises that are internally focused, such as centered breathing. This may occur for a variety of reasons, many of which are related to difficulties with letting down their guard, having over-learned avoidance of internal experiences, and/or not fully understanding the point of the exercises. It is for this reason that we have found it most helpful to begin the mindfulness development process with an in-session sitting mindfulness exercise in which clients are asked to hold an (external) object and describe to the therapist the physical, visual, and other sensory properties of the object in some detail. We suggest using an object that is common but not usually carefully thought about, such as a baseball, a wallet, an apple, etc. Following such an in-session exercise, clients would then be asked to engage in the "washing a dish" exercise described in Appendix 5.3 prior to the next session. At that point, and following a full discussion of their experience with the exercise, clients will usually be ready to begin the internally focused mindfulness exercises described in Appendices 5.4, 5.5, and 5.6.

At this point, we would like to offer some comment about self-compassion and compassion-focused mindfulness training in CART (see Appendix 5.6 for a compassion-focused mindfulness exercise). Neff (2003) has suggested that self-compassion involves mindful awareness, self-kindness, and an awareness of our common humanity. Working with populations experiencing significant clinical anger has suggested to us that all three of these components of self-compassion are very often missing in our patients. Clients often enter treatment with little, if any, history of manifesting compassionate feelings toward either themselves or others. Given these clinical observations, and in keeping with the empirical data suggesting the strong positive relationship between self-compassion and a wide array of positive psychological outcomes such as increased positive affect, social connection, and life satisfaction (Neff, Kirkpatrick, & Rude, 2007; Neff, Rude, & Kirkpatrick, 2007), compassion-focused mindfulness training is included in the CART protocol. Many clients respond as well, if not better, to compassion-focused mindfulness training than any other single aspect of this treatment. Perusal of the exercise presented in Appendix 5.6 should clarify the purpose of self- and other-compassion, which is essentially to enhance the client's capacity to experience and express positive emotions about themselves and others.

This should be the last of the mindfulness exercises, and functions as a form of "opposite action" experience, as clients are asked to respond to themselves and others in a manner very much unlike their usual day to day responses. This therefore acts to promote a very new and powerful learning experience. This exercise is likely to prompt a good deal of interesting reaction/discussion, and therapists must be sure to be encouraging and supportive of this process. For most clients, allowing space for this type of emotion is very foreign to them, and it is typically first experienced as difficult, then interesting, and finally as quite calming.

The development of enhanced mindful emotion awareness is such an important piece of the CART program, as by its very nature, mindful emotion awareness promotes the full experiencing of anger and related cognitive, affective, and physiological processes; disrupts both the cognitive and behavioral avoidance/escape process; and thus, directly targets the primary core pathological process of clinical anger suggested by the AAM. As such, it is important that therapists require both in-session and between-session practice. Clients should be asked to practice these exercises on a daily basis (or as much as realistically possible), and each subsequent CART session should begin with a discussion of the successes and difficulties with performing these exercises between sessions, and should then include an in-session mindfulness exercise. For some clients, a record of their efforts is useful, particularly those clients who appear to struggle with the exercises. In this regard, Appendix 5.7 provides a self-monitoring form, which we have called the Mindfulness Record Form. We encourage use of this form with clients who might benefit from between-session recording of their efforts.

Before we discuss the obstacles that may arise during this module, we would like to provide a couple of final points that we think are of significance. The first is that following completion of the mindful emotion awareness module, the therapist should still either begin or end each subsequent session with a mindfulness exercise, regardless of the module being worked on. Second, therapists must insure that the concepts of mindful emotion awareness are well understood, and that regular mindfulness practice is being conducted. This module is such a foundational component of CART, and therapists are cautioned that moving to the next module should absolutely *not* occur until this process is clearly under way. While we generally suggest a four-session time frame for Module 3 to be fully engaged, please note that this time frame is a best-case scenario, and that many clients require additional sessions before moving onto the next module. Further, the process of mindful emotion awareness should be seen as spanning the entire CART program, and therefore, continued practice and monitoring of mindful emotion awareness should be followed throughout.

Obstacles Often Encountered in Module 3

There are several obstacles that may be encountered in the course of Module 3. The first relates to the therapist's lack of full understanding of and/or personal commitment to the concept of mindfulness and emotion awareness. This module requires that the therapist understand that mindfulness exercises are *not* intended to promote relaxation (and with it, in many cases avoidance), but rather, a greater capacity to experience the present moment, including a variety of thoughts, sensations, and feelings that may in fact be uncomfortable. In addition, this module, and in fact the entire CART treatment process, requires therapists to be comfortable with, or at least tolerant of their clients' negative emotions, particularly anger; and even their own emotional experiences. Some therapists are themselves uncomfortable with anger and/or are afraid of having their clients become angry. This therefore can lead them to subtly avoid or sabotage efforts to promote their clients' mindful emotion awareness.

Similarly, it is critical that mindfulness and emotion awareness be presented in the correct manner to the client; that is, promoting the idea that the willingness to have/experience anger is a key component of ultimately changing problematic behavior. This is a concept that is antithetical to what most clinically angry clients have been taught to believe. If this concept is not accurately and consistently conveyed, and/or therapists cannot personally tolerate their own emotions or their clients' anger, CART is likely to be ineffective. Specifically, with regard to Module 3, therapists must ensure that clients understand that mindfulness exercises are not intended to promote a relaxed state, but instead, the goal is enhanced non-judging awareness of internal events, including the wide array of thoughts and emotions, both "positive" and "negative," that are part of the human experience.

Additionally, therapists who do not personally engage in mindfulness practice often cannot adequately understand or speak to the struggles, frustrations, and "normal" experiences of those trying to learn this skill.

Therapists not personally engaged in and/or fully understanding of the purpose of the inclusion of mindfulness training in clinical protocols tend to rush through or lack the patient persistence to follow through and ensure that the client adequately develops mindfulness skills. We therefore strongly suggest that as part of engaging in the CART model of treatment, therapists engage in their own personal use of mindfulness meditative exercises.

Another obstacle often seen in the course of Module 3 relates to a lack of client engagement and/or follow-through with between-session exercises. Of course, this requires the therapist to carefully review the use of between-session mindfulness exercises with the client at the start of each session. While non-compliance is a potential issue across all CART modules, it is particularly poignant here, as the regular practice of mindfulness and work at developing enhanced emotion awareness are core foundations upon which all subsequent components of CART are built. It is *strongly* recommended that therapists *not* move on to Module 4 until they can see tangible ongoing between-session practice and engagement with regards to mindfulness practice, specifically, and emotion awareness training, generally. If these between-session exercises are not performed, it is essential that the reasons for this be explored and discussed. The most typically stated reason is lack of time, but in fact, the most typical *actual* reasons for non-completion are lack of treatment engagement/interest, lack of understanding (i.e. the purpose of the exercises), and/or an unwillingness to do it "wrong" and "look bad" in the eyes of the therapist. It is helpful to remember that most clients referred for clinical anger have had an early aversive history in which they were often mistreated, resulting in a life strategy in which they excessively scan their environment for possible physical *and* psychological danger. Thus, the thought of possibly making errors in the course of attempting these exercises, and in turn possibly looking bad in the eyes of a therapist, will be construed by many clients as psychological danger. This will sometimes be manifested by the client as overtly expressed anger when confronted about not completing between-session exercises. Angry clients have typically learned to rapidly and automatically respond to perceptions of personal vulnerability and/or anxiety with anger, and in turn, with avoidant behavior. Therapists therefore must patiently convey their understanding of such client (typically unexpressed) concerns, gently encourage and positively reinforce effort, and use this as an opportunity for new interpersonal learning (i.e. the therapist is not a punitive judging parent/authority figure, and making mistakes does not automatically result in an aversive outcome).

Often, using additional sessions to complete these assignments in-session as a means of promoting between-session exercise completion will be necessary. In such cases, therapists are cautioned to abandon the idea that this module will be completed in four sessions. Instead, they could use the flexibility built into the CART model, and take as much time as is necessary to achieve the necessary goals of Module 3 before moving on to Module 4. We have found it helpful to present the development of this skill as analogous to the development of physical strength. In the beginning of any exercise plan, it is often difficult to get started, and easy to feel overwhelmed and find reasons to avoid putting out full effort. One can expect to be sore sometimes, and progress can be expected to be slow. Yet, regular effort almost always pays off. This analogy helps normalize the experience of beginning mindfulness practice and makes the point that consistent effort results in long-term gain.

The final obstacle of Module 3 reflects the fact that some clients may find it particularly difficult to direct compassion toward either themselves or others. Due to the early aversive histories inherent in this clinical population, and the associated attachment difficulties that have ensued as a result, positive emotions toward the self or others are often responded to as discriminative stimuli signaling possible danger (and thus triggering avoidance behavior). In such cases, these exercises may be difficult for the client, and will either be avoided, minimized, or even responded to with defensive aggression (loud verbal responses, body posturing, etc.). As was done during Module 1, therapists must patiently provide the developmental reasons for the reaction, share the importance of engaging in such exercises, and gently persist and help clients find their way to try this very new and important experience. For example, therapists may help clients view their immediate reactions to the exercise as understandable due to their past experiences, and encourage clients to see what comes next, after those thoughts pass. The following vignette provides just such an example.

T: Tell me what your experience was in doing this exercise just now.

C: Well, actually, it was difficult.

T: What do you mean by difficult?

C: It was very hard to see myself in this compassionate and kind way. I don't know, but seeing myself that way, and trying to see people in my world in that way, felt kind of strange, almost embarrassing.

T: Tell me what you mean by embarrassing. In what way was it embarrassing?

C: It's just not me . . . it felt weak. Like I was telling the world I am a pushover. I don't know.

T: Sounds like this exercise was feeling threatening to you. Like somehow you were making yourself vulnerable in some way.

C: Yea, exactly.

T: What would come next? If you just noticed feeling uncomfortable . . . and we have talked about where that comes from . . . then just stick with the exercise, notice the feelings and just let them pass, and just see what comes afterward. Maybe being compassionate with yourself and others can coexist, and you can find a place to be vigilant when you need to be and compassionate when you want to be.

C: I can try that. There is something interesting about the possibility of letting go of some of this stuff I walk around with all the time, and letting myself feel positive about myself once in awhile.

T: And maybe others too?

C: [Laughs] Yea, well, that too I guess. One step at a time.

This vignette demonstrates the obstacles and the process necessary to advance compassion-focused mindfulness training. We stress the significant benefit this mindfulness exercise and its variants can have in working with this population (such as a "loving kindness letter" written to themselves expressing positive emotions toward oneself, used as either a between-session exercise or an in-session exercise); and, we encourage therapists to stay with the process even in the face of the strong resistance that they may encounter.

Module 4: Cognitive Defusion and the Reduction of Problematic Rule-Governed Behavior

Estimated Number of Sessions to Completion: 2–3

Goals of Module 4

- The client gains an understanding of the concept of cognitive fusion and its relationship to problematic behavioral patterns.
- Enhanced client awareness of relevant internal rules (schemas) and their associated automatic (fused) behaviors.
- The client begins to defuse those rules and behaviors through the process of decentering from anger-related cognitions.

Materials Needed for Module 4

- Acceptance and Action Questionnaire-2 (AAQ-2)
- Anger and Violence Impairment Scale (AVIS)
- Valued Living Questionnaire-2 (VLQ-2)
- Mindful Attention and Awareness Scale (MAAS)
- Between-Session Emotion Monitoring Form

In Module 4, the therapist presents the concept of cognitive fusion/defusion. Cognitive fusion can be described as the tendency to react to what we think as if our thoughts are absolute truths that *must* be responded to in some way. In a sense, it would be as if we are "fused" with our thoughts. However, in actuality, thoughts and events are not the same, even though we often learn over time to react to our thoughts *about* an event as though they are equivalent to the event itself. For example, the thought, "this guy is disrespecting me, I can't work for him," is vastly different than the thought "OK, my mind is telling me that this guy is disrespecting me and that I can't work for him." In the first statement, the thought is made as an absolute statement of fact, as if it reflects some higher truth that inevitably must be responded to. On the other hand, the second statement can be viewed as simply a thought, which might be coming from a place other than fact. It is merely one of many thoughts that occur over the course of a day.

Another important distinction for therapists to help clients make is the difference between using the words "but" vs "and" as a sentence modifier. For example, the phrase, "I want to do the right thing at work to keep my job, *but* he pisses me off," suggests something very different than, "I want to do the right thing at work to keep my job, *and*, he pisses me off." The former statement suggests that the right thing to do cannot occur because of one's anger or perception of wrongdoing, while the latter suggests that the two can coexist simultaneously. This linguistic distinction is quite helpful to clients, and allows them to "defuse" automatic and immediate problematic behavior from these thoughts.

Teaching clients to regularly and consistently view their thoughts as a reflection of what their mind is telling them, as opposed to viewing their thoughts as absolute realities that must be immediately acted upon, further enhances their capacity to develop a decentered perspective about their internal experience (a treatment goal that began as part of mindfulness training in Module 3). The ongoing development of mindfulness is the foundation for the individual's capacity to defuse/decenter from his or her thought processes at this point in treatment.

Clients may struggle with idea that they do not need to control or eliminate certain thoughts (or emotions for that matter). In fact, nearly all clients find the idea that there is no such thing as a "good" or "bad" thought (or emotion) challenging to grasp. Therapists must therefore patiently discuss the impossibility of controlling or eliminating thoughts, and should remind clients that thoughts of all kinds will come and go in all of our minds. Thus, a more realistic goal is to develop enhanced awareness of these thoughts and the ability to distance ourselves from them so that they exert less automatic control over our behavior. In time, clients will most often come to understand this concept. Actually, they eventually experience a sense of relief, as all previous efforts to control or eliminate thoughts have been unsuccessful. This discussion is also a great opportunity to restate the importance of continued mindfulness practice.

Herein, clients are also helped to see that thoughts also take the form of personal rules, which are linguistic representations of clients' own personal learning histories. For example, if clients have had harsh negative experiences with emotionally and/or physically aggressive significant figures in their lives, they may have developed strongly held rules about mistreatment. These rules may look something like, "If I get close to people, I'll eventually get mistreated." As previously noted, these internal rules are often referred to as schemas (Young *et al.*, 2003), and they can direct our actions in seemingly repetitive and automatic ways. So, when put into a new situation that involves becoming even marginally close to someone that has even the remotest (real or perceived) aggressive characteristics, like someone from earlier in a client's history, the client may respond to that person based upon his or her rule (rather than the context of the immediate situation), and may subsequently act in an avoidant, highly defensive, or even aggressive manner as a means of self-protection. Therapists need to remember the ultimate function of the behaviors that follow from these rules. Specifically, these rules, and the avoidant or anxious adult attachment styles that are associated with them, are essentially self-protective in nature, and develop as a means of controlling or limiting the experience of (anticipated) negative affect. It is not uncommon for these "rules" to become the focus of discussion at the end of Module 3 when the client engages in compassion-focused mindfulness exercises, as the issues that will often make these compassion-focused exercises difficult are in fact the triggering of such rules. Therapists may use the previous examples brought up in the context of compassion work as a starting point for the discussion of the internal rules and the behaviors with which they are automatically associated. In this regard, it should become more obvious to clients why the self-compassion exercises may be difficult, and how their use may help to promote a different interpersonal style.

While it is important to express an empathic understanding as to how and why these internal rules developed (based on the client's own previously reported history), it is also important to gently point out that the consequences of the behaviors associated with these rules are more often than not quite problematic. The rules, and the automatic (over-learned or fused) behaviors associated with them, generalize to many situations in which the predicted harm is not likely to be forthcoming. For many clients, especially those living in poor, socioeconomically deprived, and dangerous environments, there is often some reality to their continuing concerns of personal safety and possible harm. In such cases, therapists must acknowledge the realities of such clients' lives, while simultaneously helping them develop appropriate stimulus discrimination by promoting an enhanced capacity to distinguish between truly dangerous and less dangerous situations. The ability to distinguish between thought-as-fact vs thought-as-what-my-mind-is-telling-me is of great importance, as it allows clients to slow down their thought-action fusion and allocate greater consideration to threat distinctions and focus attention on more prosocial values-driven choices that are available to them in any given situation. In essence, in Module 4, clients develop the capacity to distinguish between what *is* and what the mind *tells them.* We encourage therapists to ask clients to discuss several examples from their lives that reflect this concept, as we have found that these personal example presentations truly begin the process of cognitive defusion in which clients can create a distance between the content or meaning of words and the believability or absolute correctness of those words.

This is also true with words or phrases that are self-descriptive. For example, clients may tell us that they are "headstrong," "tough," or "never tolerate disrespect." At these times, it useful to use an in-session technique in which clients are asked to make a list of five words or phrases that they believe describe them best. They are then asked to cross one out (by randomly choosing a number from 1 to 5), and are asked, "If that word is not used to describe you, would it still be you?" This is repeated until there are no remaining words. Clients will usually come to see that they, as people, remain as is, even if these descriptions are no longer present. That is, as human beings, they are more than any one word or description, and that one word or phrase can *never* describe them in all situations. In essence, we as human beings change our behavior as situations dictate, and thus "what we are" at any given moment in time is based on the situation at hand. On occasion, clients will become adamant that they would no longer be who they are without a given characteristic. This clearly notes a very specific problem with cognitive fusion, as there are likely to be very rigid automatic behaviors associated with that characteristic. Obviously, this creates an important therapeutic moment. The concept of helping clients become aware that no word or description describes "them" all the time, but rather, that they are what situations require them to be, is equivalent to Hayes and colleagues' (1999) concept of "self-as-context." This is an important area to be addressed with this clinical population, who tend to have extremely rigid ideas about what they are and what they must be.

Another cognitive defusion exercise has been described by Hayes, Strosahl, and Wilson (1999) as the "milk exercise." In a variant of this exercise, clients are asked to think about the word *milk*, and all of the characteristics associated with that word. Then, clients are asked to repeat the word *milk* out loud as rapidly as possible for 30 or more seconds. When that time period is up, therapists ask clients what the word means to them at that exact moment. The usual answer is, "nothing," as the word has just become a sound after the excessive repetition. Therapists then do that same thing with a word like *disrespect*, following the exact same procedure. We have asked clients who have a difficult time with the concept of disrespect to do this exercise once a day for three to four days between sessions. The typical result is that the word is noticed more readily when thought about; and the exercise changes the stimulus function of the word to some degree so that it no longer has quite the same meaning to the client. We propose that this is part of the reason for effectiveness of traditional Rational Emotive Behavior Therapy (Ellis, 1966), in its repetitive focus on key strongly held words and phrases such as *should, must, awful,* and *can't stand.* In our view, REBT does not reduce the frequency of these words in the client's thought process, as much as it lessens the power that the words have over behavior. In essence, we suggest that when effective, REBT defuses/decenters clients from the automatic and behavior-driving function of such words.

In working with aggressive populations, the internal rule/thought process associated with what often appears to be automatic aggressive behavior (as a means of avoiding or escaping negative affect), frequently involves the issue of (dis)respect or closely related concepts/words. The following vignette provides an example of cognitive defusion with "disrespect" as a primary issue of clinical attention.

T: Why don't you tell me what happened with your Probation Officer this week?

C: I got to her office 15 minutes late . . . traffic was really bad . . . and then she came out and gave me an attitude, really disrespectful, you know? And then, she kept me waiting on purpose for another hour. No way I'm taking that kind of crap from anyone.

T: Tell me how she gave you an attitude? And what was disrespectful about it?

C: She just gave me a dirty look.

T: What made it a dirty look?

C: Come on man, you know what that looks like. Why else would she have been so late?

T: Lots of looks can mean lots of things to different people. And, you've told me before she's real busy all the time. Did you expect her to give you a hard time?

C: Well, yea, I was late.

T: I know from what we have talked about several weeks ago, you were frequently treated quite badly, even when not deserved, when you were younger, so you learned to expect some pretty harsh treatment. I know that you still expect people to treat you that way, so I wonder if you really got an "attitude" from your PO, or your mind was just telling you that you were, based on your history?

C: She gave me an attitude . . . I guess . . . but, I don't know . . . it was just a look, so, umm, I don't know.

T: That's OK, just something we need to consider and work on; noticing the difference, or at least considering the difference, between what our mind tells you vs what may really be happening. Let's say the PO did look at you. That is probably a fact. What it means? Whether or not it was disrespectful? That's your mind talking to you based on the rules that you have about people.

C: What do you mean?

T: Well, your history suggests that you have developed an unspoken rule, something like, "People are going to hurt or take advantage of me, so I have to be on guard all the time." When something happens, whether real or just in your mind, that triggers this rule, you think about being disrespected, and you get pretty angry and aggressive . . . just like you did with your ex-girlfriend, when you interpreted her behavior as disrespectful.

C: People *do* hurt you if you're not careful.

T: Yes, sometimes, but you expect it all the time. So, you're always on guard and then respond with pretty aggressive behavior as a way of warding them off and not feeling hurt. Now look, I'm not expecting you to simply agree and change everything, but we need to work on slowing yourself down so you can learn to tell the difference between real threat and the threat your mind interprets a little too easily.

C: I understand, but I don't know what to say about it.

T: Let's just talk about it and see where it takes us.

C: OK, I understand, and it does make some sense, but I don't know.

This type of discussion can take many forms, but it inevitably does occur. It is an important part of the CART treatment, as anger clients have very rigid rules as a means of self-protection, and often their own anger signals external danger. Therapists are encouraged to utilize the Between-Session Emotion Monitoring Form at the outset of each session in this module as a way of enhancing clients' awareness of their thought processes, and its (often) fused connection to a variety of avoidant behaviors.

Learning to decenter from their internal rule systems and ultimately defuse behavior from these internal cognitive processes are important strategic goals in the CART program. In addition, the combination of enhanced mindfulness and cognitive defusion reduces the pernicious ruminative process that serves to avoid (i.e. cognitive avoidance) the full experience of anger, and also serves as a motivating operation for aggressive behavior (i.e. behavioral avoidance). As such, while efforts at cognitive defusion are the main focus of attention in Module 4, it is imperative that therapists maintain their vigilance to clients' regular and ongoing practice of mindfulness, as these processes significantly build upon one another.

As noted in previous chapters, while CART does focus on cognitions in this module, there is a significant difference between how CART views cognitive products when compared to traditional cognitive behavioral therapies. As is the case with all acceptance-based behavioral therapies, CART seeks to change the *relationship* we have with our thoughts, as compared with the traditional CBT goal of changing the *content* of our thoughts. In CART, we make no effort to suggest that there are right or wrong, logical or illogical, rational or irrational thoughts. Rather, there are a wide variety of thoughts that flow through our minds, which can be noticed and allowed to pass without requiring action. Some are accurate reflections of reality, and some are not. But in any event, we must develop the capacity to notice and reflect upon (decenter from) our thoughts before acting upon them. From this perspective, CART makes no effort to utilize cognitive restructuring and/or traditional cognitive reappraisal as techniques. While it is certainly possible, and probably likely, that the decentering process leads to some reappraisal of situations, there is no effort made to make these changes in our clients, nor does CART suggest that this is a necessary component of treatment. In fact, as we posited earlier in our discussion about REBT, it has been suggested by some theorists (Teasdale, 1999b) that the process of decentering is the primary mechanism of action in traditional cognitive therapies, instead of the presumed/theorized modification of cognitive content typically posited in cognitive therapies (Beck & Shaw, 1977). In essence, it has been suggested that when cognitive restructuring does work, it is unlikely due to a change in the *content* of thoughts, but rather, the process of cognitive restructuring requires individuals to distance or *decenter* from their thought process as part of the restructuring process. CART and other acceptance-based behavioral therapies have chosen to emphasize the decentering aspect of cognitive therapeutic work, and not focus on the thought-content change aspect.

The following vignette is an example of a therapist who is confusing the goal of decentering from thoughts from the more traditional goal of cognitive change.

T: Tell me what went through your mind when your boyfriend just stared at the TV while you were talking to him.

C: I thought, "he's not listening, he doesn't care and I don't have to take this disrespectful crap from him or anyone."

T: How do you know he wasn't listening to you?

C: He wasn't looking at me, wasn't saying a word . . . and was acting like I wasn't there.

T: So, from that you interpreted disrespect?

C: Yes.

T: What else could it have meant?

C: I don't know, what do you mean?

T: What if he was tired, or was really listening and didn't have anything to say?

C: You mean what if I saw something that wasn't there?

T: Or just interpreted it incorrectly. How would you have felt if you thought about it differently?

C: I don't know. He always says I see things that aren't there. He always tells me that if I can just think differently about stuff I would be less angry. So, you're saying that maybe he's right?

In this example, the therapist has taken a decidedly change-based approach, and has in fact suggested that by changing what the client thinks, she may in fact feel better. There is a problem here on two levels. First, while noticing thoughts and making room for alternatives is a reasonable goal, there is a suggestion in this vignette of a correct/incorrect appraisal of situations. In CART, our position is that thoughts are not correct or incorrect. Rather, they just occur, and are to be noticed and considered. The therapist in the above vignette has set up a scenario in which correcting the content of thoughts becomes a goal. Second, the therapist promoted a connection between correct/incorrect thoughts and how one feels, with the implication that feeling less angry is the goal of treatment. Both of these implications are unworkable, and additionally contradict of the empirical data presented in Chapter 1. Notice the contrast between this last vignette and the previous one in which the client's cognition is approached in a different manner. While some, particularly traditional CBT therapists, may suggest that these are the same processes, we strongly disagree. As we have both been intensely trained in and have extensively utilized both approaches, we therefore suggest that there is a very different feel and a very different purpose of the two approaches. The traditional cognitive restructuring model that seeks to change the content of cognitions in the service of reducing anger is wholly inconsistent with the goals of the CART program, and should not be used in the context of this particular treatment approach.

Obstacles Often Encountered in Module 4

Interestingly, the most likely obstacle in Module 4 does not lie with the client. Rather, the greatest challenge in the successful completion of this module lies with the therapist. The obstacle is the ability of the therapist to her or himself accept the position that thoughts are not good or bad, healthy or unhealthy. This is often especially problematic with therapists trained in traditional cognitive behavioral therapies, where changing "negative" thoughts to more "positive" or "realistic" ones is the central goal of psychological treatment. We have found that therapists often give mixed messages in this regard. In such cases, therapists may "talk the talk" of accepting and decentering from the full range of thoughts, yet at the same time, they communicate a more subtle message that some thoughts are correct or good, and others are incorrect or bad. To minimize this occurrence, we suggest that prior to beginning the CART protocol, therapists: (a) become fully comfortable with the tenets of acceptance-based behavioral therapies; and (b) personally utilize the acceptance/decentering approach to their own thoughts, rather than the reappraisal model suggested by traditional cognitive therapies.

Module 5: Understanding Anger and Anger-Avoidance

Estimated Number of Sessions to Completion: 3

Goals of Module 5

- The client gains an understanding that the emotion of anger is a normal and unavoidable aspect of life, learns about its function, and learns the problems associated with seeing anger as something to be feared and avoided.
- The client gains an understanding of the common misconceptions about anger, which are that anger inevitably leads to aggression if not controlled, that venting is both healthy and necessary, that other people are the cause of anger, and that being angry and displaying anger are helpful.
- The client gains an understanding of the costs of his or her efforts to avoid the experience of anger, including costs in interpersonal, career/financial, health, and energy domains.
- The client develops an enhanced capacity to (increasingly) tolerate anger, and thus come to experience and understand anger better.

Materials Needed for Module 5

- Acceptance and Action Questionnaire-2 (AAQ-2)
- Anger and Violence Impairment Scale (AVIS)
- Valued Living Questionnaire-2 (VLQ-2)
- Mindful Attention and Awareness Scale (MAAS)
- Between-Session Emotion Monitoring Form

In Module 5, clients should continue to use the skills and knowledge acquired through all previous modules and begin the task of understanding and relating differently to their anger. The goal of this module is essentially for clients to stop seeing their anger as an inherent problem that needs to be controlled or eliminated, but rather, as a normal and expected part of the human experience. Clients should come to see becoming angry as normal . . . not dangerous, not intolerable, and not requiring avoidance or escape. Therapists will help clients understand the place anger has had in their personal histories, and importantly, will differentiate the costs and benefits of experiencing anger vs the costs and benefits of extreme automatic efforts to avoid or escape the experience of anger.

In this module, therapists systematically discuss the nature of anger and how the emotion of anger can be used *effectively* as a vehicle for action. This process actually began in previous modules, especially in Module 3 in which emotion awareness was being enhanced. Yet, it is extended here, with an emphasis on the many experiences of anger and how it is inevitable and natural, and can be used as a signal for a problem to be solved and not an immediate danger to be confronted. The following vignette provides a good example of this process.

T: Let's talk about the experience you told me about earlier, the one regarding the taxicab.

C: The guy drives me to my stop, then says he forgot to put the meter on, and the fare is $15. I take this cab ride all the time and it never costs more than $7 or $8. I was so freaking mad I thought I was going to hit him. I think the only reason I didn't is the stuff we've been doing . . . ya know, about disrespect. I noticed that I was thinking about that and just decided to let it go, and pay him the 15 bucks. It wasn't worth hitting him, and it's not the kind of person I want to be.

T: Well, I'm glad to hear that you didn't hit him automatically . . . especially since that would have certainly put you back in jail, and it's certainly great that you were aware of what your mind was telling you. And, you're right that it doesn't fit with the values we have discussed for you. But, while I think that is a great step forward, the goal for you still seems to be not letting yourself be wronged. I think this is a great time to talk about the actual purpose of anger, and why it is normal for human beings to get angry sometimes.

C: OK, I think you mentioned something about that before. But I'm a little confused.

T: Let's go through this together. Anger does tell us there might be danger, or, there might be some situation we need to respond to. Now, you did a great job of being mindful of your anger, and the thoughts that you had while feeling angry. Your choice of walking away rather than hitting him was also a good one. But, what else could the anger have led you to do?

C: I see what you're saying, but I'm not sure.

T: That's not too surprising, because in your life, you've learned to walk away or fight, and we'll get to that later in our treatment. But for now, let's just look at what the anger was telling you. It was telling you that you were mistreated and you should respond in some way.

C: Like telling him he is overcharging me, and just give him the money I know the ride should have cost?

T: Exactly! Did you just think of that now?

C: [Laughing] No, my mother actually told me that when I told her about what happened.

T: That was one option. Now look, I know you haven't developed these kind of middle-ground type skills previously, and like I said, we'll get to that, but for now, just see that the anger itself was not bad, it was a reasonable signal. You didn't try to escape the feeling by hitting the guy, but you chose a better way of escaping the feeling by walking away. A better choice, but it still left you feeling somewhat taken advantage of.

C: I see what you mean. I did just want the whole thing, including the anger, to just go away.

T: Give yourself some credit though. Much better awareness and choice of action based on your values, but we still have some work to do.

This vignette is illustrative of several important points. First, it highlights the potential value of anger in motivating behavior, and as such, is important for our clients to see. Remember, they typically have been told most of their lives that anger is bad, and the capacity to see it as neutral is important in the overall success of CART. Second, we begin to see the lack of behavioral choices available to these clients given their lifetime of avoiding or escaping from anger. The lack of necessary skills is often most obvious during this module. However, skills training is still premature, as they have not yet developed the necessary capacity to fully experience the emotion of anger without the need to avoid or escape. While it is tempting to begin the process of skill development at this point in time, it would be highly premature, and doomed to fail, as these new skills require a much greater tolerance of anger than clients would typically have at this point in the CART program. In the previous vignette, it can be readily seen that while walking away was more pro-social, it was still an act of avoidance, as the capacity to tolerate anger has not been developed enough for new skills to be effectively utilized. While it was a good step, and demonstrated that enhanced mindful awareness and cognitive defusion has had an impact, it shows that the client is ready for the next step, which is to understand the scope of his avoidance, and the enhancement of the capacity to tolerate anger.

In addition, during this portion of Module 5, common misconceptions about anger (often reinforced in many cultures), such as its lack of utility, its natural association with aggression, and its need to be vented, are discussed in detail. This module begins the process of normalizing the experience of anger and by doing so creates a treatment environment that supports and tolerates the full, healthy experience and expression of anger. In addition, clients increasingly enhance their capacity to experience (and tolerate) anger without the need to avoid, escape, or otherwise reduce the feeling. Continuing on with the previous vignette will more clearly make this point.

C: This week I had a similar situation, I guess. My girlfriend just wouldn't stop nagging me. She was having a bad day or something, and just wouldn't stop. Complaining about everything and anything. I felt myself becoming angrier and angrier as she kept saying really nasty stuff to me. But, like with the cab driver, I noticed what I was feeling, and just decided to walk out.

T: What did you say to her during this time and at the time you left?

C: At first I started yelling. Asking her to just stop. You know, I didn't even think about doing the stuff I used to do.

T: You mean pushing her?

C: Yea, nothing like that. But she wouldn't stop, and I couldn't take it. I thought I was going to explode, so I just walked out. We didn't talk for two days after that.

T: Again, I do want to commend you on being more aware. You used to tell me you didn't feel anything.

C: I remember.

T: And, you didn't get physical, which is extremely important. But, like you said, it does have a similarity with the cab driver. Do you see what it is?

C: Yea, I just walked away.

T: And, you did yell at her, which is another way of trying to escape from your angry feelings. Why did you walk away?

C: Because I couldn't take it . . . I knew if I stayed I would explode.

T: You're partially correct. Yes, in both cases you walked away, so you were able to keep yourself from becoming violent by removing yourself from the situation. It worked, but only because you found another, better, way of escaping how you were feeling.

C: What choice did I have?

T: Before I answer that, let me just ask you a question; what if you couldn't walk away for some reason?

C: I honestly have no idea.

T: That's the problem. At this point, doing the right thing by your life and the values that you have established for yourself depends on you being able to escape the feeling of anger. Yes, you are much better at knowing when you are feeling it, but you still seem to be afraid of it. Like believing that you would explode. What if I told you that while it feels uncomfortable, you could handle feeling angry? That you would feel it, which makes you feel hot and sweaty, and tense, but that if you stayed with it and didn't run from it, you could be angry *and* do the right thing?

C: That's hard to believe.

T: You already did it to a certain degree. You waited a while before you walked out. This isn't the last time that someone will say things or do things that you don't like and you can't control. So, let's imagine for a minute what your life would be like if you could just tolerate the discomfort. Have you ever had any physical problem you had to tolerate until you got better?

C: Yes. I had knee surgery. The pain was tough, but it was what it was. I had to still go to work, and eventually the pain went away.

T: Exactly, it hurt, but you still had to do the right thing without running away from it.

C: Ha, there was no place to run.

T: Well, let's see if we can approach your anger the same way. It's tough, it's uncomfortable, but it's going to be there from time to time. Let's talk about how you can not run away, not try to avoid or escape, and simply have the anger. Then after that, we can figure out how to get you better at communicating while being angry, and not two days later.

C: Sounds like a plan.

In this module, in addition to developing an understanding that anger is normal and not in and of itself dangerous or bad, clients should develop an understanding of the concept of emotional (i.e. anger) avoidance, come to see the various ways in which they avoid angry feelings, and develop an understanding of how this avoidance contributes to the problematic behavior that has brought them in to treatment. In this regard, we have found it useful for therapists to help their clients see that while avoidance of anger may work to reduce discomfort in the short run, it rarely has positive benefits in the long run (as seen in the previous vignette).

It seems most useful for the discussion of avoidance to begin with the more easy-to-identify behavioral avoidance strategies, such as walking out of a room when becoming angry, yelling at or threatening someone, physical aggression such as breaking or throwing objects, and overt violent behavior such as pushing, hitting, etc. All of these strategies have the intent of in some way reducing or eliminating anger by terminating the anger-producing situation or behavior of others. Of course, clients are likely to manifest many overt behavioral variations of this, ranging from the obvious to the somewhat less obvious, but they can most often easily be distinguished by their function (changing the triggering stimulus in order to avoid or escape from anger). Therapists should point out the avoidance strategies that they have noticed when working with clients, and then ask clients if they can think of other typical behavioral avoidance strategies they have used. Clients have probably never viewed their behavior as anger avoidance before, but rather, as simply the way they act when angry, "pissed off," or "stressed out." This discussion taps into a core component of the CART treatment program, which is the idea that the behavioral avoidance of anger is the problem, and not the anger itself. Interestingly, at this point in therapy, most clients can readily connect their problematic behavior to the anger they have experienced, and more often than not are willing to consider that their behavioral patterns are largely due to a desire to make the feelings stop, and not because of the feeling itself.

The next component of Module 5 is a somewhat more difficult component, which is the discussion of more subtle cognitive forms of avoidance. In this portion of Module 5, therapists present the idea that when we ruminate (repetitively think, over and over again) about getting revenge on someone who we think has wronged us, or when we think over and over again about how we will respond differently the next time we are treated unfairly by someone, we are actually *avoiding* being angry. This may seem counterintuitive to many clients and non-clients alike, because during these ruminative periods we do not necessarily feel good. Yet, it is important to educate clients that research has shown that our neurological systems react differently when angry than when ruminating (Segerstrom *et al.*, 2000). Rumination blocks the full experience of anger. How? By keeping us in the past (thoughts of revenge over past maltreatment) or the future (preparation for the next maltreatment). In neither case are we actually *living* in the present, living our current lives. That is why we often refer to rumination as *concentrated avoidance*. It allows someone to avoid present-moment emotional experiences by living in yesterday or tomorrow. Further, just as being hungry makes it more likely that we will actively pursue food (sometimes above all else), ruminating sets the stage for us to act more aggressively than situations may dictate (i.e. motivating operation). That is, it sets us up to overreact. This more subtle, yet no less pernicious form of avoidance is often more difficult for clients to wrap their heads around, but is no less important. Therapists may point out that regular mindfulness practice has been shown to be an effective treatment of rumination, as mindfulness exercises promote present state awareness, and encourage clients to notice and let go of ruminative processes in the service of staying present-focused. As clients become more mindful (i.e. aware) of, and decentered from their ruminations, they are able to refocus on the present and act in a less automatic and more functional manner.

One of the most important aspects of this module is the introduction of the distinction between behavioral choices in the service of anger vs behavioral choices in the service of values. In the discussion of emotional avoidance, both overt behavioral avoidance and more subtle cognitive avoidance, therapists should engage in a full discussion of the short-term gains (anger being reduced) vs long-term costs (e.g. relationship, legal, financial problems) inherent in how we choose to respond to our emotions. At this point, therapists shall note how avoidance behaviors are most often contrary to the life values identified earlier in treatment. In contrast, it should be pointed out that the previously identified values can best be achieved when tolerating anger and still choosing to act in a manner that is consistent with what matters to us most in the long run. Ultimately, the only reason that our clients, or anyone for that matter, will tolerate discomfort is the pursuit of something more important. Going back to a previous analogy, people who complete physical therapy following an injury do so because having a functional and normal life is more important in the long run than the short-term discomfort of physical therapy. There are many such examples that clinicians can employ, and it is important that clinicians connect with clients in this important area. From this point through the remainder of treatment, it is important for therapists to contrast behavioral choices made in the service of personal values vs those made in the service of short-term anger reduction or avoidance. This becomes the anchor for clients to use in their behavioral choices.

Our experience in the clinical milieu suggests that this is the most critical stage of the CART process. When clients understand that they have been avoiding anger, see the short-term gain of this avoidance, can acknowledge the long-term costs of this behavioral pattern, and can then recognize that getting what they have previously identified as the life they truly value requires tolerance of the discomfort inherent in feeling angry, treatment will almost always end successfully. When this latter goal is achieved, it is time to move on to Module 6, which readers will soon see is the obvious next step in the anger tolerance process. However, once again, we caution therapists to stay with Module 5 as long as necessary for the above components to be fully in place.

Finally, as this is the halfway point in the CART program, it is a valuable time to carefully assess the changes in weekly scores of the AAQ-2, AVIS, VLQ-2, and MAAS. At this point, one could expect small to moderate decreases in the AVIS and AAQ-2 scores, some larger changes in the MAAS scores, and little or no change at this point in the VLQ-2 scores. This pattern of self-report change would be expected based on the current stage in the CART program. Some minor improvements in the AAQ-2 and AVIS will likely be noted, as clients are beginning to slow down their reactions to situations and begin the process of enhanced emotional awareness. The MAAS should show some stronger improvements, as ongoing mindfulness practice and the therapeutic focus on mindful awareness should naturally lead to enhancements in this area. The VLQ-2 should remain relatively unchanged, as we have just set the stage to begin the process of enhancing committed behavior in the service of personal values. If the MAAS scores do not reflect improved mindful awareness and attention at this point in treatment, therapists should pause and consider the possibility that mindfulness practice is not occurring as needed, and a step back to Module 4 is strongly recommended.

Obstacles Often Encountered in Module 5

The obstacles most often encountered in Module 5 directly relate to the core problems being addressed. Namely, to many clients experiencing clinical anger, emotions are viewed as highly toxic. The concept of tolerating feelings such as anger is extremely difficult to accept. This is not necessarily due to a precontemplative stage of change, or a resistance to the therapist, but is most likely to simply be due to the fact that these clients have spent their entire lives doing whatever they could to avoid or escape from unpleasant emotions. With such clients, whose response to emotion is somewhat analogous to a physical allergy in which non-pathological substances are responded to as though they are highly dangerous to the body, non-dangerous (normal) emotions such as anger are responded to intensely, as though the client is in imminent danger. With these clients, the number of sessions in Module 5 may be greater than the three-session usual time frame. Multiple sessions may be required in which each step of this module is slowly and compassionately presented and discussed. Additionally, such clients often score in the average range on the variety of self-report assessments that are utilized pre-treatment, as even the process of acknowledging emotion on these self-report instruments is unacceptable.

Of course, this client obstacle creates an obstacle for therapists as well . . . in the form of impatience. We have found that it is during this module that some therapists, especially those who are inexperienced, new to acceptance-based interventions, or new to the use of a modular-based therapy approach, tend to give up on the protocol too readily, seeing the client obstacles as insurmountable. Thus, such clinicians inappropriately change therapeutic direction. We suggest that once again, patient persistence is required, with an understanding that this module gets to the core of the psychopathology inherent in clinical anger, and thus, for some clients, additional time and patience on the part of the therapist is required. The greatest obstacle for therapeutic improvement lies in (a) giving up on the necessary treatment sequence too readily, and either (b) inappropriately sequencing the CART modules, or (c) giving up on the CART program altogether.

At this point, readers have likely noticed that CART modules are logically connected, and to a certain extent, separation into distinct modules is somewhat arbitrary, as one leads directly and interconnectedly into the next. This is especially true as we move from Module 5 into Module 6.

Module 6: Acceptance and Anger Regulation

Estimated Number of Sessions to Completion: 3

Goals of Module 6

- The client will increasingly develop the capacity to tolerate/accept the presence of anger (and the hurt/rejection with which it is often associated).
- The client will develop the capacity to distinguish between anger-driven behavior and values-driven behavior.
- The client will develop the capacity to modulate (i.e. down-regulate) anger when necessary—not to *feel* better, but to allow for behavior in the service of personal values.

Materials Needed for Module 6

- Acceptance and Action Questionnaire-2 (AAQ-2)
- Anger and Violence Impairment Scale (AVIS)
- Valued Living Questionnaire-2 (VLQ-2)
- Mindful Attention and Awareness Scale (MAAS)
- Between-Session Emotion Monitoring Form

The ultimate therapeutic goal of Module 6 is the further development of clients' capacities to experience anger without needing to resort to historically over-learned avoidance or escape behaviors, a process that began in Module 5. In Module 6, clients and therapists continue to explore the workability/effectiveness of the variety of strategies previously used to avoid or escape from feelings of anger and hurt. In this context, therapists reinforce the idea that the lack of success in controlling anger and hurt has not been due to personal failure or absence of adequate strategy, but rather, has been due to the impossibility of the goal itself. The reality is that people get angry and feel hurt, and nothing can eliminate that fact. Additionally, the reality is that the pursuit of this goal has led to more negative consequences than the experience of anger ever would.

Encouraging non-judging acceptance of emotional experiences as normal parts of the human experience, and with it the willingness to remain in contact with these experiences, also increases the ability to utilize information conveyed by emotions such as anger. Thus, during this module, clients will continue to develop a full understanding of the various thoughts, feelings, and physical sensations associated with anger and hurt. They will also begin the process of modifying the stimulus functions of anger and hurt by increasingly and purposefully entering into situations that produce anger, without the usual behavioral avoidance strategies. Enhanced acceptance/tolerance of anger will promote a greater distinction between emotion (anger/hurt)-driven behavior that has been the source of many of the client's life difficulties, and values-driven behavior, which can promote an enhanced quality of life.

In Module 6, we contrast the concept of experiential acceptance with that of experiential avoidance. Therapists work to help clients move to a place of greater acceptance/tolerance of anger, including thoughts, feelings, and physical states that were previously assumed to be bad in some way. Instead, clients continue to hear the message of non-judging acceptance of one's experience . . . accepting the fact that emotions of all kinds (including anger) invariably occur, and that they are neither good nor bad, just realities of life. In addition, clients learn that these periods of anger have a beginning and an end, and are not perpetual or intolerable. This is important, in that clients previously saw the likely course of anger as perpetually increasing up to the point of some internal or external explosion. A discussion of the reality that anger, as with all emotions, has a beginning, a middle/peak, and an end, has rarely been carefully considered until now.

Herein, clients are also presented with the possibility that rather than struggling to control or eliminate thoughts and feelings (which ultimately cannot be consistently done anyway), a more powerful strategy is the acceptance of these feelings while simultaneously applying one's efforts at dealing effectively with whatever issue or task is at hand. Thus, in dealing with a difficult relationship issue, work problem, or other frustrating situation, the focus is on handling the issue in a manner consistent with life goals and values, and is not based upon the immediate desire to feel better and make the situation triggering those feelings disappear. In essence, as we have mentioned numerous times, one can function appropriately *and* be angry at the same time.

It is important that in these discussions, therapists not imply that we all must simply accept unwanted life circumstances, even though on occasion this does become necessary. This is a very frequent misunderstanding of the concept of acceptance. Rather, the term *experiential acceptance* is intended to convey a willingness to experience and tolerate emotions that may sometimes be painful in the service of pursuing values that are personally meaningful.

At the point in Module 6 where clients understand the concepts presented thus far, therapists should move on to the use of *in-session anger exposure exercises*, using triggering external (and internal, in many cases) stimuli that are likely to produce strong or intense anger as the next step in the development of emotional acceptance/tolerance. While most typically seen in anxiety treatment, exposure exercises serve an extremely valuable function in the treatment of clinical anger. Importantly, the primary focus of these exposure exercises is the emotion of anger itself, and not a specific situation or activity. The specific situation or activity is simply a trigger from clients' lives that is most likely to result in the experience of anger.

This can be a very challenging part of treatment for clients, as after all, the experience of anger is what they have sought to avoid their entire lives. Yet, it is critical in the full development of anger tolerance, and for new learning to replace the automatic emotion-driven behavior that was so problematic for clients prior to treatment. In addition, therapists must communicate to clients that the purpose of exposure exercises is not immediate reduction of anger, although this may occur. Rather, the goal is for clients to experience their anger fully. In doing so, they learn that anger is in fact tolerable, break the automatic patterns of avoidance, and subsequently embark upon the development of new prosocial behaviors.

In-session exposure exercises allow the therapist to facilitate the client's full experiencing of anger during the exercise, while also allowing for post-exposure processing of the experience with the therapist. The specifics of the exposure exercises will inevitably vary from client to client. We suggest that, similar to what is often done when working with anxious clients in preparation for exposure, therapists develop a hierarchy of anger producing situations, from least to most difficult, and use those as a guide for exposure exercise selection (Figure 5.1). In our experience, seven situations allow for a good range of anger triggering situations. We suggest beginning in-session exposure work with situation number five, allowing for the two "easiest" situations to be later used by clients on their own outside of therapy (real world exposure exercises are described below), and suggest that the two most difficult exposures to be used as part of the Relapse Prevention module later in CART (Module 9). Therapists should also ensure that at least two situations of the hierarchy involve close interpersonal situations (i.e. family member/intimate partner). Appendix 5.8 provides guidelines for the use of anger exposures. Please note that part of the guidelines in Appendix 5.8 includes the use of an adapted version of the "empty chair technique" originally developed as part of gestalt therapy (Korb, Gorrell, & Van De Riet, 1989) and currently used as part of contemporary emotion-focused therapy (Greenberg, 2004). When used as a form of interpersonal exposure as described in Appendix 5.8, the empty chair technique is highly effective in promoting anger tolerance and modifying automatic emotion-driven behaviors previously associated with that anger, specifically in the context of important and highly emotionally charged interpersonal situations/relationships.

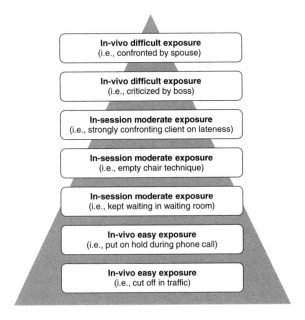

Figure 5.1 Anger Exposure Hierarchy

Once in-session exposures have effectively begun, therapists will work toward moving clients toward systematically engaging in *real-world exposures* outside of the therapy session. These real-world exposures allow clients to develop a sense of autonomy, enhance the skills that they have been working on in therapy, and build confidence that they can truly tolerate real-world anger. Therapists should use the two or three easiest items from the exposure hierarchy to help design appropriate real-world exposure exercises, and clients should be encouraged to complete the Between-Session Emotion Monitoring Form immediately following completion of each real-world exposure exercise for review and processing during the next therapy session. The following vignette provides an example of a common post real-world exposure session in which the exposure experience is discussed, its purpose clarified, and its outcome reinforced.

C: I did the anger exposure during the week.

T: That's great. Before we review the Between-Session Emotion Monitoring Form together, why don't you give me a brief summary of how it went?

C: OK. I sat down with my wife and talked about the way her family treats me, and like I predicted, she started attacking me, calling me names, putting me down . . . basically everything that I knew she would, and everything that I knew would get me angry.

T: So you did get angry?

C: Very angry. And she went on for, I don't know, 15–20 minutes. It felt like days, she was just getting more and more wound up, yelling louder and louder, and I just sat there. I tried saying something in the beginning, but she just yelled over me, so then I sat there and just listened. I felt real angry the whole time . . . didn't scream or cuss or anything, didn't walk out, and I didn't lay a hand on her of course. She does have some good reasons to be angry at me, with all that's gone on. I know that. But the anger never got better . . . it stayed pretty intense the entire time.

T: I think you did great. I'm proud of you for giving that a try.

C: But the anger didn't get any less even though I just sat there.

T: Remember that we talked about first, being more aware when you get angry . . . you did that. Second, being aware of what your mind is telling you when angry and what it feels like physically, were you able do that?

C: Yeah. I thought about how I couldn't stand it [laughs], but I guess I did, and my face got so hot, like I had a sunburn.

T: That's great, your awareness of what you were feeling, thinking, and how your body was reacting was excellent. Did you do anything to avoid the feeling?

C: For a minute, I started thinking about what I should do, like leave or scream or tell her to go to hell and break something, but I kind of realized I was thinking that and tried to concentrate on what she was saying. You know, some of the things weren't wrong. Said in kind of a nasty way, but her comments about how I drove her closer to them because of the way I have acted, and now when I decide to try and change I expect her to pull away from them. She has a point.

T: By sticking it out, you allowed yourself to experience anger for a prolonged period of time, without running away physically or mentally, you were aware of your thoughts, feelings, physical reactions, *and* even when your automatic avoidance began to kick in, you refocused onto what was happening at that moment . . . your wife talking to you. To top it off, you even listened long enough to see a point your wife was making even in the midst of being angry. We never talked about anger *going away* during these exposures. In fact, we talked about the goal of these exercises being greater tolerance when experiencing anger. Just like the exposures we have done during our sessions. The anger didn't go away, but you were able to stay with it. You tolerated it without having to run away from it. If you remember, we said that the ultimate goal of exposures is for you to learn that you can handle it, and learn that it isn't dangerous. It seems to me like you learned that a little bit, and more.

Ultimately, anger exposures are the point in the CART program that clients begin to utilize the skills that have developed to date when in real-world challenging situations, and therapists now get to see: (a) what needs to be further developed, (b) what skills will ultimately need to be learned, (c) how well clients understand the goal of anger acceptance/tolerance, (d) how well their anger awareness has developed thus far, and (e) to what degree they can make a direct effort to no longer utilize the pernicious avoidance and escape behaviors that have been a part of their lives for so long.

While the ultimate goal of CART is the development of greater anger acceptance, and the development of more values-driven prosocial behaviors in the place of emotion-driven avoidant/escape behaviors, there are some circumstances in which overly intense episodes of anger may overwhelm anger tolerance and subsequently interfere with optimal behavioral responding. Therefore, therapists may at times need to help clients develop appropriate values-driven self-soothing skills, as a form of emotion modulation, to be judiciously used during such hyper-intense periods of anger. In such cases, behavioral approaches to down-regulate anger by the use of a brief momentary coping response should be presented to clients. It is important that this self-soothing technique be carefully considered prior to use, as therapists do *not* want to promote alternative means of avoidance. Rather, therapists should promote this skill as a form of emotion modulation in the service of mindful awareness of the emotional experience, rather than in the service of avoiding or escaping from the emotional state. That is, as a means of "taking the edge off" so the anger can be fully experienced and the emotion-driven avoidance behavior not occur. It is also important that these efforts be introduced *after* anger-related experiential acceptance has already been effectively enhanced to the point where anger can most often be tolerated without the use of self-soothing. In essence, this emotion modulation skill should not be presented early in this module, and should only be introduced when circumstances clearly dictate its appropriateness. In cases in which clients have a tendency to become excessively angry in response to specific stimuli to the point that loss of behavioral control often follows, introducing a self-soothing technique such as a brief progressive muscle relaxation exercise (Benson & Klipper, 1976) can have value. The goal in such circumstances is a reduction of intensity so that clients can then stay in contact with the remaining anger, and in turn engage in values-driven behavioral choices. The following vignette offers an example of an in-session use of brief progressive relaxation as a self-soothing technique.

T: So you got the decision that you were losing custody of your children today?

C: Yeah, its overwhelming . . . and I am soooo mad, I can hardly think straight. I don't know at all what I'm going to do [client gets up and starts pacing].

T: What is going through your head right now?

C: Doc, not now OK, I can't do this [client starts screaming curses].

T: Let's try to bring you down a couple of notches like we talked about last week. Come on, sit down and let's give it a try.

C: [Client takes a deep breath and sits down]

T: Just close your eyes and take some slow deep breaths, in through your nose and out through your mouth. Try to focus your attention on your breathing.

C: [Client breathes deeply for about 30 seconds]

T: Now, keep breathing in and out, and tighten your feet for a moment . . . hold it [5 seconds] . . . now release the tightness . . . and keep breathing deeply [10 seconds]. Now do the same thing with your calves. Now clench your fists and do the same thing. And now with your shoulders. Tighten up and hold it [5 seconds] . . . keep breathing . . . now release the tightness, and keep breathing deeply [10 seconds] . . . now open your eyes, and let's talk. How do you feel?

C: Still angry, but a little better.

T: That's the point. This very brief exercise can take the edge off. We're not trying to make it go away at all, but you did need to get it down just a bit so we could talk about this.

C: Thanks man, I'm still really angry, but I do feel a little bit more in control.

Note that this is not a full, extensive relaxation exercise. Instead, it is a brief, easy-to-use exercise for use when the level of anger is such that rational decision making is unlikely. The brevity of the exercise makes it easy to remember, and easy to use in difficult situations. There are some clients who are so temperamentally easily and intensely aroused, that this brief self-soothing exercise is useful. The significant caution, of course, is that this exercise should not be introduced too early in treatment, and the therapist must carefully monitor its use so that it does not function as just another anger-avoiding behavior.

The development of anger acceptance through discussion, in-session exposure, and real-world exposure exercises, and the enhanced differentiation between anger-driven (avoidance/escape) and values-driven behavior sets the stage for the next module, in which increasing commitment to consistent values-driven behavior is the primary goal. It is imperative that therapists not move on to the next module until all of the elements of Module 6 have been completed and clients are now substantially more tolerant of being angry, describing that anger, and refraining from the cognitive and behavioral avoidance/escape strategies that were previously and automatically utilized.

Obstacles Often Encountered in Module 6

For many clients, engaging in exposure exercises is often the most difficult component of the entire CART program. These exercises require that they confront their most feared emotion (i.e. anger), and do it first in front of a therapist who they may not want to displease. As we have discussed earlier in the CART program description, to many of these clients, experiencing anger is much like an allergy. Thus, we are asking them to do what they have fiercely avoided for many years. The process of effectively utilizing these exercises once again requires a persistent and patient approach by the therapist. It is crucial that therapists accurately convey that the goal is the experience itself and not feeling better from it. Therapists must stress that clients will probably not feel good doing this, but will grow stronger from it. Again, we have often used a physical strength training analogy, in that during weight training, we push ourselves more and more, we get tired, and we often ache afterward, but little by little we become stronger. Clinicians should empathize with the desire to avoid these exercises, and must also be aware of subtle safety behaviors in-session (i.e. changing the subject, making jokes), which can be used to avoid or interrupt the full experience of anger.

Aside from the natural obstacles that clients present when completing exposure exercises, therapists may actually become an obstacle based on their own fear of engaging in exposure exercises. This may be due to an actual fear of clients' anger and the behavior that may occur with it, or due to their own discomfort with having to sit with clients while they experience so much intense feeling. In any case, therapists should be self-aware and recognize when they themselves are avoiding these exercises or allowing clients to avoid these exercises due to their own issues/discomfort. It is not only our clients who are uncomfortable in the presence of anger. Sometimes, we, as therapists, become aware of just how difficult angry emotions are for us, when in the context of anger exposure exercises. As effective in-session and real-world anger exposures are critically important to the overall success of CART, therapists must be mindful of their own reactions and behaviors, not avoid their own issues that may be brought to the forefront, and respond accordingly when they become aware that their own thoughts or feelings with regard to anger are becoming an obstacle to therapeutic success.

Module 7: Commitment to Values-Based Behavior

Estimated Number of Sessions to Completion: 2

Goals of Module 7

- The client develops a clear connection between previously identified values and specific behaviors to be increased.
- The client continues to develop the understanding that experiencing intense anger can (and often must) occur at the same time as the need for effective values-driven behaviors (through the use of values-driven experiential exposure).
- The client develops a behavioral activation plan to record and monitor specific values-driven behaviors.
- The client learns to identify skill deficits needing correction, to further enhance values-driven behavioral choices.

Materials Needed for Module 7

- Acceptance and Action Questionnaire-2 (AAQ-2)
- Anger and Violence Impairment Scale (AVIS)
- Valued Living Questionnaire-2 (VLQ-2)
- Mindful Attention and Awareness Scale (MAAS)
- Committing to Life Values Exercise Form

In the first six CART modules, the focus of therapeutic attention has been on the development of mindful awareness of anger; defusion of the words or internal rules automatically driving behavior; an understanding about the various anger avoidance/escape behaviors automatically used to gain relief from anger at the expense of personal values; and greater acceptance and tolerance of the emotion of anger. In Module 7, all of the knowledge and skills developed thus far are utilized to enhance values-driven behaviors in place of previously utilized emotion (anger)-driven behaviors. In this portion of the CART program, therapists work to enhance clients' commitment to attaining what they want out of life through the activation of specific values-directed behaviors.

This CART module is intended to help clients develop a consistent approach to engaging in those behaviors that optimize what really matters to them, and help them become the type of people they hope to be and live the lives they would like to have. While once again noting the distinction between emotion-driven and values-driven behaviors, clients are encouraged to increase their willingness to act in accordance with their stated values *while* feeling angry or hurt. Of course, this cannot be accomplished without the skill development in previous modules, which allows clients to understand, tolerate, and utilize their emotions (i.e. anger) more effectively. Herein, clients are encouraged to continue the real-life exposures utilized in Module 6, and systematically confront, with new behavioral options, situations previously avoided. These new behavioral options should be based upon clients' own personal values. In so doing, new emotional meanings are developed in response to previously avoided situations, and clients increasingly gain a sense of personal effectiveness. A critical aspect of this module is the utilization of a behavioral activation plan to systematically identify and increase client behaviors that are consistent with identified personal values, often occurring *while experiencing* angry feelings. Finally, as chronic emotion dysregulation has most likely taken the form of behavioral avoidance and has typically resulted in deficits in necessary interpersonal skills, during this module, therapists will inevitably notice specific skill deficits that are likely to interfere with desired positive interpersonal outcomes. Thus, in the process of developing a consistent values-driven behavioral activation plan, therapists catalogue communication, conflict management, and/or problem-solving skill deficits in need of development for optimal interpersonal effectiveness, which will be the focus of therapeutic attention in the next module (Module 8).

In the first part of Module 7, therapists should once again review the personal values first discussed in Module 1 via use of the VLQ-2. At this point, these values should be reviewed and consideration should be given to making changes deemed appropriate by the therapist. At this point of the CART program, it is not uncommon for clients to begin to see life and its possibilities differently. It is also helpful for therapists to once again note the difference between goals and values, as clients occasionally lose the distinction from time to time until the concept is truly solidified.

Once clients have developed a solid idea about their values, that is, what they want life to be about, therapists now move to a discussion of the concept of commitment. We begin by differentiating motivation from commitment. Namely, *motivation* reflects wanting something, while *commitment* reflects one's willingness to actually behave in ways that can lead to what one wants, even when it's uncomfortable to do so. We thus define commitment as the regular and consistent engagement in those specific behaviors and activities that are in the service of one's personal values. With the stage appropriately set, therapists now introduce the Committing to Life Values Exercise Form (see Appendix 5.9), which now replaces the Between-Session Emotion Monitoring Form for weekly use during this module. In this exercise, the client:

- connects personal values to associated short- and long-term goals
- connects values and goals to specific behaviors necessary to promote the identified goals and values
- regularly monitors naturally occurring (real-world) situations that require behavior in the service of values and goals.

When first introducing the "committing to life values" exercise, therapists should work with clients to complete the form using a recent situation as an example. Clients are then asked to complete the form between sessions to monitor events and the presence or absence of behaviors related to the identified values and goals. Table 5.3 provides an example of a completed between-session Committing to Life Values Exercise Form.

The following vignette is an example of a therapist and client completing this exercise during a session.

T: Now that we've talked about it, let's actually go through the form and see if we can fill in the sections so you can see how to use it between sessions.

C: Sure.

T: OK, let's start with a specific personal value that we've already identified. Let's use "be a good husband and father," which you've mentioned before. Sound good?

C: Yep, definitely.

T: So, we write that in on top. Now, let's talk about some short- and long-term goals, you know, some specific achievable things associated with that value.

C: How about making a point of spending more time with them as a short-term goal, and being more involved in school and family stuff as a goal that will take more time to see some results.

T: That's perfect, so let's write that in the next two lines. Now, what do you think are the specific behaviors that would be necessary?

C: Oh that's obvious. The things I do when I get angry, for sure.

T: Let me rephrase that for you a little bit . . . you mean the things you do when angry in order to make people stop doing whatever it is they are doing, so you stop feeling angry. Or, the things you do to just escape feeling angry.

C: [Laughing] Yes, I know that's what I do, just thought I'd say it the short way.

T: [Laughing] Ahh, just wanted to be sure. Let's right that down . . . I'll write it as, "change behavior that avoids or escapes feeling angry into behavior that engages with family even when angry." OK? By the way, we should change "spending more time with family" to "spending more time with family even when angry," don't you think?

C: Yea, that's good. That's the tough part.

T: Yes it is, but isn't it tougher to watch your relationships get more distant even though you say you want to be a good father and husband?

C: Absolutely. This is important.

T: OK, so now let's talk about a situation that has occurred during the past week or so that we can use as an example, and that will be how you use the form going forward.

C: Um, OK . . . uhh, last week my wife told me there was a school play, which I forgot about, and made plans to hang out with my friends and watch football. She started pushing me about it and I got pretty angry.

T: OK, so the situation was a school play that you had forgotten about. Fits right in with the good father value you established, doesn't it?

C: Yes, and I started getting angry about being pushed about it, and that I had to cancel my plans. Wanted to just tell her to go without me and leave the house.

T: Well, there's your obstacle. Getting angry and immediately acting on it in order to feel better instantly.

C: Yea, but, I just sat there a few minutes, like we talked about. Thought about what I really should do, and I called my friends, cancelled my plans, and went to the play.

T: Great. So, the action taken was to go to the school play. What would be the short- and long-term goals?

C: Well, the short-term goal would be see my daughter's play . . . I can't remember ever going to one. The long-term goal would be getting closer to her and showing my wife that the two of them matter to me.

T: OK, good job. Now, just use this form between our sessions, and write down situations like that . . . no matter what choices you made. No one's perfect, so you'll have some successes and some that work out less well, but, over time, you'll do more and more things that conform to what your values and goals are. The whole purpose of this exercise is that you can use this as a form to remind you of the specific behaviors you want to increase . . . that really matter to you, and also keep a record of what you actually do and see your own progress. It also gives us something to focus our sessions on each week.

Table 5.3 Committing to Life Values Exercise Form (Case Example)

Personal Value: To be a good husband and father

Short-Term Goal Associated with Personal Value: Spending more time with family even when angry

Long-Term Goal Associated with Personal Value: Being more involved in school and family activities

Behavior(s) Required to Pursue Value and Goals: Change behaviors that avoid or escape being angry into behaviors that connects me with my family even when angry

Potential Obstacles: Long history of automatically behaving badly when angry and pulling away from my family

Situation: A school play that I forgot about and made other plans

Action Taken: Thought about it, then cancelled my plans and went to school play

Situation: Wife wanted to go out and I was tired

Action Taken: Talked to her about it, she told me it was important to her, and I decided that I should go out with her even though I wanted to stay in.

Note that, in creating this form during a session, the therapist is setting up a behavior plan for the client in the week ahead. It is helpful if therapists create one of these for each identified personal value, to record increased behavior in all identified values areas. We suggest that two areas be developed in the first session of Module 7, and the remainder in the next session. The completed between-session forms should then be reviewed at the beginning of each subsequent CART session, even following the completion of Module 7.

In the course of this exercise, it often becomes obvious that the client is lacking in certain skill sets to effectively work toward stated values. For example, clients might note the desire to be a good relationship partner, but may lack the necessary communication skills (often as simple as conveying thoughts, feelings, and needs in an appropriately assertive way, rather than in a harsh aggressive way, or not at all). These skill deficits should be noted, as suggested earlier in the CART program, as they are addressed in the next CART module. When clients are actively and consistently engaging in committed actions in the service of their values, Module 7 is complete, and we are ready to move on to Module 8.

Obstacles Often Encountered in Module 7

In Module 7, the most common obstacle faced by therapists is the lack of client completion of the between-session exercises and forms. While some clients will claim that they engaged in the behaviors, and just didn't have time or forgot to complete the forms (and in fact they do often complete the tasks without completing the forms), therapists must work to ensure that the forms are complete. These exercises and the completion of necessary forms provide a great deal of information for clients and therapists, and they allow both clients and therapists to monitor progress, note skill deficits, and often lead to important information. Discussing these situations long after they occur provides some information, but not the level of detail that can be gained from immediate completion, which takes a very short amount of time. As each session of this module should begin with a review of these forms, when the forms have not been completed, the first task of that session should be to review the situation(s) that have occurred during the week, and have clients (not the therapists) complete the forms. Of course, this is not a good use of time, and should only occur if clients fail to complete the forms between sessions. Yet even when this happens, therapists should discuss the lack of previous completion of the forms as an obstacle, and stress to clients that they are expected to come to the next session fully prepared.

Less frequently, but on occasion, we will find that clients are not creating situations that allow for these new behaviors. In such circumstances, therapists need to work with clients so that they understand that the purpose here is not to passively wait for such circumstances to present themselves, but rather, to actively create opportunities to engage in values-driven behaviors. In this regard, therapists may need to help clients see situations in which to try their new behaviors, or look for missed opportunities of which clients are not even cognizant. This is an important component of the CART process, and must therefore be carefully attended to so to promote the necessary commitment to values-based behavioral activation.

Module 8: Developing Effective Interpersonal Problem-Solving Skills

Estimated Number of Sessions to Completion: 2–3

Goals of Module 8

- Enhance interpersonal problem-solving skills.
- Enhance communication and assertiveness skills.
- Enhance conflict management skills.

Materials Needed for Module 8

- Acceptance and Action Questionnaire-2 (AAQ-2)
- Anger and Violence Impairment Scale (AVIS)
- Valued Living Questionnaire-2 (VLQ-2)
- Mindful Attention and Awareness Scale (MAAS)
- Interpersonal Problem Solving Form

The primary therapeutic task of Module 8 is the development of the fundamental problem-solving and interpersonal skills necessary for the ongoing pursuit of previously identified personal values. It is likely that a number of skill deficits will have been obvious in previous treatment modules, as clinical anger clients have historically utilized over-learned avoidance and escape behaviors rather than proactive skill-based behaviors to respond to a wide array of social situations. As such, clients will more often than not need to develop specific skills relating to problem solving, communication, and/or conflict management. These skills are taught and practiced within therapy sessions and ultimately utilized between sessions, with concomitant feedback and additional practice serving to shape these necessary behaviors. These skills are systematically shaped in order to promote the continued (effective) use of values-driven behaviors in clients' lives. At this point in the CART program, these skills can be more effectively learned, as clients should by now have developed the emotional tolerance to function adaptively without the need to utilize emotion-driven behaviors as a means of avoidance or escape. The importance of the skill development in this module lies in the fact that utilization of more effective "positive" interpersonal behaviors in turn increases the likelihood that clients will be naturally reinforced by their environment and will thus remain values-directed in their behavioral choices, even while experiencing emotional discomfort.

In understanding the skill deficits inherent in clinical anger populations, we refer the reader back to the AAM presented in Chapter 2. Clients experiencing problems with anger have most often come from early environments that would best be described as chronically aversive and/or harsh. In this regard, clients experiencing clinical anger are similar to those clients who experience chronic depression, which evolves from very similar early environments (McCullough, 2000) and includes significant deficits in developing "if–then" reasoning. Given their aversive and often unpredictable historical environments, both chronically depressed and clinically angry populations do not develop an adequate capacity to effectively interpret their environment and draw accurate conclusions about likely outcomes based on specific behaviors. Rather, they view the world as random and unpredictable, and outcomes as unconnected to their behavior. The development of effective interpersonal skills begins with an effort to help clients experiencing clinical anger better understand the connection between action and outcome, as well as understand the relationship between specific behavioral choices and desired outcomes. Many of us take this process for granted, as most people have developed the necessary action-outcome connection. Yet, this connection is more often than not lacking in anger clients, and as such, this becomes a necessary target of therapeutic attention in Module 8.

We begin the process of skill development by sharing with clients the goal of this module, with an eye toward a discussion of a recent situation in which these deficits can be readily demonstrated. Such situations are not uncommon for clients, and it is most likely that therapists will readily remember an appropriate recent situation by which to begin the skill building process. The following vignette is an example of just such a conversation with a client in the first session of Module 8.

T: Jenny, now we begin the next phase of our program . . . we call it the interpersonal skills building portion of treatment. Remember during an earlier part of therapy that we talked about once you could handle experiencing anger better that we would eventually get to putting some skills in place so that you would be able to respond better to difficult situations in your life?

C: Yeah I do . . . it was a while ago, but I remember something about that.

T: Good, because that's what we're going to work on next. Let's start by focusing on a recent situation in which you got angry, let yourself be angry, and did not try to escape the feeling, but also didn't really get what you would have wanted out of the situation.

C: How about the stuff we talked about last week with my boss?

T: That would be fine . . . let's review that. As I recall, he put you on a shift that you didn't want, and that you were too "senior" for. When you tried to talk to him about it, he interrupted you and told you to stop complaining and get back to work. You became angry, wanted to spit at him as I recall, didn't . . . thankfully, and just walked away, but really felt mistreated.

C: That's it . . . totally. And I think about it whenever I see him.

T: OK, now I think the time is right for you to learn how to directly deal with things that need to be dealt with, *while* you feel angry, and without resorting to the aggressive stuff that got you in trouble.

In this first part of the vignette above, the client was presented with the therapeutic goal ahead, and the therapist then presented a recent situation that would seem to call for some improved communications skill. This first part of the module focuses on setting the stage and preparing clients for what lies ahead. Next begins the process of actual skills training. While there have been many presentations of interpersonal skills training programs within professional psychology (D'Zurilla, Chang, &

Sanna, 2004; Linehan, 1993), in CART, we have integrated components found in various interpersonal skills training programs into an approach developed specifically with the needs of clients experiencing clinical anger in mind.

As noted in Chapter 2, McCullough (2000) has suggested that chronic depression is characterized by an early aversive history, culminating in significant difficulties in understanding and responding to interpersonal situations. The Anger Avoidance Model has similarly suggested (backed by empirical data) the early aversive childhood experiences and social skill deficits in clinical anger clients. As such, in CART-based interpersonal skills training, we begin with a systematic effort to: (a) enhance our clients' capacities to accurately and effectively understand situations; (b) determine specifically what they would like the outcome of those situations to be; (c) connect specific behaviors likely to result in those outcomes; and (d) develop the skills necessary to increase the likelihood that those behaviors, and hence the desired outcomes, will occur.

The first component of CART's interpersonal training is intended to help clients clearly distinguish between facts and opinions/beliefs/assumptions, as well as between desired values-based outcomes and actual outcomes, with regard to interpersonal situations. This process can be most readily done with the use of the Interpersonal Problem Solving Form (see Appendix 5.10). The process begins with identifying a recent situation, which will be used as a vehicle to demonstrate the use of the IPS form, and also serves to begin the in-session task of implementing interpersonal skills training. What follows below is a continuation of the previous vignette in which the purpose of interpersonal skills training was presented.

T: OK, so let's begin by taking a look at this form that we use as part of this segment of the treatment. We're going to go through the situation we briefly reviewed, and fill in each part of this form based on that situation. Then, after you understand how it's used, I'll ask you to complete it a couple of times before our next session.

C: Yea. What do I do first.

T: Let's begin by writing in the situation we just reviewed. How would you briefly describe it?

C: My boss gave me a shift that he knew I didn't want and I didn't deserve.

T: OK, write that down on top. Now let's write down *only* the facts about the situation . . . what we call the Five Ws.

C: Alright, um, well it was last Monday, while I was at work. A new schedule comes out every Monday, and, what's left . . . uhh, the "what," OK, he gave me a shift he knew I didn't want . . .

T: Let me stop you for a minute . . . who, where, when, and why seems about right. But, let's take a look at the "what" for a moment. How do you know that he knew you didn't want this shift?

C: How could he not know? I've been there for five years.

T: How long has he been your boss?

C: About two years I guess.

T: Well, you may be right, but since it's not a fact, and just an assumption you are making, let's leave it off for now.

C: I get it . . .

T: OK, next, what other thoughts, opinions, or assumptions did you make about the schedule?

C: I'm not sure if this is a fact or assumption, but I did think that he knew that I had seniority over a few of the guys who got better shifts, and he was doing it on purpose to screw me.

T: I hear two assumptions . . . that he knew you have seniority, and that he was trying to screw you.

C: Well, if he didn't know, he should have.

T: Maybe so, but this is still an assumption . . . What we are trying to do here is separate the clear absolute facts from how you interpreted the situation, the reasons for the situation, and the motivations of others. The point is that we want you to be clear about these differences because ultimately the goal will be for you to consider the facts and make decisions based upon them.

C: OK, I see that.

T: Let's go to the next part of the form . . . What did you really want to make happen in this situation? What outcome would have been what you wanted, and also consistent with your values?

C: I guess I would have wanted to get my shift changed . . . being home at night really matters to me and my family, you know?

T: OK . . . now write that on the form. Next, tell me what you did to get what you wanted.

C: Actually, not much. I stormed out . . . cursed pretty loudly as I left too. And, since then haven't said a word to him.

T: OK, let's write that down, too. So, I would imagine that the actual outcome of what you did has been that nothing has changed. You still have the shift you don't want.

C: Right.

T: OK, now we write that down as well. So, what do you think you would have needed to do to get the outcome you wanted?

C: I'm not sure anything would have worked. Besides he knew that I didn't want this shift.

T: Well maybe, but, like we talked about before, that is an assumption, maybe correct, maybe not. But, what *might* have worked?

C: I don't really know.

In this portion of the vignette, we first see the difficulty the client is having with distinguishing between fact and assumption, a difficulty that is very common and often needs a good deal of work to overcome. We also see an inability to recognize that there were *possible* approaches to getting the desired outcome. As we have noted previously, this is characteristic of this clinical population, in that for reasons of chronic childhood maltreatment and resultant difficulties with emotion regulation, clients with clinical anger have significant deficits in the capacity to recognize that their actions can in fact impact situations. The vignette then continues with this issue:

T: OK, well, let's think about it, and just focus on the facts, not the assumptions. In order for your boss to even consider changing the schedule, you would have had to let him know that you didn't want it, that your seniority should give you first choice in shift, and to let him know that this decision negatively affected your home life and that it upset you.

C: But he had to know.

T: Maybe, but maybe not. The bottom line is, you can't be sure, and regardless of whether you are correct or not, you have every right, and maybe even an obligation to yourself, to do what you can to possibly change a bad situation. Even if it doesn't work, you did what you could. At this point, all you can say is that you did nothing to make it worse.

C: [Long pause] . . . well, I guess you're right. But what if I start to talk to him and he gives me an attitude and tells me to shut up and just go to work.

T: If that happens, you will be angry, you will accept your anger as reasonable, and will act in a manner that is in your own best interest. And, I have to point out, you would be in no worse situation than you are now. The same shift, but at least, if you do this, there is a chance that things could change.

C: I don't know if I have ever just calmly talked to someone when they do something I don't like.

T: I know, and that's why we're here working on this stuff. So, you can write in "speak to your boss about the situation" in the "needed to do" column of our form. And in the last column of the form, the one about obstacles, you indicated that your anger might be an obstacle, so list that. Now you are ready to go out and try doing this during the upcoming week . . . let's practice how you might do this.

In the latter part of the vignette, the client and therapist complete the form, and then move on to practice the new behavior in which the client is being asked to engage. It must be emphasized that identifying appropriate new behavior is not sufficient, as these clients have not experienced appropriate assertive communication before, and thus, some in-session role-play-oriented practice is most often necessary. In this regard, we provide our clients with a distinction between aggressive, assertive, and passive behavior in the following way: Aggressive behavior is where, for what-ever reason, you act as though your feelings and your needs are important and no one else's are. Passive behavior is when, for whatever reason, you act as though someone else's feelings and needs matter and yours do not. Finally, assertive behavior is when you present your needs and feelings directly and respectfully in a manner that communicates what you feel and what you need, while also letting the other person know that his or her needs and feelings matter as well. While there certainly is a continuum between these three descriptions, we seek to help our clients communicate as frequently as possible in a manner consistent with assertive behavior. This is also a critical component of conflict management skills in which the ability to hear the needs, concerns, and feelings of others, and balance them with one's own needs, concerns, and feelings is essential. Finally, it is necessary to help clients generate alternative possibilities for their responses to situations, and carefully review the possible outcomes of each prior to deciding on a choice of action. Once again, this lack of problem-solving skill is often missing in such clients, and clinicians must help them become better at this fundamental skill.

The therapist should review the Interpersonal Problem Solving Form in each session dedicated to interpersonal skills training, and utilize this form as a vehicle by which new learning can occur. If this form is not com-pleted between sessions, therapists and clients should complete the form using between-session material, as suggested in the previous vignette, and this module should not be seen as complete until clients can successfully complete this form on their own between sessions and begin to utilize enhanced interpersonal skills in their daily lives.

At this point, the substantive portion of the CART program is com-plete, and we move to consolidate learning and prepare clients for treat-ment termination in the next and last module.

Obstacles Often Encountered in Module 8

There are two common obstacles to the successful completion of Module 8. One is a familiar refrain—that is, the failure of the client to engage in both the activities and completion of the required form between sessions. Therapists must understand that, in many respects, this is an overwhelm-ing task to many clients experiencing clinical anger, in that the consid-eration of fact vs assumption, and careful consideration of actions that may result in their desired outcomes, are often quite foreign to them. In fact, these clients have most likely spent the greater part of their lives not adequately seeing the connection between their own actions and later outcomes. It is therefore particularly important for therapists to assess the degree to which these activities are either being avoided because: (a) they are difficult, or (b) they are simply not fully understood. The lat-ter case requires additional time and explanation, while the former case reflects a clinical issue to confront. Is the client simply not making time or accepting the importance of developing these new skills? Or, is the client avoiding the discomfort of approaching life in a new way? If the problem lies in avoidance, therapists should rely on reaffirming the importance of tolerance/acceptance of that discomfort in the process of pursuing valued outcomes, in contrast to the old habits of avoidance in the service of short-term comfort. This may require a step back, as it is very possible that such clients, despite the efforts of the therapist, do not fully understand or have not fully grasped the skill set of appropriately analyzing situations, determining desired outcomes, and selecting appropriate behavioral responses intended to achieve those outcomes.

If, however, it appears to be more of the latter problem relating to commitment and/or time management, therapists should instead carefully and with patient persistence once again discuss the importance of developing these skills and connecting/anchoring these efforts with clients' personal values.

Module 9: Integration, Relapse Prevention, and Treatment Termination

Estimated Number of Sessions to Completion: 2

Goals of Module 9

- The identification of anger-inducing triggers and a discussion of possible lapses.
- The in-vivo practice of potential anger-inducing triggers.
- The development of ongoing action plans for continued use of CART principles and strategies.
- Proactive treatment termination.

Materials Needed for Module 9

- Acceptance and Action Questionnaire-2 (AAQ-2)
- Anger and Violence Impairment Scale (AVIS)
- Valued Living Questionnaire-2 (VLQ-2)
- Mindful Attention and Awareness Scale (MAAS)
- Interpersonal Problem Solving Form
- Post-CART Practice Plan Form

We now embark upon the final CART module. In this module, as has been the case throughout treatment, therapists will begin each session by completing the AAQ-2, AVIS, VLQ-2, and MAAS, followed by the usual beginning of an in-session mindfulness exercise. At this point in treatment, therapists should note improved scores on the AAQ-2, AVIS, and MAAS, suggesting increased psychological flexibility (as a result of reduced experiential avoidance), reduced negative life impact of anger and associated behaviors, and an increase in mindful attention and awareness. Interestingly, our clinical research lab has found that if additional measures assessing anger itself have been given as outcome measures (i.e. ADS, STAXI-2), small decreases in the experience of anger may or may not be noted, as reduction of anger has actually not been the goal of CART. In fact, for many clients who have presented with inhibited anger, by this point in treatment an increase in experienced anger may be noted on relevant self-report measures. In addition, therapists should note increased values-driven behaviors on the VLQ-2, as clients should at this point be more consistently engaged in behavior that is directly and purposefully intended to be in the service of identified personal values. If these changes are not apparent, therapists should consider whether some additional time needs to be spent on the relevant previously completed modules prior to beginning Module 9. If, however, these positive changes are noted, therapists and clients are ready to move on to the final CART module.

In this final module, we continue to monitor and provide feedback on the Interpersonal Problem Solving Form early in each session of Module 9, as a way to continue building upon interpersonal skill development. Next, clinicians revisit the previously identified hierarchy of anger producing situations list developed in Module 6, with a focus on the two most challenging/difficult situations identified on that list. Therapists should now go back to the first two (most difficult) situations on that list, which were suggested to be left uncompleted until this final module, and: (a) engage in in-session exposures to these situations, and (b) follow in-session exposures with assigned between-session real-world exposures to these situations, if possible. With anger regulation/tolerance further developed, with an enhanced commitment to values-driven behavioral choices, and with newly developed interpersonal skills in place, clients are now able to more effectively confront their most difficult potential anger-inducing situations, and as such, move closer to being ready to finish their course of psychological treatment. The manner in which these exposures should be performed is exactly the same as was described in Module 6. This is an important component of Module 9, and of significant importance, it is the effective completion of these exercises that signal a client's readiness for treatment termination.

These exposures also allow therapists to review the entire skill set that has been included in the CART program. In this portion of Module 9, therapists should review all of the primary skills of the previous eight modules and discuss with clients how each of these module skills have been incorporated into their lives. This review should be more than a historical retrospective, but rather, should be seen as an important part of the preparation for treatment termination, in that it should lead to a very careful and detailed discussion of how clients plan to continue their use of CART principles and skills once treatment ends. It is useful for therapists to help develop a very specific plan for when, where, why, and how clients will utilize what they have learned in CART in their continued pursuits of a valued life. This plan is an essential part of Module 9 and should be carefully constructed with the client. The Post-CART Practice Plan Form contained in Appendix 5.11 provides a structure for this discussion, and can be used as an ongoing guide and recording form for clients. For example, it helps clarify when and how they will utilize mindfulness exercises, what thoughts their minds still tell them from which they must decenter, when they are likely to experience anger and how they would like to behave when confronting that anger, and what their most important values are and how they need to behave to move toward those values on a regular basis, to name but a few possibilities. Therapists should explain this form to clients and help them understand that continued use of the CART program's techniques and strategies are necessary for continued growth and development. We have found it useful here to once again use a comparison to diabetes to help clients understand this point. Diabetes is a disease that at this point in time has no cure, and if it is ignored can be extremely debilitating and result in death. However, if individuals understand their diabetes, and accept that daily management of their diabetes requires that they do very specific things on a regular basis (medication, diet, checking blood sugar level, etc.), they can live a relatively normal and healthy life. Similarly, given their histories and genetic hard wiring, which cannot be changed, our clients must address some psychological processes on a daily basis in order to maximize the quality of their lives. As such, managing one's life by regularly and systematically engaging in mindfulness exercises and remaining willing to confront anger-inducing situations while behaving in a manner consistent with personal values, is necessary in a manner that is similar to the diabetic patient's day-to-day medical management requirements. We have found this comparison to be easily understood and helpful in making the crucial point that the upcoming end of formal treatment should not be seen as the *end*, but rather the *beginning* of a different chapter in the ongoing pursuit of a meaningful life.

It is following this review and future post-treatment plan development that a discussion of upcoming treatment termination should begin with clients. It is likely that brief mention/discussion of upcoming treatment termination has occurred earlier in the CART program, as clients regularly, and appropriately, want to know how much longer treatment will last. So in this regard, preliminary aspects of treatment termination discussion and contemplation have more than likely already occurred. However, as CART moves close to being completed, issues related to treatment termination move front and center. It has been our experience that there are several guiding principles for therapists to consider in the process of treatment termination, as follows.

1. Treatment termination must be presented as reflecting clients' successes. Clients have worked hard, have been open to viewing life and the problems that brought them to treatment differently, and have been willing to act differently in order to move closer to a valued life.

2. Treatment termination does not suggest or imply that future contact with the therapist for one or two "booster" sessions cannot occur. In this regard, we often present a dental example in that when one completes a course of dental treatment, there is no assumption that a new dental problem will never emerge. Here, it is suggested to the client that the therapist is available if issues, be they similar or different, emerge in the future.

3. Clients experiencing clinical anger have most often experienced difficult childhood relationships in which emotional and/or physical neglect/abuse resulted in expectations of abandonment in close relationships. When abandonment issues have been identified, it is imperative that therapists use treatment termination as an opportunity for clients to experience a healthy relational outcome, and in appropriately conducting a proactive and fully processed treatment termination, this new relational learning takes shape. Therapists should take the time needed to engage clients in this discussion and make certain that clients have effectively processed the upcoming termination and show no signs of a problematic response before termination is complete.

4. Whenever possible, there should at least one session following the discussion of treatment termination to gauge reactions and responses.

While therapists must ensure that clients are responding appropriately to issues surrounding treatment termination, therapists must also ensure that they themselves are responding appropriately to termination. These discussions are often difficult. Such issues include (but are not limited to): (a) facing our own relationship-ending schemas; (b) dealing with the loss of clients with whom we have established a bond, and who are often reinforcing to us through their improvements; and (c) any issues that are an elephant-in-the-room with clinicians, such as letting go of clients who are financially supporting our practice through the fees that they pay. These are all issues to which therapists are not immune. As such, it is imperative that therapists moving through the treatment termination process be mindful of their own reactions and work to ensure that they do not avoid these discussions or unnecessarily prolong treatment for their own personal reasons.

Obstacles Often Encountered in Module 9

The most common obstacles in effectively completing Module 9 fall within two broad themes. The first relates to clients whose rejection sensitivity/abandonment schemas make treatment termination a real-life exposure that must be understood and processed the same way that other anger-related schemas were processed in Modules 6 and 9. For these clients, the appropriate ending of the therapeutic relationship will nevertheless trigger discomfort and a stimulus to automatically engage in previously (over-learned) avoidant interpersonal behaviors. If therapists are aware of and sensitive to these schemas, the termination process actually enhances the growth and personal development of clients. The problem surfaces if termination is treated superficially and is not seen as potentially a very real stimulus for maladaptive interpersonal behaviors. If recognized and understood as reflecting rejection/abandonment sensitivity, therapists will, at this final point in the CART program, find that the knowledge and skills put in place throughout the program will allow the issue to be addressed in a constructive and positive way, more quickly than might initially have been thought. It has been our experience that when addressed at this point in treatment, the issues related to treatment termination can be processed effectively, as the termination process itself allows for constructive and interpersonally appropriate new learning.

The second broad theme noted as an obstacle for effective completion of Module 9 relates to the therapist's own personal issues, as noted earlier. Most importantly, therapists who are themselves uncomfortable with discussing termination, either due to their own relationship issues, or due to discomfort in simply having the termination discussion with clients who might possibly react negatively, tend to avoid the issue and either have more sessions than are necessary, or shorten the termination discussion to an unrealistically brief period of time. While there is no simple solution to this problem, we suggest that therapists be reminded once again that to be effective using the CART model, they must work toward the same mindful, accepting, committed action approach to life that they expect their clients to adopt.

Concluding Comments and Treatment Efficacy

With the step-by-step description and discussion of the CART program complete, we conclude this chapter by reinforcing and accentuating a number of strategies that therapists should remember in moving through the nine CART modules, and finally conclude with a brief discussion of the treatment efficacy data of the CART protocol. Below are some of our final thoughts on critical key points for clinicians to remember.

- CART comprises nine modules and *not* nine sessions. As previously described, CART has been designed to maximize therapist flexibility based upon client needs and treatment context. As such, the nine CART modules have been presented with a usual number of sessions necessary for completion. Once again, we stress that these numbers are to be seen as a general guide and not an inflexible prescription for treatment length.

- While Module 2 emphasizes the awareness and appropriate response to clinically relevant behaviors, it is important to reinforce the idea that these behaviors are very likely to appear throughout the nine-module CART treatment, and will rarely be restricted to early sessions. While we have in fact found that these issues are most likely to manifest early in treatment (and hence the particular focus/emphasis on CRBs in Module 2), therapists must always maintain vigilance for CRB1s early to mid-treatment and CRB2s mid- to late treatment, as these in-session clinically relevant behaviors should always take precedence over any preplanned session content and be responded to as indicated. We have noted that, often, therapists—especially those who are inexperienced or simply new to CART—will become so focused on their planned session strategies and techniques that they ignore or simply do not notice important clinically relevant behaviors occurring in session.

- Effective use of CART requires that therapists systematically utilize regular assessment/measurement of appropriate psychological processes. While we have introduced instruments that we have found to be theoretically appropriate, well designed, and clinically useful, therapists can most certainly utilize measures of their own choosing. If therapists intend to utilize different measures than those discussed herein, we suggest: (a) choosing measures that are directly related to the processes that are being targeted and the outcomes that are desired; (b) choosing instruments that are reasonably short and do not take up important treatment time; and (c) choosing instruments that have been shown to be sensitive to change, thus providing clinicians with accurate feedback regarding treatment progress.

- Therapists should remember the core role that regular mindfulness practice has in the success of CART. As such, it is important that therapists remember that each session should begin or end with a brief mindfulness exercise, chosen based upon client readiness. Remember, the introduction and use of mindfulness exercises should generally be structured from external focus (e.g. washing a dish) to internal focus (e.g. centered breathing), and from brief (e.g. mindful breathing) to somewhat longer (e.g. self/other compassion exercise) exercises. For many clients, beginning a session with a mindfulness exercise creates the context appropriate for good session content and discussion that follows.

- Following the mindfulness exercise, or at the beginning of the session if the mindfulness exercise is done at end of the session, therapists should commence with a review of the between-session exercise that was assigned. These exercises should be assigned each week, and provide: (a) the opportunity to begin each session in a manner that creates direct connection to the previous session. That is, rather than beginning with "How was your week?" or some similar normal conversation, the therapist begins with a discussion of the assigned exercise, thus creating a natural and seamless connection from session to session. This also allows the module-relevant therapeutic goals to be the prime focus of each treatment session; (b) the opportunity for between-session practice, feedback, and correction; or (c) the opportunity to address a client's lack of true understanding or willingness to change/add a particular behavior, or characteristic avoidance of something new and challenging. In any case, this review is often ignored by therapists who are not use to or comfortable with structured treatment protocols.

- Some sessions inevitably provide the opportunity for a premature discussion of situations/issues unrelated to the module to which therapists should be attending. In such cases, the situations/issues that are presenting themselves will be more closely related to the processes/goals to be addressed in future modules. In such cases, therapists must first and foremost understand the full module structure of CART so that they in fact recognize issues that are more closely related to activities intended for future modules. Second, clinicians must demonstrate patience and resist the temptation to move ahead too quickly or change the CART module sequence. CART has been developed with a very careful scaffolding of processes and treatment goals, and reorganizing them is highly likely to create problems in the sequenced learning of skills that is the foundation of the CART program. We have found that premature movement from one module to the next and/or impatient restructuring of the module sequence is a common reason for lack of treatment success.

- The CART protocol has been developed as a transdiagnostic treatment approach for clients whose anger and its associated behaviors are the central focus of treatment. It goes without saying that there will be many diagnostic combinations that are presented to clinicians working with clinical anger clients. Clinicians must always consider when, how, and at what point of treatment to address issues relating to these other diagnostic entities, although research has consistently demonstrated that effectively treating a primary psychological issue most often results in the reduction of other psychological difficulties most often associated with other diagnoses (Farchione *et al.*, 2012). The issue of comorbidities, and when and how to integrate treatment components that may be appropriate for different diagnostic groups, will be addressed in greater detail in Chapter 7.

Treatment Efficacy

The CART program is being continuously evaluated in our clinical research laboratory. We have presented data on a group of clients court mandated for non-domestic violence (Gardner & Moore, 2010) and additional data with regard to the treatment of clients who have been court mandated for domestic violence (Gardner, Moore, & Dettore, 2013).

Study 1

The first study, intended to be used for protocol development and modification as needed, included 193 clients who were court referred for a variety of non-domestic violence offenses (such as simple and aggravated assault) for treatment using the CART protocol. Non-domestic violent offenses are defined as violent offenses that do not involve family members, partner, girl/boyfriend, etc.

In this first CART evaluation, from an attendance standpoint, there was a relatively high attrition rate prior to session 4 (75%). Gondolf and Foster (1991) reported that, in an anger management program for domestic violence populations, the no-show rate for intake sessions was 73%, and that 86% of their sample never returned after their *first* session. So, the attrition rate of 75% *by* the fourth session likely represents several issues. First, when referred by the court system, clients are often told that they will be attending an anger management *class*. Thus, many clients enter treatment with the expectation that their mandated intervention will be a "class" and not formal psychological treatment, and thus, the expectation is that the time they will put into this process will be exceptionally brief and many balk at the idea of more than the initial intake session. In addition, even when a "class" was not mandated, quite often a specific (and often very brief) number of sessions were mandated, usually two to four. Thus, since many clients fulfilled their treatment mandate *by the courts* in two to four sessions (even though the CART protocol was not finished), very few of these particular clients continued past the required mandate. This creates a situation in which "attrition" is difficult to truly gauge.

The premature attrition issue may be circumvented by providing education regarding the program to clients prior to their initial intake sessions. In fact, subsequent to this first study, we have found that such a procedure dramatically reduces early attrition. Interestingly, the best predictor of early attrition (i.e. immediately following intake) was elevated scores on the AAQ, reflecting high levels of experiential avoidance/lack of psychological flexibility. The best predictor of premature termination once actual CART treatment sessions began was elevated scores (above the 75th percentile) on the Hurt and Rejection subscale of the Anger Disorders Scale.

When looking at the data of the CART program completers, statistically significant differences were found on several ADS measures across sessions. Scores on the subscale that measures a participant's reactions to perceived social rejection or threats to self-esteem (Hurt/Social Rejection

Scale) were reduced by 41% from initial intake to session 8 ($p < .05$, $d = .41$). Differences were also found on the subscale that measures angry rumination (Rumination Scale), as participants' scores were reduced by 25% from the first to the eighth session, representing a statistically significant finding ($p < .05$, $d = .47$). On the Resentment subscale, which measures an individual's attitude of hostility based on the belief that life is unfair to them, statistically significant differences were obtained when comparing sessions 1–8, as scores were reduced by 30% ($p < .05$, $d = .32$). There was also a statistically significant improvement on the Scope of Anger Scale, which represents an individual's tendency to respond with anger when faced with eliciting situations. Between initial sessions 1–12, a 42% reduction was noted ($p > .05$, $d = .67$). Most importantly, the subscale measuring the tendency to actively express anger through physical aggression (Physical Aggression Scale) demonstrated the greatest significant difference from sessions 1–12, as scores were reduced by 49% ($p < .01$, $d = .89$).

These results provided preliminary evidence for the viability of CART in a real-world clinical setting. These data suggest that the 48 clients who completed the CART program at that time made significant gains as defined by scores on the ADS. While the attrition rate in this first study was problematic, our experience leads to the unmistakable conclusion that the primary factor for this attrition was not the treatment itself, but rather was due to unreasonable expectations of one- to four-hour "classes" for "anger management" found frequently in the judicial system. Clients know that this is an option for them and often choose to go down that route as an easier and less time-intensive (and often less costly) way of fulfilling their sentencing mandates. Thus, such individuals never make any real commitment to psychological treatment.

In addition, the medium to large effect sizes found in this study, while good, were still not what we had hoped for. While one reason for this finding was certainly the low-powered, relatively small sample, the fact remains that the effect sizes were not as good as expected. The one exception to this was maybe the most important—that is, the effect size with regard to the reduction of physical violence as a behavioral response to anger, which was both the strongest of all outcomes, and is in line with treatment outcomes found in anxiety and depression treatment studies. Further, both interestingly and importantly, our clients showed little change in physiological arousal and overall experience of anger as measured by the ADS, a finding which is significant in that: (a) CART does not target these processes, and as such, the lack of change in them is quite predictable; and (b) the changes in rumination, and especially physical aggression, occurred in the absence of reductions in the subjective experience of anger and anger arousal. These are fully expected outcomes from CART, and likewise as expected, are contrary to traditional cognitive behavioral models.

In addition to the Anger Disorders Scale used as a primary outcome measures noted above, we incorporated measures that would reflect the process of CART. For this purpose, we utilized the DERS. Results indicate that, as would be predicted by the Anger Avoidance Model and targeted by CART, clients demonstrated significant and strong changes in the desired direction in emotion regulatory processes of emotional understanding and clarity, acceptance of emotions, the availability of strategies to respond to emotions, and reduced impulsivity. Thus, we see a pattern in which aggression and rumination, which are both viewed as avoidant processes by the AAM, are reduced, not in association with the reduction of the experiential and arousal components of anger itself, but rather in association with enhanced emotion regulatory processes.

Study 2

In a structured open-trial, which is presently ongoing, 45 adult clients representing a diverse Caucasian, Latino, and African American sample, were mandated for domestic/intimate partner violence treatment (often referred to as "batterers intervention/counseling"). It should be noted that these clients were *not* given specific session length mandates, but rather, were all given open-ended treatment mandates, a much better means of assessing outcome and treatment tolerance. At intake, clients completed a variety of self-report measures related to level and scope of anger, violent behavior, personal distress, difficulties in emotion regulation, and psychological flexibility. In addition, reoffense rates of treatment participants were made available. With regard to the most important outcome variable, which is overt violent behavior, of the 45 clients who began the CART treatment, 32 completed at least eight sessions (71%). Results indicated that, at five months post-treatment, one (3%) of the CART program completers had reoffended, while five of thirteen treatment *non*-completers had reoffended (38%) within five months of treatment termination. No pre-treatment differences between program completers and non-completers were found. CART program completers also showed significantly enhanced psychological flexibility/experiential acceptance, emotion regulation, and social role functioning, along with a significantly reduced scope of anger-triggering situations (Gardner, Moore, & Pess, 2012). It is important to note once again that, in contrast to the studies using traditional CBT interventions noted earlier, which found a 30–40% recidivism rate within six months of arrest for interpersonal violence (Stover, Meadows, & Kaufman, 2009), only one of the 45 CART participants who have to date completed the open trial has reoffended (as of press time, five months post-treatment completion). While additional data collection and follow-up continue, this open-trial provides strong support for the CART protocol in working with violent offenders, especially interpersonally violent offenders. With protocol development representing Phase 1 of CART development, this open trial represents Phase 2 of an outcome research program that will soon culminate in a randomized controlled trial (Phase 3) comparing CART with traditional CBT interventions.

Study 3

A second open trial of CART was also recently conducted using a developmentally modified group CART protocol provided in an urban school system within a low SES community (Dettore, Lee, & Gardner, 2012). In this study, 12 African-American 5th-grade males (ages 10–12), who were assigned to a self-contained public school class and previously classified by the school district as emotionally disturbed (demonstrating chronic levels of physical and verbal aggression with frequent school suspensions), took part in a nine-session group-based CART program. The CART program followed the same sequence as the adult protocol, with developmentally appropriate modifications of language, examples, and exercises. Following the intervention, these students demonstrated significant increases in concentration, academic functioning, and higher order cognitive skills, and reduced levels of aggressive and impulsive behaviors, as measured by teacher self-reports. Of note, classes receiving treatment-as-usual (i.e. classroom behavioral consultation) showed no such increases. While self-report improvements are certainly a positive sign for clinical research, possibly the greatest indicator of treatment success, however, is the fact that the school district has requested that the CART program be extended throughout their school system and across multiple age groups. This age-modified CART program will be further discussed in Chapter 6.

While the research data in support of CART is still evolving, it is nevertheless substantial. Empirical findings to date suggest that CART: (a) results in behavioral outcomes that appear to be superior to those found in studies utilizing traditional treatments; (b) results in self-report effect sizes at least as strong as, and in some respects stronger than those found among traditional cognitive behavioral interventions for this challenging clinical population; and (c) the mechanisms by which CART appears to work are consistent with theoretical predictions, and in keeping with the foundations of the Anger Avoidance Model (through the enhancement of emotion regulation skills and development of behavioral flexibility). We are excited for future efficacy studies to add valuable data to those collected thus far.

Now that the modular CART protocol has been presented in a step-by-step treatment format, the next chapter discusses some important special considerations that warrant consideration, such as client–therapist issues (culture, SES/privilege, and gender); treatment context (setting, mandated offender status, finite session availability); comorbidities (especially PTSD, depression, and personality disorders); family/couple engagement in treatment; individual vs group treatment; and age considerations.

Appendix 5.1

Decisional Balance Form

Name: Date: Age:

Occupation: Gender:

Please list details for each of the following:

Specific Problem Behavior:	
Benefit(s) of Current Behavior:	
Cost(s) of Current Behavior:	
Benefit(s) of Changing Behavior:	
Cost(s) of Changing Behavior:	

Appendix 5.2

Between-Session Emotion Monitoring Form

Triggering Situation (Person, Place, Event):
What I was thinking?
What I was feeling?
How was my body reacting?
What did I do when I was experiencing this emotion?

Appendix 5.3

Washing a Dish Exercise

Choose a relatively quiet moment to select a dish and place it in an empty sink. Just look at the dish for a moment and become aware of the color, shape, and texture of the dish. You may become aware that other thoughts come into your mind while performing this exercise. This is inevitably going to happen as numerous thoughts come and go in our head all day every day. Simply notice them, notice the tendency to fight them, and let them be. Gently bring yourself back to the task of focusing on the physical aspects of the dish.

Now, pick up the dish and allow comfortably warm water to pass over it. Notice the sensations of the water, its temperature and the feel of the dish as the water passes over it. Once again, you are likely to notice a variety of thoughts unrelated to this task. If so, please notice without judging them as good or bad, right or wrong, but simply an activity in your mind that comes and goes like waves intermittently hitting up against a shore line. The specific thoughts you are having do not matter, just your ability to notice and focus on the feelings and sensations that the water and the dish create. Allow yourself to feel the sensations in more and more detail. In this way, you continually strengthen your concentration.

Now, wash the dish with whatever mild detergent you normally use, and become aware of the additional sensations of smell and touch that emerge from this activity. As you continue to mindfully wash this dish, notice any external sounds and any internal thoughts as though they are simply words or symbols on a tickertape, and gently bring your attention back to the task of washing the dish. Having a variety of thoughts is normal, so be patient with yourself. The fact of the matter is the mind will always tend to wander. Remain in the moment with washing the dish and you will increasingly enhance your attention.

After about 5 minutes, wipe off the dish, stop the water, sit down, and briefly describe in the space provided below the experience you just had. Include all thoughts, reactions, and actions that you took during this exercise.

Initials:
Date:
Time:
Place:

_____
_____
_____

Appendix 5.4

Brief Centering Exercise

This brief exercise will help you focus on the immediate moment. You will also begin the process of developing the skill of mindful attention. This exercise should take you about five minutes to complete. Just like with any other exercise or activity, before you start, remember that success requires the development of specific skills, and a commitment to working on the development of these skills is the first step to success.

Please find a comfortable sitting position. Notice the position of your feet, arms, and hands. Allow your eyes to close gently. [pause 10 seconds] Breathe in and out gently and deeply several times. Notice the sound and feel of your own breath as you breathe in and out. [pause 10 seconds]

At this time, focus your attention onto your surroundings. Notice any sounds that may be occurring. What sounds are occurring inside the room? What sounds are occurring outside the room? [pause 10 seconds] Now focus your attention on the areas where your body touches the chair in which you are sitting. Notice the physical sensations that occur from this contact. [pause 10 seconds] Now notice the spot where your hands are touching the front of your legs. [pause 10 seconds] Now notice any sensations that may be occurring in the rest of your body and notice how they may change over time without any effort on your part. [pause 10 seconds] Don't try to alter these sensations, just notice them as they occur. [pause 10 seconds]

Now, let your thoughts focus on why you have chosen to pursue this program. [pause 10 seconds] See if you can notice any doubts or other thoughts without doing anything but noticing them. Just notice your reservations, concerns, and worries as though they are elements of a parade passing through your mind. [pause 10 seconds] See if you can simply notice them and acknowledge their presence. [pause 10 seconds] Don't try to make them go away or change them in any way. [pause 10 seconds] Now allow yourself to focus on what you want your life to be about. What is most important to you? What do you want to do with your skills? [pause 10 seconds]

Remain comfortable for a few more moments and slowly let yourself focus once again on any sounds and movements occurring around you. [pause 10 seconds] Once again, notice your own breathing. [pause 10 seconds] When you are ready, open your eyes and notice that you feel focused and attentive.

Reprinted with permission from *The Psychology of Enhancing Human Performance: The Mindfulness–Acceptance–Commitment (MAC) Approach* (p. 75), by F. L. Gardner and Z. E. Moore, 2007, New York, NY: Springer. Copyright 2007.

Appendix 5.5

Mindfulness of the Breath Exercise

This brief exercise will help you expand upon your mindfulness skills, and will allow for further development of mindful awareness and attention. This exercise should take no more than 20 minutes to complete. It is suggested that this exercise be completed at a slow pace.

Please find a comfortable position to sit. Notice the position of your body, particularly your legs, hands, and feet. Allow your eyes to close gently. [pause 10 seconds]

Take several deep breaths and notice the air going in and out of your body. Notice the sound and feel of your own breathing as you breathe in [pause] and out [pause]. Allow your focus of attention to be on your abdomen rising and falling with each breath. [pause 10 seconds]

As you continue to breathe in and out, imagine that there is a pencil in your hand and that you are drawing a line upward with each inhale, and then a line downward with each exhale [pause 10 seconds]. Imagine the picture that these lines would create [pause 10 seconds].

As you slowly continue to breathe in and out, notice that you may become aware of a variety of thoughts and emotions that enter and leave your mind. Simply notice them as though they are part of a parade, gently allow them to pass and once again focus on your own breathing and all the sensations that come. [pause 10 seconds] Having a variety of thoughts and emotions is not incorrect or in any way a problem, but simply reflects the reality of the human mind. There is no need to change, fix, or in any way attempt to control these experiences. Simply note the parade of thoughts in your mind and refocus on your own breathing. [pause 10 seconds]

Allow yourself to continue to breathe gently in and out, focusing your thoughts on the physical sensations of each breathe that you take. Whenever you are ready, slowly open your eyes, become fully aware of your physical surroundings, and continue your day.

Appendix 5.6

Compassion-Focused Mindfulness Exercise

Begin by simply noticing your breath. You do not have to do anything but breathe in and out. Simply be aware and attentive to the physical sensations of breathing in and breathing out. [pause]

Now imagine that you are a deeply compassionate person. Think of the qualities that a compassionate person would have. [pause]

Now imagine yourself with each of those qualities. Imagine yourself as a person that understands your own difficulties and the difficulties that others experience. [pause]

Notice yourself doing this in a non-judgmental way, with the confidence to be sensitive to the shortcomings of others and the ability to tolerate life's difficulties. [pause]

Now imagine being warm and kind. Imagine speaking to someone who has frustrated you in the past, and notice the tone of your voice. Imagine reaching out to that person with warmth, and experience what that might be like. [pause]

Now imagine that you have lost interest in condemning or blaming yourself or others for past events, and are now wanting to do the best you can to help yourself and others move forward in what is often a difficult situation. Hold on to your warm, confident feeling. [pause]

It doesn't matter if you believe that you have these qualities or not, just imagine that you have them. See in your mind yourself having them, and work with them. Simply allow your inner compassion to come to you slowly and steadily. [pause]

Breathe deeply once again . . .

Appendix 5.7

Mindfulness Record Form

What mindfulness exercise was practiced?

When and where was it practiced?

For how long was it practiced?

Please record the experience(s) you had during and after the exercise.

When do you plan to practice next?

Appendix 5.8

Guidelines for the Use of Anger Exposures

- Anger exposures should be utilized only in the appropriate module and after all prior skill sets are mastered
- Anger exposures should be carefully considered and planned before beginning a session
- Exposure should be explained to the client, with an emphasis on its value as a form of "opposite action" to difficult triggers in their lives. The focus should be on: (a) the development of tolerance of the experience of anger, and (b) the development of new ways of responding to situations when and while angry
- Exposure exercises are most effective when the connection between developing these skills and the pursuit of personal values is clearly understood
- The therapist should leave ample time to debrief the client following exposure exercises, whether done in or between sessions
- The traditional "empty chair technique" can be utilized as an interpersonal exposure by carefully selecting the imagined chair occupant as someone who is a clear and consistent trigger for poorly expressed anger
- Exposure exercises are best delivered in a graded fashion, with increasing difficulty. In-session exposures are best utilized prior to asking the client to engage in unsupervised between-session exposures

Appendix 5.9

Committing to Life Values Exercise Form

Name: Date: Age: Occupation: Gender:

Personal Value:

Short-Term Goal Associated with Personal Value:

Long-Term Goal Associated with Personal Value:

Behavior(s) Required to Pursue Value and Goals:

Potential Obstacles:

Situation:

Action Taken:

Situation:

Action Taken:

Appendix 5.10

Interpersonal Problem Solving Form

- Situation (specifically describe target situation in detail):
- Facts (who, where, when, why, what):
- Opinions (thoughts, opinions, or assumptions about the situation):
- Values-Based Outcome Goal:
- Actions Taken to Achieve Goal:
- Actual Outcome:
- Alternative Actions:

Appendix 5.11

Post-CART Practice Plan Form

This form is to be used to help plan, monitor, and guide you following completion of the CART program

What are the key elements of CART that would help me on a regular basis?
(Such as mindfulness exercises, cognitive defusion exercises)

When will CART be used?
(Select specific times for CART program practice)

Where will CART be used?
(Indicate specifically where the practice/utilization of CART exercises will be done)

How will CART be used?
(Indicate the areas of your life that will be best served by regular attention to CART principles and practices)

Key Obstacles/Triggers
(Indicate the specific obstacles to continued growth and development, including particularly troublesome triggers and/or situations to be worked on)

Values and Targeted Values Directed Behaviors
(Indicate the specific valued life directions that you want to be sure to continue to actively pursue)

6 Special Considerations

Now that we have provided a step-by-step description of each CART module's goals and associated techniques, this chapter discusses a variety of issues that warrant special consideration when considering or conducting the CART protocol (or any empirically informed psychological intervention, for that matter). While some issues presented herein require consideration at the outset of treatment (e.g. treatment context; individual, couples, or group treatment; age appropriateness of treatment), others require constant attention during the course of treatment (e.g. cultural factors). For simplicity, the issues that we think are most likely to require attention/consideration are grouped below. The order is arbitrary and does not suggest that one issue is more or less important than any other. In fact, the relative importance of any of these issues will vary from client to client and situation to situation.

Client–Therapist Issues: Culture, SES/Privilege, and Gender

In our contemporary, multi-national society, it is fairly certain that all clinicians will ultimately come face-to-face in the treatment room with someone who is not like them by virtue of race, religion, culture, socioeconomic status, etc. Effective clinicians must develop an overarching method and personal comfort with these inevitable individual differences.

In working with clients referred for problems related to clinical anger, the behavioral manifestations of mistrust, interpersonal sensitivity, and a general difficulty with relating to people seen as being in a position of authority, are frequent clinically relevant behaviors. In this regard, differences in culture, gender, and probably most importantly, socioeconomic status, and the privilege and lifestyle that inevitably go with these variables are frequent issues requiring direct discussion. This is typically most easily done in the context of Module 1 of the CART program. Let us provide a real-life example. When needing to refer a new African-American client to a CART therapist working in an urban violence reduction program, an African-American therapist was randomly assigned to work with this new client. During intake, the client was dismissive and overtly hostile when asked about his presenting problem, family history, and current life circumstance. When the therapist pointed this out and sought a discussion, the client pointedly remarked, "You're asking these questions, but what do you know about the kind of life I'm describing? You're educated, dress real nice, probably have money, and have no idea about the life I have, so why are you making believe you are like me or can understand anything about me?" The therapist was shocked by this, and had assumed that the fact that they were both African-American would somehow shield her from dealing with this type of response.

The reality is that therapeutic consideration of race and culture, without understanding and considering the context of socioeconomic status and privilege, is not likely to be anything other than an academic exercise. In fact, in our experience, the issue of socioeconomic status/ privilege is often the overriding consideration in working with clinically angry clients, the majority of whom come from poor and often marginalized families and communities in which substance use and criminal behavior are rampant. Therapists must convey appropriate empathy along with a genuine level of interest in clients' racial, cultural, and socioeconomic status and differences, without presenting these individual differences as an inevitable treatment obstacle or themselves as an expert in them. In the example provided above, a response of, "You're right, I have had a different background than you and have not experienced your life or reality, but I can feel for you and would like to understand better. And, on the other hand, maybe there are some things that I can offer to you that you can benefit from as well," might be an effective and honest response to a challenge that many clinicians will face.

It is likewise important that clinically relevant cultural issues be identified and addressed. Issues relating to personal discrimination (especially in the process of navigating the judicial system and/or employment), family relations (e.g. internal and external stressors often found in mixed marriages, first vs second generation-in-America family conflict), religious customs (e.g. role of male/female/husband/wife), and a multitude of similar issues should be identified and addressed where appropriate. Clinicians must walk a line in which these issues are not ignored, and are given their rightful place in treatment planning, but at the same time not make them into the overriding feature of treatment, which they rarely are. Additionally, clinicians should do their best to walk into such difficult discussions with honesty and with the capacity to suspend their own judgments and even personal beliefs. An example of this was a female doctoral student trainee who was working with a very observant Muslim couple, for whom the roles of husband and wife were ordained by their beliefs, and not open for discussion or change. This presented a very real challenge to this clinical trainee, who had very clearly established personal opinions about these issues that were in many respects in stark contrast to her patients' beliefs.

One challenge that we, and our students and trainees, have frequently faced is the reality that there are numerous situations in which clients' lifestyles with regard to anticipation of harm, overt demonstration of anger, and/or aggressive behavior in their community, may in fact be functional within the context of very difficult and dangerous personal life circumstances. In such cases, we have found that clinicians lose credibility and treatment often fails when they pursue a general life change approach (following which we may seem at best naïve and at worst uneducated) by suggesting that complete lifestyle alterations are necessary, possible, or even desired. Rather, they can help clients see that their over-generalized response strategies (having a single response style regardless of situation) are not in the service of what they want in life, and that stimulus discrimination (developing a different response strategy for use in different life circumstances) may be more useful. Thus, learning to respond differently to anger and perceived threat at home and with family may warrant a different response than the response to perceived threat "on the street." This distinction enhances clinician credibility, is more likely to engage clients in treatment, and is often vastly more functional given the context of clients' life circumstances. In our experience, one of the biggest challenges to effective therapy with clinically angry populations is not based on skill or technique, but rather, is the likelihood that the client's environment will support and ultimately reinforce the change that we promote in-session. Targeting those areas that are likely to promote and thus reinforce appropriate change is substantially more likely to result in positive treatment outcomes.

In addition to culture and SES, when dealing with clients referred for violent behavior, and particularly interpersonal violence (IPV), the issue of gender may certainly have a much more pronounced impact on treatment and its likely outcome than in other clinical settings. It is clear that, in such situations, therapists of the opposite gender are quite likely to have their own personal reactions to individuals who have committed these offenses, and clients may very well respond to the gender stimulus characteristics in their behavioral responses to therapists. In such cases, we encourage clinicians to once again refer to Module 1 in order to fully understand and embrace the tenets of behavioral–interpersonal treatments before commencing work with perpetrators of IPV. In essence, we suggest that clinicians will need to be mindful of their own reactions (emotional and behavioral) to clients as well as remain cognizant of the gender-based behaviors that may be elicited by clients during the entire CART protocol, particularly during the early sessions. Without this self-awareness and interpersonal focus, it is unlikely that treatment will progress adequately. The process of treatment-generated stimulus discrimination, noted above, begins with the behavioral interchange between therapists and clients, and it is here that the foundation of treatment change begins for individuals who engage in interpersonal violence. Consistent with both the Anger Avoidance Model and previous research (Jakupcak, Lisak, & Roemer, 2002), a recent study conducted in our treatment facility suggests a strong relationship between deficits in emotion regulation, anger, and interpersonal violence, as deficits in emotion regulation increase the likelihood that individuals will use interpersonal violence as a dysfunctional attempt to regulate anger (Gardner, Moore, & Dettore, 2013). As therapists will often have stimulus qualities (i.e. aspects of themselves based upon gender and/or behavioral style) that trigger angry responses similar to the response to individuals in non-treatment situations, the relationship between therapists and clients naturally allows for enhanced emotion regulation to be learned and developed within the context of a safe therapeutic environment.

Treatment Context: Setting, Mandated Offender Status, and Finite Sessions Available

There are several aspects of the therapeutic context that are particularly likely to influence treatment with clinically angry populations. The first and most obvious is *treatment setting*. It certainly creates a different environment, with different client responses, if psychological treatment is provided in prison, hospital, or outpatient settings. Each, by definition, has different elements of a power differential. As previously noted, in a population that is generally suspicious and sensitive to issues of power and control, the treatment setting can provide a treatment issue that must be considered and understood. For example, issues of confidentiality and treatment goals are likely to be different based upon setting. We have found that a single (one-time) discussion of confidentiality (and its limits) and treatment goals is not sufficient, and that frequent reminders and discussions (in the context of Module 1) should be expected to occur before clients truly understand the role of the therapist and the therapeutic relationship. Similarly, the issue of *mandated offender status* requires a good deal of consideration before beginning CART. Indeed, most people come to treatment in some "mandated" way. Certainly, couples are rarely in full agreement on the need/benefit of couples/marriage counseling. Adolescents and children rarely, if ever, announce to their parents that they require psychological treatment, and most adult outpatients arrive at therapy with either friends or family members encouraging or even insisting that treatment be undertaken. From this perspective, a "mandate" for treatment is not at all unusual.

That said, certainly when one is mandated for psychological treatment as part of a probation/parole/court mandate, the treatment context begins with important concerns that need to be carefully considered and discussed. There are two specific issues that should be addressed from the perspective of both ethical practice and treatment effectiveness, as follows.

1. *The relationship between clinician/agency and the legal system.* While this may be obvious in a prison, in other settings it is certainly not. For example, a particular facility may be an agency that accepts referrals from the local department of probation and parole, but is not in any way part of or affiliated with that department of probation and parole. That reality is not always understood or even believed by mandated clients at the outset of treatment, and requires concerted and often repeated explanation.

2. *Confidentiality.* Limits to confidentiality must be provided within the informed consent for treatment, but also explained in detail… and done several times, to ensure full understanding. For example, it is not uncommon when treating court/probation mandated clients for feedback related to attendance/compliance to be required by appropriate court personnel at various intervals, and it is also not uncommon for progress and/or termination reports to be required. While it is not typical for specific treatment session content to be requested, clients do need to recognize that the court/probation department may request information at any time based upon case-specific issues and requirements. Clients must fully understand the release of information they sign, as well as the informed consent for treatment. While this is true with all patients regardless of setting, we have found that this clinical population is in need of careful and repeated discussion of these issues. It is clearly more difficult to gain trust and enhance openness in a "court-mandated treatment" circumstance, but over time and with genuine honest and open communication (along with necessary therapist qualities of empathy and professionalism), clients can come to recognize that despite the limitations to confidentiality, the clinician is trying to help them function better in the areas that really matter to them. While the mandated offender status can never be seen as irrelevant, it can be made to be a non-interfering reality that does not have to impede treatment in any way. One additional point should be made with regard to "mandated offenders." It is often very difficult to get individuals mandated for treatment to complete clinical measures honestly *before* they understand the issues noted above and become comfortable with the agency and clinician. Unfortunately, these measures are often required at the outset of treatment. While there is no easy solution to this dilemma, our suggestion based on years of experience with this issue is to spend time first explaining the relationship between the agency, clinician, and legal system; and importantly, the limits to confidentiality (e.g. the specifics of what, when, and how information will be requested by the relevant legal agency). Taking some extra time to slowly, patiently, and honestly describe and discuss these issues is likely to result in somewhat more honest self-report measure completion, and more importantly, allow treatment to begin with a more solid foundation.

The final contextual issue requiring some discussion is the circumstance, and in some cases clinical reality, of therapeutic environments in which a fixed and/or finite number of sessions are available/required, and thus the flexibility of the modular approach is challenged. We have presented CART as a nine-module psychological treatment, with no absolute cap on number of sessions. When clinical realities require a more time-limited framework (e.g. six-session treatment mandate), we suggest one of two alternatives. If the time requirements allow for six to eight sessions, we suggest that depending on whether six, seven, or eight sessions are available, the following modules can be combined into single sessions if necessary: (a) Modules 1 and 2 (psychoeducation, values identification and motivation enhancement; and using the therapeutic relationship to recognize and modify clinically relevant behavior) may be combined into one treatment session; (b) Modules 6 and 7 (acceptance, emotion processing, and anger regulation; and commitment to values-based behavioral choices) may be combined into a single session; and (c) Modules 8 and 9 (developing effective interpersonal problem-solving skills, and integration of concepts and relapse prevention) may be combined into a single session. When this type of reductive modification is required, it is imperative that clinicians cull the main points of the combined modules *based upon the clinical needs and realities of the client*. While there is no absolute guideline as to how this must be done, we caution that clinicians must have a sound understanding of the fundamental treatment goals and processes inherent in the CART protocol and must strive to modify the treatment in accordance with these foundations as well as clinical realities. One final caution is that these modifications should be undertaken only when external demands require this to be done, and *not* simply for ease and/or a desire to present a shorter treatment, as the modified treatment strategy is experimental at this point, with little empirical support.

In circumstances in which five or fewer sessions are available, we suggest that clinicians may want to focus on Module 1 (psychoeducation, values identification, and motivation enhancement), Module 4 (cognitive defusion and the reduction of problematic rule-governed behavior), Module 5 (understanding anger and reducing emotional avoidance), and a combination of Modules 6 and 7 (acceptance, emotion processing, and anger regulation; and commitment to values-based behavioral choices). The same cautions with regard to reducing CART into smaller units, as noted above, would be operational in this circumstance as well.

Comorbidities: PTSD, Depression, and Personality Disorders

Given the fact that the CART protocol is intended for individuals for whom aggressive/violent behavior and/or under-/over-inhibited anger have been manifested in a clinically relevant manner (clinical anger), a logical question is how to effectively and appropriately intervene when clients present with symptom constellations that result in a *DSM* diagnosis of disorders such as depression (major depressive disorder or chronic depression/dysthymic disorder), posttraumatic stress disorder, or personality disorders (most typically the Cluster B types or unspecified personality disorder). To answer this question, we first discuss the nature of the current diagnostic system and its shortcomings, and then move on to a brief discussion of the current focus on transdiagnostic psychopathological processes and unified-transdiagnostic treatment protocols that cut across diagnostic groups.

As discussed in Chapter 1, there is no "anger disorder" within the current *DSM*. As such, clients who present with difficulties involving the emotion of anger, including the broad range of cognitive, subjective, behavioral, and physiological sequelae of this emotion, when diagnosed, are given diagnoses that range from mood disorders, to posttraumatic stress disorder and other anxiety disorders, and to personality disorders of various types. In fact, one of our recent studies revealed that *DSM-IV-TR* personality disorder NOS (not otherwise specified) was the most common single diagnostic classification given to clients presenting for the treatment of clinical anger, although it even still represented only one-fifth of all diagnoses given (Dettore, Kempel, & Gardner, 2010). Of course, even if there was in fact an appropriate single diagnosis for clinical anger, we would be left with the question of how this would guide treatment. Recent advances in experimental psychopathology and clinical psychology in general have consistently demonstrated that there are several transdiagnostic processes, such as *rumination, difficulties in emotion regulation*, and *dysfunctional avoidance* that are at the core of many, if not most, psychological disorders (Kashdan *et al.*, 2006). These findings, along with evidence suggesting that comorbidities across emotional disorders are a function of core common components of these disorders (Brown & Barlow, 1992), lead to the conclusion that psychological treatments are better served by targeting these specific core transdiagnostic *processes*. In essence, we should strive to treat the pathological processes involved in these numerous disorders, rather than simply the topographical features (signs and symptoms) of diagnostic groups (Barlow *et al.*, 2010).

In this regard, CART is not intended to treat a formal diagnostic category or class of client problems, but rather is based upon empirically informed strategies and techniques, and organized around specific transdiagnostic treatment objectives that are relevant to a clinical anger population. That said, we also recognize that certain psychological problems meeting criteria for diagnoses have specific problem areas that require specialized interventions. For example, individuals experiencing a constellation of signs and symptoms consistent with a diagnosis of PTSD might see a clinician for the treatment of anger/violence, but may still require that traumatic events be appropriately processed and confronted, consistent with most empirically derived treatments for PTSD. In such circumstances, it is relatively easy to integrate the specific treatment components necessary for PTSD into the CART protocol. Mindful awareness, enhanced emotion regulation/emotion processing, exposure to emotion triggering cues, acceptance of emotional experience, and commitment to personal values as a means of reducing dysfunctional avoidance (all part of evidence-based interventions for PTSD) are all integral components of CART.

We would like to expand on the noted relationship between and importance of anger in PTSD for a moment, because we think it requires some specific discussion and consideration. It is clear from recent research that difficulties with the experience and expression of anger are strongly associated with PTSD, and in fact, such difficulties make the course of the disorder and the treatment of it substantially more problematic. Recent research has suggested that a diagnosis of PTSD was associated with significantly greater difficulties with the emotion of anger than was any other anxiety disorder diagnosis (Olatunji, Ciesielski, & Tolin, 2010). Research has further found that unemployed veterans suffering from PTSD evidenced greater problems with anger versus those who were employed, even when the researchers controlled for PTSD severity (Frueh *et al.*, 1997). Importantly, it also appears that clients suffering from PTSD who also manifest anger difficulties experience significant interpersonal difficulties, including violent interpersonal behavior (Jakupcak & Tull, 2005; Jordan *et al.*, 1992). Anger has also been associated with a myriad of serious negative complications for those suffering from PTSD, such as substance abuse (DeMoja & Spielberger, 1997) and physical health concerns (Helmers, Posluszny, & Krantz, 1994). Additionally, it appears that excessive anger is likely to negatively impact the treatment of PTSD (Cahill *et al.*, 2003). The reason for this may be found in a study by Foa and colleagues (1995) in which female assault victims with PTSD who reported greater levels of anger prior to intervention were apt to display less fear expression during exposure-based reliving of the traumatic episode, and in turn benefitted less from exposure-based treatment than clients lower in anger severity.

What these important data suggest is that the treatment of anger seen in PTSD should be considered a critical target. We have found that utilizing CART as a first line intervention with clients presenting with PTSD where anger is a primary symptom, is an effective first component of treatment. Further, we have found that more traditional exposure-based interventions for PTSD are easily and appropriately incorporated during Module 6, which emphasizes emotion exposure. Integrating traditional prolonged exposure for PTSD into CART allows for a more complete experiencing of emotion and avoids the problem of anger difficulties inhibiting full fear experiencing, as noted by Foa and colleagues (1995).

On another note, the core elements of CART are also appropriate for use with Cluster B personality disorders and mood disorders, with additions and/or modifications not based on diagnosis, but rather only as per the treatment needs of the specific client. An important point to remember is that modifying the CART protocol for use with various diagnostic groups is not necessary for most clients. That is, as a unified/transdiagnostic protocol, CART was designed to be effective for the varying needs of clients experiencing anger and violent behavior across many psychological diagnoses. While aspects of clinical anger are the primary outcome goals, the treatment focus is on core transdiagnostic processes such as rumination, dysfunctional avoidance of internal and external experiences, cognitive fusion, etc., which in turn make the issue of diagnostic group appropriateness less relevant. CART should therefore be seen as part of the recent trend toward more unified or transdiagnostic psychological treatments. Of course, clinical work requires flexibility, and clients being referred for anger-related treatment often present with issues that require immediate attention, such as active substance abuse, high levels of depression, and/or suicidality. In line with appropriate clinical practice in which client safety is of greatest concern, it is recommended that in such cases, the clinician focus first on the aspects of the client's condition that is of the highest risk, and then transition into the formal CART protocol when indicated.

Family/Couples Engagement in Treatment

When providing workshops and in-service trainings of CART, we are frequently asked about the feasibility and pragmatics of utilizing CART within a couples or family framework. While the basic theoretical and empirical framework certainly suggests that CART could be viable in a family-focused treatment, to date we have not seen any studies nor have we as a clinical and research group engaged in any systematic study to determine its workability and effectiveness in a family setting. That noted, we have had several opportunities to use the CART model as the foundation of couples work, in situations in which both partners were argumentative, emotionally dysregulated, and engaged in either verbally aggressive and/or more overt violent behavior with each other. While the specifics of the CART modules were modified to be appropriate for a couples counseling intervention, the broad modular approach was still taken. Psychoeducation (Module 1) was provided as prescribed in the beginning of treatment, followed by the focused use of clinically relevant in-session interpersonal behaviors between both the couple and the therapist, as detailed in Module 2. Mindful self-awareness (Module 3) was then presented and developed in both partners, which included mindful listening exercises in which the awareness of, and the capacity to remain in contact with the words and emotions of one's partner as he or she was talking about increasingly important and challenging issues was then introduced. This module ended with mindful relational exercises in which partners would mindfully hold hands and look at each other without breaking eye contact, and in so doing developed a greater sense of intimacy and compassionate connection. As per Module 4, relational rule-governed behavior was noted, and cognitive defusion exercises were utilized as indicated in the standard CART program. Modules 5 and 6 were then sequentially incorporated into treatment, through which anger, anger avoidance (and associated behaviors that include aggressive/violent behaviors), and enhanced tolerance/acceptance of the experience of anger and other related emotions were the focus of therapeutic attention, much as it would be in the individually based CART program. The final stage of treatment included a focus on values-directed relationship behaviors; commitment to ongoing and regular behavioral choices in the service of these values (regardless of transitory thoughts or emotions) consistent with Module 7; basic relational skills such as conflict management and reflective listening (as noted in Module 8); and finally, relapse prevention work as per Module 9. While there have been no empirical studies of couples-focused CART, the cases in which it has been utilized have proceeded smoothly, with outcomes that appear to be as good, if not better, than more traditional couples interventions. Once again, while this has been our clinical observation, any conclusions await formal empirical scrutiny.

We would like to make the recommendation that, for most couples who are not experiencing/displaying excessive amounts of anger-avoidant aggressive/violent behavior, traditional empirically supported couples interventions such as integrative behavioral couple therapy (IBCT; Jacobson et al., 2000) and/or emotion-focused couples interventions would appear most appropriate, as they have a large body of empirical support and are easily tolerated by most couples. However, in those cases in which anger/aggressive behavior is a central and overriding clinical feature across both partners, we suggest that couples-focused CART can be appropriately utilized. The feedback from therapists who have used this approach with couples presenting with extreme anger/aggressive behavior is that the CART principles are easily and seamlessly woven into a couples format with little need to adapt the basic modules other than the simple ways noted above.

Individual vs Group Treatment

Similar to the topic of couples-focused CART, many individuals attending CART workshops or in-service training have asked whether CART is suitable for group interventions. While there is no a priori reason to assume that CART could not be utilized in a group setting, experience has suggested to us that several problems may arise that can complicate the use of CART in groups of adult patients. As such, we strongly suggest that clinicians carefully consider the likelihood that the issues presented below may be relevant to their therapeutic situation or context. These issues include: (a) context and population, (b) member psychopathology, and (c) personality disorders.

Context and Population

In many areas across the globe, gang affiliations are not uncommon, especially when working in, or as a referral network for, the judicial system. Since it is often not openly discussed when mandated for treatment, the potential to have group members from competitive/antagonistic gangs is not at all unlikely. Yet, this is often not known in advance. Such circumstances are clearly not appropriate for treatment situations, at best make effective treatment impossible, and at worst may create a highly dangerous situation. In addition, given that this is a population for whom vulnerability is a strong stimulus for avoidance, it has been our experience that group settings do not easily allow for the safety and comfort required to create an environment that supports the learning of appropriate anger tolerance/acceptance and expression. Rather, many stimulus functions will pull for exactly the behaviors we are looking to modify.

Member Psychopathology

If group treatment is the chosen or requisite intervention modality, the question of best fit for effective group work is an obvious and long-standing clinical issue. Our experience is that group members should have generally similar issues and treatment goals for CART to be effective as a group treatment program. We certainly believe that primary substance abuse clients, psychotic clients, highly bipolar clients, and suicidal clients be excluded from the CART group format. We suggest that more effective, and more empirically supported interventions are available for clients with these particular disorders. As noted previously in this chapter, this is certainly not to say that there needs to be diagnostic homogeneity. Rather, core issues should center around anger dysregulation and its various processes, along with the behavioral excesses with which they are often associated.

Personality Disorders

As previously described, the clinical population that is most likely to include anger-related concerns spans many disorders, such as mood disorders, anxiety disorders, and Cluster B personality disorders (e.g. narcissistic personality disorder). Yet, there are several additional points to be made in this regard. The first important point is that while most of the patients referred for treatment at our facility have characteristics of the various Cluster B disorders (i.e. antisocial, borderline, histrionic, narcissistic), in most cases they do not meet full criteria for a diagnosis. In any event, whether diagnosable or not (which we view as relatively unimportant), the fact is that in most cases, these individuals can certainly benefit from CART treatment. The second point is that there is one major and one minor exception regarding the appropriateness of CART with personality disordered populations. Specifically, the major exception includes patients who primarily and *strongly* meet criteria for a diagnosis of antisocial personality disorder, and the minor exception includes *highly* dysregulated (and highly dysfunctional) patients meeting criteria for borderline personality disorder, whose symptom structure includes parasuicidality, severe depression, and/or issues related to possible self-harm. For ease of discussion, let's consider each of these exceptions separately. As most clinicians know, antisocial personality disorder remains essentially intractable, and our treatment outcomes in this regard are no different. One reason for the poor treatment response to CART in people meeting full criteria for antisocial personality disorder is that by and large, unlike patients who manifest the other Cluster B syndromes, individuals who meet criteria for antisocial personality disorder do *not* experience emotion dysregulation in quite the same manner as other Cluster B disorders. We tend to see these antisocial individuals as not manifesting *reactive* aggression/violent behavior, in which anger is a substantial component. Rather, they typically manifest a more *predatory/ exploitive* type of aggressive behavior (we have previously referred to this as "instrumental aggression"), which is seemingly unconnected to inhibited or expressed anger and related emotion dysregulation. Again though, less severe antisocial personality disordered patients have been responsive to the CART program.

The other exception is decidedly much less significant, and includes those borderline personality disordered clients who are severely dysregulated, highly dysfunctional, and whose symptomatology includes severe levels of depression, parasuicidality, and/or other issues related to possible self-harm. Such patients may be more appropriately treated within a structured and complete Dialectical Behavior Therapy format (Linehan, 1993). Yet, we have found that many less severe clients with borderline personality disorder do quite well in the CART program, so we do not want to give the impression that all borderline personality disordered clients will be of poor fit with the CART program. On the contrary, many borderline clients do very well in CART treatment, as do a wide array of Cluster B personality disordered clients. Finally, we often see clients who manifest characteristics of narcissistic personality disorder, and have found that their interpersonal sensitivity and self-aggrandizing behavior are very much related to deficits in emotion regulation. Thus, individuals meeting criteria for narcissistic personality disorder or manifesting characteristics of that disorder are good candidates for CART. This is additionally true for histrionic patients, for precisely the same reasons. In essence, we generally conceive of CART as appropriate for any disorder that includes anger as a centerpiece of difficulties in emotion regulation.

Age Considerations for CART

While CART was originally conceived and developed primarily as a treatment protocol for late adolescent and adult populations, as noted in Chapter 5, it has also been modified for use with younger populations. To date, there has been one completed study (Dettore, Lee, & Gardner, 2012) utilizing CART in a school-based program for 5th-grade children (aged 10–12) in a class for severely behaviorally disordered youth. The child-based program included each of the fundamental components of all basic CART modules into seven revised modules, as follows.

- Module 1: Student Motivation—essentially an age-appropriate version of values identification and monitoring.
- Module 2: Psychoeducation—essentially covering the questions of what anger is, why it is normal, and why it does not have to be a problem.
- Module 3: Mindfulness Training—using child-adapted mindfulness exercises.
- Module 4: Decentering—helping children view the mind as "story teller" and not always as "fact giver."
- Module 5: Emotion Exposure—essentially allowing the children to experience anger eliciting situations (in-session), such as competitive activities, without demonstrating the usual problematic aggressive behaviors.
- Module 6: Interpersonal Skills Training—focused on emotional expression, listening skills, and conflict resolution techniques.
- Module 7: Wrap Up—a review.

It should also be pointed out that clinically relevant interpersonal behavior was included in the protocol and focused on throughout the program, although it was not given its own unique module.

Results indicated substantial improvements in teacher ratings of inattentive symptoms ($d = .54$), learning problems ($d = .94$), executive functioning deficits ($d = .64$), learning problems combined with executive functioning deficits ($d = .94$), and aggressive behavior ($d = .52$). Most importantly, the school district requested that the program be continued and expanded to other age groups within their district. Additionally, within a clinical treatment setting, this same basic format, with activities and exercise once again being adapted for age appropriateness, is currently being utilized in younger children (aged 4–6) who have experienced significant maltreatment and who are demonstrating aggressive/violent behavior. Early results are positive. In both the 5th grade and early childhood intervention programs, CART was/is being delivered in a group format, with no problems in delivery.

In short, the results collected to date certainly suggest that CART is an intervention that can readily be adapted for children of varying ages, beginning in early childhood, moving through latency age, and into adolescence.

Conclusion

Clinicians working with populations experiencing clinical anger have a number of issues that require special consideration. These issues include interpersonal, intrapersonal, and contextual concerns that must be carefully considered and skillfully attended to in order to effectively deliver CART and compassionately provide culturally sensitive and ethical practice with this challenging population. With the theoretical basis of CART presented, the goals and processes of pre-treatment assessment discussed, the CART protocol itself presented in step-by-step detail, and special issues often found in clinical practice when working with this population noted and considered, the next and final chapter provides a full case study from referral to treatment completion. We hope that it allows readers to gain a true and complete sense of the clinical issues frequently confronting CART clinicians, and the strategic and technical aspects of the CART protocol.

7   Case Study

We are so pleased that you have traveled through the CART program with us thus far, and think that a great way to wrap up this text is to provide a full case study that walks through the assessment, conceptualization, and treatment of an actual (sanitized) client presenting with clinical anger and its associated behavioral manifestations. We hope that this case study illuminates the entire CART program from start to finish, and energizes clinicians to incorporate CART into their professional armamentarium.

Identifying Information

Nicolette is a 28-year-old, married, African-American female who was referred by a local Department of Probation for "anger management" following a recent arrest and conviction. Nicolette holds an associate's degree from a local community college. She is employed part-time as a cashier at a local arts and crafts store, and lives with her husband. She describes herself as "spiritual but not religious." She and her husband married five years ago, and they presently do not have children.

Presenting Complaints/Reason for Referral

Nicolette's presenting complaints included intense episodes of anger, impulsivity, and the negative consequences of her behaviors when angry. She reported that her anger has resulted in substantial interpersonal and occupational problems. Specifically, Nicolette endorsed being verbally aggressive at work and physically aggressive with her husband. She was referred for court-mandated "anger management" following arrest and conviction on a charge of disorderly conduct.

Precipitating Factors and History of the Problem

Nicolette was arrested approximately one year ago following admitted verbal aggression toward a police officer. The day Nicolette was arrested, her husband had been pulled over by a police officer a few blocks away from their home for a driving infraction, and was found to be driving without a license. Nicolette's husband was forced to leave the vehicle with the police. When Nicolette learned what had transpired, she decided to retrieve the vehicle from the police. When Nicolette spoke with the police officer, she perceived that he had responded rudely to her. She reportedly began yelling and cursing at the police officer, and would not leave the facility when asked. During her court hearing, Nicolette was mandated to "anger management" and 400 hours of community service.

Nicolette reported that her aggressive behaviors commenced during middle school. She stated that her first physical altercation occurred when she was 11 years old, when she grabbed a classmate by the hair, punched her, and repeatedly kneed her in the face. Nicolette indicated that aggressive behaviors such as this continued throughout high school. After skipping several classes in 11th grade, she was suspended, and both her mother and the principal urged her to seek psychological treatment. Nicolette refused these suggestions, and the current mandated treatment is the first time she has sought (or been required to undergo) psychological services.

Several of Nicolette's adolescent behavioral patterns have continued throughout her young adulthood. She reported that when she perceives that her husband has lied to her, or in some way is disrespectful to her, she frequently reacts by throwing objects at him, such as bottles, glasses, and chairs, or by punching him repeatedly in the side of the head, arms, or stomach. Nicolette reported that these physical altercations with her husband have occurred as frequently as once per week. The most recent violent encounter between them was reportedly less than 1 week prior to the start of treatment. At that time, Nicolette reported that her husband tried to walk away from her during an argument, and she responded by grabbing his hair, pushing him to the ground, and repeatedly punching him. She denied that she or her husband have required medical treatment because of their physical encounters, although she stated that he has been cut or scraped with minimal bleeding as a result of their fighting in the past. Regarding feelings of regret for fighting with her husband, Nicolette stated, "I don't like to hurt him, but when he mistreats me he needs to learn a lesson."

In addition to her physical aggression, Nicolette reported that she is frequently verbally aggressive and impulsive. She stated that while at work, she "tells off" various co-workers when they frustrate her. Additionally, Nicolette has had over 20 different jobs in the past four years. She stated that when she becomes bored, irritated, or angry at work, she leaves immediately.

She has attempted to manage feelings of distress through substance use, namely smoking cigarettes, using marijuana, and drinking alcohol with friends. Nicolette reported that she is now completely clean of substances, stating that she quit smoking cigarettes two months prior to entering treatment, and that she quit drinking and smoking marijuana six months prior. Nicolette indicated that quitting cigarettes was difficult for her because she had smoked consistently since she was 15 years of age (up to a pack of cigarettes per day). She also stated that she had made previous efforts to quit that were unsuccessful. Nicolette denied that alcohol and marijuana use were ever a problem in her life.

Developmental and Historical Information

Nicolette was born and raised in a relatively poor inner-city environment. Her mother works in the billing department of a local retail store, and her father is a mechanic at an auto dealership. Nicolette's sister, who is one year her senior, works with her at a local arts and crafts store. Nicolette's family psychiatric history is positive for anxiety (panic attacks), which Nicolette reported in her father, and anger, which Nicolette reported in her mother.

Nicolette stated that she suffered from asthma as a child and was hospitalized several times per year during preschool and elementary school for asthma attacks. She also indicated that children teased her while she was suffering from asthma attacks in both preschool and elementary school. She denied suffering from anxiety or depression as a result of these negative peer interactions, but reported that these experiences taught her that, "people could be mean."

Nicolette reported that her father punished her throughout elementary school by hitting her on her buttocks or legs with a leather belt. She stated that her father would hit her 10 to 15 times with a belt when he believed that she had done something wrong. Nicolette stated that she was hit with a belt for approximately seven years (kindergarten through 6th grade), at least once per week. She reported that she often cried during the beatings, and claimed that she never required medical attention as a result of this punishment. According to Nicolette, her parents taught her that "when you do something wrong, you deserve to get beaten." She appears to have adopted this punitive attitude in her interpersonal relationships, as evidenced by her physical aggression toward her husband.

The community culture in Nicolette's neighborhood would appear to have reinforced her current attitudes regarding disrespect and aggressive responding. She indicated that you had to be "tough" in her neighborhood or people would publicly humiliate you either verbally or physically. She reported that her mother exhibited "toughness" while she was growing up, as evidenced by the way she spoke to others and by the way others seemed to go out of their way to leave her alone. Nicolette aspired to be like her mother, and by middle school, reported that she had established herself as someone not to be "messed with." Nicolette indicated that if she "walked around smiling and being nice all the time" people would perceive her as being weak. In this way, being tough was reinforced in Nicolette's environment. She also learned that by demonstrating toughness, she could avoid feelings of disrespect and its associated intolerable consequences, such as public humiliation and physical pain.

Nicolette met her husband while they were working at a retail store together seven years ago. She has experienced frustration regarding this relationship and reported chronic feelings of distrust and anger toward her husband. She claimed that her husband refuses to talk about, or outright lies to her, regarding details about his day, such as where he goes after work and what he had for lunch, and frequently ignores her when home. Nicolette denied suspicions of infidelity. Several months ago, she became so infuriated with her husband that she left their home and stayed with a friend for an entire week. She then returned to her husband because she believed his pleas that he would treat her better. Nicolette also indicated that she returned to her husband because she has a "big problem" in being alone, and needs to get in contact with someone during times that she is alone or she feels as though she "might go crazy." Since this time, Nicolette reported that their relationship has improved, but that he still treats her badly and that she still becomes "furious" with him.

Assessment Measures

Nicolette's intake evaluation included the Anger Disorders Scale (ADS) and State Trait Anger Expression Inventory-2 (STAXI-2), which are both self-report assessments that specifically examine symptoms of clinical anger. These measures suggested that Nicolette is likely to outwardly express her anger (93rd percentile, higher order reactivity/expression subscale of ADS; 85th percentile, anger expression-out subscale of STAXI-2) and that her anger is provoked across a wide array of situations (94th percentile, anger provocations subscale of ADS). Nicolette also indicated that she has been experiencing "anger problems" for a prolonged period of time (99th percentile, duration of anger problems on ADS). These self-report measures further indicated Nicolette's difficulty with regulating her anger, and assessment scores were congruent with her verbal report. In addition, Nicolette's score on the physiological arousal scale (97th percentile; ADS) suggested an intense physiological response when angry. Finally, her ADS scores on the hurt/social rejection scale (98th percentile), suspiciousness scale (84th percentile), rumination scale (78th percentile), and coercion scale (86th percentile) were all consistent with her verbal report, and were suggestive of someone who experiences rejection very easily, is distrustful of others, ruminates about past and potential future slights, and uses aggressive behavior to coerce others.

Self-report assessments that examined general distress were also congruent with her verbal report. As Nicolette reported, she experienced minimal anxiety and depression, as indicated by a Beck Depression Inventory-2

(BDI-2) score of 5, and a Beck Anxiety Inventory (BAI) score of 3, both of which fell in the minimal range of these affective states. Nicolette's scores on the Outcome Questionnaire (OQ-45), which broadly assesses symptom impairment, and on the Quality of Life Inventory (QOLI) also fell in the average range, suggesting that she was not experiencing significant overall subjective distress. Nicolette's Childhood Trauma Questionnaire (CTQ) scores fell in the moderate range of physical and emotional abuse, which is congruent with her verbal description of her parents' childhood parenting styles.

When looking more specifically at her skills in and approach to emotion regulation, some interesting findings emerged. Nicolette's scores on the Difficulties in Emotion Regulation Scale (DERS) indicated that she lacked adequate coping strategies, emotional understanding, and emotional clarity when experiencing distress (all above average).

Behavioral Observations

Nicolette dressed appropriately and appeared engaged during the interview. Likewise, her affect was appropriate to the conversation. Nicolette did not appear to suffer from any cognitive deficits, as her memory, insight, and ability to form logical conclusions seemed to be adequate. Nicolette's physical coordination also appeared average.

Nicolette reported one long-term health concern (asthma). She suggested that, at the present time, her asthma is under control, noting that she has not suffered an asthma attack since high school. Nicolette stated that she uses an inhaler for her asthma when exerting significant physical strength.

Nicolette had at first indicated no true motivation for treatment ("I'm only here because I have to be"), but was nevertheless cooperative and attentive. She presented with a pleasant demeanor, but demonstrated a wide range of emotions during the interview. Specifically, she became tearful when discussing her relationship with her husband and her difficulty regulating her anger. On the other hand, when reviewing an incident in which someone said something hurtful to her, Nicolette raised her voice and her facial muscles clearly tightened, suggestive of easily triggered anger.

Diagnostic Formulation

Based on her intake evaluation, Nicolette demonstrated sufficient symptoms to meet criteria for personality disorder NOS based on *DSM-IV-TR* criteria (APA, 2000). Specifically, she demonstrated a pervasive pattern of: (a) impulsivity, (b) irritability and aggressiveness, (c) consistent irresponsibility, (d) difficulty regulating her affect and high affect reactivity, (e) frantic efforts to avoid abandonment, and (f) entitlement to be physically punitive toward others, as well as her lack of empathy. This symptom picture has characteristics of Cluster B disorders such as antisocial personality disorder, borderline personality disorder, and narcissistic personality disorder, but she did not meet full criteria for any of those specific disorders.

In regards to Nicolette's psychopathological processes, consistent with the Anger Avoidance Model, her most salient problem is anger dysregulation and the behavioral avoidance and escape behaviors that naturally follow.

Case Formulation

Nicolette's difficulties can easily be understood by viewing her life through the lens of the Anger Avoidance Model. As discussed in Chapter 2, a core component of this model is the premise that many individuals who experience clinical anger are "avoidance/escape aggressors" (Gardner & Moore, 2008, p. 908), in that their aggression serves the function of helping them avoid/escape angry feelings. This model fits Nicolette's pathology well because it captures her anger avoidance behaviors, such as physical and verbal aggression, as well as the function of her expectation and scanning for evidence of maltreatment (i.e. hostile anticipation). Several components of the model seem clearly present, including her early aversive history, biological vulnerability, hypervigilance to threat, intense experience of anger, emotion (anger) dysregulation, and anger avoidance strategies.

Based on the AAM, Nicolette's current difficulties are likely to have originated from her early aversive history and biological vulnerability to experiencing intense affect. Nicolette's aversive history includes her father frequently using a belt to discipline her, frequent hospitalizations because of her asthma, and being bullied during preschool and elementary school. In addition, throughout her childhood, Nicolette's mother reportedly demonstrated the benefits of appearing tough, as people knew not to aggravate her. Taken together, these early life experiences may have taught Nicolette that the world is unsafe, people are not to be trusted, people should be punished if they demonstrate disrespect, and that one can protect oneself from others by being alert and appearing tough. Nicolette may also have inherited a biological vulnerability to experiencing intense affect from her mother, who frequently exhibited anger, and her father, who frequently exhibited anxiety.

Her early learning history appears to have impacted the way in which Nicolette views the world. Nicolette scans her environment for threatening stimuli, and is hypervigilant to possible signs of danger or disrespect from others. When Nicolette experiences feelings of vulnerability or disrespect, she likely feels as though she has been personally violated because she associates vulnerability and disrespect with intolerable consequences, such as humiliation and physical pain. When Nicolette perceives that she has been disrespected, she feels threatened, becomes agitated, and experiences intense anger, which in turn are poorly understood, differentiated, or tolerated/regulated.

By way of example, if she perceives that her husband has lied to her or if a co-worker talks to her in a way that she interprets as disrespectful, she experiences clear discomfort. For instance, Nicolette reported that when angry, her body temperature rises and she feels "heated and mad." Overcome by emotion, Nicolette likely lacks the ability to understand, process, and experience anger (Gardner & Moore, 2008), and in fact views the presence of anger as a sign that external danger is present. She seeks to avoid the full experience of anger by ruminating about previous negative events and also by replaying in her mind the event that triggered her anger (cognitive avoidance). Additionally, Nicolette seeks to avoid or escape from experiencing her anger by physically and/or verbally aggressing against her threatening stimulus (e.g. her husband, co-workers) in order to achieve situations modification/control.

The short-term benefits of Nicolette's aggressive behavior is that she can accomplish what she wants by exhibiting these behaviors. She is able to force her husband or co-workers to back down from an argument, and she is able to defend her image of being a tough individual. The long-term consequences of Nicolette's anger, however, are deleterious. By continuously using physical and verbal means to exert control over her environment, she has increased her marriage and job instability and has gotten into trouble with the law.

Treatment Goals

Consistent with Contextual Anger Regulation Therapy, Nicolette's treatment plan included the main objectives of: (a) increasing her motivation to engage in behavior change; (b) increasing her awareness of, and capacity to defuse from the internal rules that at present automatically direct her behavior; (c) increasing her awareness and tolerance of emotional arousal; (d) increasing the frequent utilization of values-driven behavior, even when experiencing intense anger (and simultaneously reducing the frequency of emotion-driven behavior); and (e) maintaining treatment gains and preventing a relapse of physically or verbally aggressive behaviors.

Treatment

Module 1: Psychoeducation, Values Identification, and Motivation Enhancement

After an in-depth discussion of the court-mandated reason for referral, including the inherent limits to confidentiality in such referrals, the clinician spent a good deal of time presenting the Anger Avoidance Model, with an emphasis on drawing a clear connection between the parenting style and community attitudes that Nicolette experienced as a child, the seeming biological disposition to experience emotions intensely, the constant scanning for evidence of impending maltreatment, and the reinforced use of aggressive behavior to feel safe and reduce the intensity of anger. In the context of this discussion, the clinician also made a point to validate the historical development of the use of aggressive behavior as a means of feeling safe and secure, but also pointed out the frequent consequences of that behavioral style.

During this first module, which required two sessions, increasing Nicolette's motivation to engage in behavioral change was a primary treatment goal. A frequent problem often seen when working with clients experiencing clinical anger is the tendency for therapists to move too quickly into a change phase of treatment before the client is psychologically prepared. While Nicolette was motivated for treatment in general, she was reluctant to change her anger control strategies, such as verbal and physical aggression. In response, the clinician patiently discussed how the perceived safety from maltreatment that her behavior was intended to create, never really occurred. At that point in the module, the clinician engaged Nicolette in a discussion of what she truly wanted her life to be about (i.e. values), and pointed out how the behaviors in which she engaged were really intended to reduce anger and control other people so that they would not do things that led to her anger, rather than in the pursuit of her personal goals and life values. This is the point where the first session ended, and Nicolette was asked to complete the Valued Living Questionnaire-2 (VLQ-2) at home to help determine those things that really mattered in her life.

Nicolette came to the second session (of Module 1) on time, and had completed the VLQ-2 as requested. In reviewing the VLQ-2, it was clear that Nicolette desired to be a good relationship partner, have a "drama-free" relationship, and eventually have children. She also indicated that she wanted to have a job that was enjoyable and meaningful. Finally, she indicated that she wanted to be a good friend and be a support and comfort to those close to her. This discussion led to a conversation about the degree to which these values have been met in the past, and the reasons for her not being able to consistently strive for these values. The distinction between *goals* and *values* was discussed, and a decisional balance was verbally performed that compared the advantages and disadvantages of maintaining her current behavioral style vs modifying that style in such a way as to promote a pursuit of her own stated values. Within this discussion, the clinician presented the possibility that anger itself may not be her primary problem, despite its occasional intensity (as she had thought for a very long time), but rather, her primary problem may be her efforts (often frantic and extreme) to avoid or make the anger go away.

Session 2 of Module 1 concluded with a discussion of the expectations inherent in therapy going forward with regard to appointments, payment, between-session exercises, and clinician availability for between-session phone calls in the event of an emergent situation.

Module 2: Using the Therapeutic Relationship to Recognize and Modify Clinically Relevant Behavior

Nicolette arrived 30 minutes late for session 3 (Module 2). The clinician calmly reiterated that her session was 50 minutes long, that Nicolette would only have 20 minutes left for this session, and that session promptness was important for the treatment process to move forward, as each session was arranged for a "50-minute dose." Nicolette immediately began yelling, "This is bullshit, what are you trying to do?" After the clinician pointed out that the rules are the same as had been discussed the previous week, Nicolette got up and walked to the door, paced around, and then angrily yelled, "You think I care if you call my probation officer, but I don't give a shit." The clinician said nothing, and Nicolette, after shaking her head back and forth vehemently, sat down, and looked away from the clinician. The clinician then calmly pointed out that Nicolette was, for the most part, doing the same thing in-session that she does outside of sessions, which is interpreting an event as a personal affront, even if it is explainable in some other way; immediately responding with intense anger; and acting in a way that attempts to control the situation and make herself feel better. Additionally, it was presented that this pattern is exactly what had been discussed in a previous session. Consistent with the goals of Module 2, this is an effort to use clinically relevant in-session behavior as a reflection of the problems that the client faces outside of therapy. The therapist made no effort to "correct" this behavior, but rather simply pointed out the relevance of the noted behavior. After a brief pause, the clinician also noted that ultimately, despite the similarities, Nicolette did not walk out, throw anything, or engage in any additional verbal aggressiveness. Nicolette acknowledged that she came close, but knew it wouldn't "do any good." The clinician noted that her final decision was in the service of pursuing her values and not simply an emotion-driven behavior. By this time, the session time was over, and a new appointment was scheduled for the following week. While the likelihood of future clinically relevant in-session behaviors was very strong, and understanding that they would need to be attended to whenever they occurred during therapy, the clinician nevertheless planned to move on to Module 3 at the beginning of the next session.

Module 3: Developing Mindful Emotion Awareness

Nicolette arrived for session 4 (the first session of Module 3) 15 minutes early, and was asked to complete: (a) the Anger and Violence Impairment

Scale (AVIS), to assess on a week-to-week basis the degree to which anger and violent behavior are negatively impacting her life; and (b) the Mindful Attention and Awareness Scale (MAAS), to assess the degree to which she is aware of and attentive to her internal and external experiences.

Since reinforcing appropriate behavior is as important as extinguishing inappropriate behavior, the clinician first commented on the timeliness of Nicolette's arrival. Following this, the assessment results were reviewed, which suggested that Nicolette was (as expected) still experiencing difficulties related to her anger and violent behavior (see AVIS case results, Table 7.1). In addition, according to her MAAS scores, it was clear that Nicolette was quite inattentive and unaware of her internal and external experiences. The foundation of this session consisted of a discussion with regard to the importance of developing an awareness of, and ultimately the capacity to be with and learn from, one's internal experiences. The remainder of the session consisted of a description of mindfulness (contrasted to mind*less*ness), the exercises that help it develop, and its importance. The client was presented with the "washing a dish" exercise as a between-session assignment to begin this process.

Table 7.1 Nicolette's AVIS

The following questions ask about your experience with anger and aggressive or violent behavior over the past week. For each question, please circle the answer that best describes your experience of anger and aggression/violence *over the past week only.*

---

1. **During the past week, how often have you felt angry?**
   a. No anger this past week
   b. Became angry only once or twice this past week
   c. Became angry occasionally (several times) this past week
   d. *Became angry frequently (daily) this past week*
   e. Became angry constantly (several times every day) this past week

2. **During this past week, when you felt angry, how intense was the anger?**
   a. Very low intensity. My anger was barely noticeable
   b. Mild intensity. My anger was not too uncomfortable
   c. Moderate intensity. My anger was uncomfortable. At times it affected my ability to relax and/or concentrate
   d. Severe intensity. My anger was very uncomfortable. It made concentrating on anything else very difficult
   e. *Extreme intensity. My anger was overwhelming. It was nearly impossible to focus on anything else*

3. **During the past week, how often did you avoid situations or people because of feeling angry or concern about becoming angry?**
   a. Not at all. I did not avoid anything because of anger or concern about becoming angry
   b. Infrequently. I avoided people or situations once or twice, but usually confronted difficult situations
   c. Occasionally. I avoided people or situations a few times due to anger or concern about becoming angry

    d. *Frequently. I often avoided people or situations due to anger or concern about becoming angry*

    e. Almost all of the time. I avoided people or situations due to anger or concern about becoming angry constantly

4. **During the past week, how often did you engage in aggressive or violent behavior (screaming, cursing, threatening, throwing objects, or physical acts/fights)?**
   a. Not at all. I did not engage in aggressive or violent behavior
   b. Infrequently. I engaged in aggressive or violent behavior once or twice
   c. *Occasionally. I engaged in aggressive or violent behavior a few times*
   d. Frequently. I often engaged in aggressive or violent behavior
   e. Almost all of the time. I engaged in aggressive or violent behavior constantly

5. **During the past week, how much did your anger, concern about becoming angry, or aggressive/violent behavior, interfere with your ability to do the things necessary for work, school, or home life?**
   a. None. My anger, concern about becoming angry, or behavior did not interfere with my life
   b. Mild. My anger, concern about becoming angry, or behavior led to some interference with work, school, or home life, but most necessary things still got taken care of. My life has generally not been affected
   c. Moderate. My anger, concern about becoming angry, or behavior definitely interfered with work, school, or home life. Most things still got taken care of, but not everything, and some things were handled less well. My life has been affected somewhat
   d. *Severe. My anger, concern about becoming angry, or behavior has strongly affected work, school, or home life this week. Many things didn't get handled like they should. My life has definitely been affected*
   e. Extreme. My anger, concern about becoming angry, or behavior has become overwhelming. I have been unable to function consistently or adequately at work, school, or home. I have experienced or appear about to experience clear consequences such as loss or threat of loss of job, school status, or family life.

    During the two subsequent sessions of Module 3 (sessions 5 and 6), the clinician and Nicolette continued this process with a discussion of the between-session exercise and practiced a centering exercise during session 5, and the therapist introduced the "mindfulness of the breath" exercise in session 6. In addition to the practice and discussion of these exercises, her occasional frustrations with them (i.e. "but I keep getting distracted," "it's so boring") were patiently discussed in terms of normalizing her experience and understanding that her reaction was actually an important part of the process of enhancing non-judging awareness, attention, and tolerance.

Module 4: Cognitive Defusion and the Reduction of Problematic Rule-Governed Behavior

After administering the AVIS and MAAS once again, it became evident that Nicolette was beginning to show early signs of improvement, demonstrating regular, albeit not daily (as desired) practice of mindfulness exercises. The therapist therefore decided to move on to Module 4. In session 7 (first session of Module 4), the clinician introduced the idea that what we think about when faced with certain situations is learned, and some of our thoughts (and internal rules) drive us to immediately act in ways that attempt to protect us from feeling bad. Sometimes these automatic behaviors are helpful, and sometimes they are not. The clinician and Nicolette discussed some of her thoughts in response to situations and the rules ("I can't let anyone disrespect me") that direct her immediate behavior. A discussion then ensued covering how this rule might have been learned, how it at times serves to protect, and how it can result in negative consequences (e.g. when the rule and associated behavior are invoked too readily, across too many situations in which it is neither relevant nor called for). The clinician then presented the concept of defusion/decentering, the process by which Nicolette can learn to notice and view her thoughts as "what her mind is telling her," which does not have to reflect a factual and immediate threat. This therefore gives Nicolette time to reflect and choose her actions as opposed to automatically acting, seemingly without choice. Nicolette appeared to understand the distinction, and seemed eager to begin the process. The clinician then proceeded to present to Nicolette the possibility that many of the aggressive behaviors toward her husband were based upon this automatic response to internal rules. Nicolette was able to see how this was the case, and a discussion regarding the benefits of slowing down the process and decentering from what her mind tells her followed.

Nicolette was then asked to continue her mindfulness practice between sessions, while paying attention to the variety of thoughts, feelings, and physical sensations that come and go. In addition, she was asked to complete the Between-Session Monitoring Form to help her understand the range of thoughts and emotions that occur when confronted with difficult situations, to be discussed at the next session.

In session 8 (the second session of Module 4), Nicolette and the clinician discussed the form, which she did complete, albeit with only one situation. This situation reflected a time in which someone on a bus bumped into her and "didn't care, didn't apologize, and acted like I wasn't even there." This triggered the "disrespect" related thoughts that had previously been discussed. Nicolette reported that she was aware of what she was thinking, was aware that she became very angry, began to get "red in the face," and decided that she would write it all down when she got off the bus. The therapist reinforced her effort to remain present with the internal experiences without responding, and her effort to record the incident. The remainder of the session was used to discuss what her mind was telling her, and how she could notice it as such and allow it to be, despite her increasing anger, and without doing anything about it. Notice that there was no effort to discuss the likelihood that her interpretation was correct or incorrect, or to suggest different ways of thinking about the event, as would be typical in traditional forms of cognitive behavioral therapy. Rather, the effort was to simply notice, be present, and reflect with no action required. Nicolette appeared to understand, and willingly noted several historical situations that might have been handled much more effectively with this approach. Nicolette was subsequently asked to complete the Between-Session Monitoring Form once again prior to the next session, and to also take one minute each day and say the word "disrespect" to herself over and over again for the entire minute. Nicolette laughed at this suggestion, and the clinician let her know that the purpose was to allow her to see that eventually the word was just a sound, and that after awhile, hearing it would be more readily noticed, and less immediately reacted to. Nicolette agreed to do this for one minute per day.

Module 5: Understanding Anger and Anger-Avoidance

Session 9 began with a discussion of between-session assignments. It was clear to the clinician that Nicolette had completed the form (using two relevant situations), practiced her mindfulness exercise several times and each day, and engaged in the defusion exercise asked of her. As such, it was decided to move on to Module 5.

Using the between-session information collected, the clinician presented the idea that the emotion of anger is a normal and unavoidable aspect of life, and the reality that the biggest reason that anger has caused difficulty for Nicolette is not the *experience* of the emotion itself, but rather, the fact that it has been seen and responded to as something to be feared and avoided. In addition, the clinician presented, as a fallacy, the idea that anger inevitably leads to aggression if not controlled, and the fallacy that venting is both healthy and necessary. Within this discussion, the personal costs of Nicolette's efforts to avoid the experience of anger were addressed, including interpersonal, financial, and health-related costs. The clinician proposed to Nicolette that an essential goal of CART treatment is the enhancement of her capacity to (increasingly) tolerate anger, and by doing so, allowing for more values-based choices of action to follow. This session ended with the clinician and Nicolette determining two situations to approach (and not avoid) during the coming week. These situations were to: (a) purposely go onto a crowded bus or train (which was often avoided) even if it meant missing appointments, as it frequently results in her becoming angry at people and their "rudeness," and (b) express her concerns to her husband, while also hearing his perspective. She was asked to notice her thoughts and feelings, and make no effort to change any of them. Rather, she was encouraged to simply be aware of them, remain in the situation, and focus as best she could on partaking in an appropriate conversation. These situations were discussed in some detail in preparation for Nicolette to approach them, not necessarily with the goal of a positive outcome, but rather, with the goal of simply being present in these situations while noticing and not avoiding or escaping in any way.

Session 10 (second session of Module 5) was subsequently devoted to a discussion of both of the assigned activities. Nicolette reported that she did in fact engage in both assigned situations. She indicated that she became very angry in both situations, in direct response to both strangers and her husband behaving in ways that reflected "disrespect." Nicolette stated that she noticed her use of this word in her head, which she indicated had less of a powerful effect on her than in times past. In addition, she noted the course of her angry feelings, as they built up and maintained until well after the situation ended. Nicolette indicated that she hated such feelings, but was able to tolerate them without responding in any way. She reported that, as hoped for, she was able to remain in both situations, and did not do anything to escape or avoid the situations. However, it did become clear to the clinician that Nicolette lacked the skills necessary to effectively deal with such situations. She was not able to easily express her thoughts and feelings to her husband, nor respond well to his comments. While she tolerated the situation, she was still ineffective therein. This was noted and discussed, and the clinician promised that some skill building in this regard would be undertaken later in treatment. Nicolette was asked to simply be present and notice internal experiences without responding over the course of the week (between sessions), with an understanding that relevant situations occurring during the week would be the focus of the next session. As Nicolette was able and willing to engage in direct efforts to begin confronting and responding differently to situations that previously were high risk for aggressive responding, it was determined that she was ready to move on to Module 6.

Module 6: Acceptance and Anger Regulation

Given that the goals of Module 6 include further development of the capacity to tolerate/accept the presence of anger and the capacity to distinguish between anger-driven behavior and values-driven behavior, session 11 (the first session of Module 6) began with a discussion of relevant between-session incidents. Nicolette presented a number of situations during the week in which she allowed herself to confront situations that she knew would trigger anger, and not make an effort to avoid or escape. One incident in particular was discussed, in which a co-worker at a local coffeehouse (where she takes customers' orders) made a disparaging remark about her work. Nicolette became furious, and while she was able to maintain awareness of her internal experiences and not react with aggression of any kind, when on a break several hours later she began thinking about the incident over and over again, ruminating about how she should have responded or would respond to the co-worker if she did it again. As she was ruminating about the event, she thought about quitting and going home, a scenario that had occurred numerous times in recent years. Nicolette chose to spend a minute using the "centering" exercise, noticed what her mind was telling her, and pushed through the day. After reinforcing her efforts, including the use of the "centering" exercise to decenter from her ruminative thoughts, the clinician used this opportunity to distinguish between emotion-driven behavior, which would include a choice such as quitting her job, from the values-driven choice of staying on the job that she and her family need. It was discussed that in reality, the reason to tolerate negative emotions like anger is so that one can live a fuller and more complete life in line with one's values. This led to an extended conversation of past situations in which emotion-driven behavior was contrasted with values-driven behavior. Session 11 ended with Nicolette being asked to continue to approach and not avoid or escape from difficult situations that trigger anger, and in addition, notice the array of behavioral choices available to her in these situations.

Session 12 (the second session of Module 6) began with a review of the between-session situations that Nicolette experienced. She first noted several minor situations at work in which she allowed herself to feel angry, notice but not respond to her thoughts and feelings, and ultimately chose to act in a manner consistent with her value of being a provider for her family. Nicolette also reported a situation at home in which she found out through a chance meeting with an acquaintance that her husband had been out with his friends one day after work rather than working late as he had indicated. She stated that she became instantly enraged, and that this anger maintained and even increased for several hours before her husband arrived home. By the time he arrived at home, Nicolette reported that she was so angry that she "couldn't take it any more," and the moment he entered the door, she threw a book at him. She then began screaming (calling him names) and left to spend the night with a friend, after never even telling him why she was so angry. This situation was discussed, and Nicolette indicated that while she had wanted to remain present and have a rational conversation, her anger "was overwhelming." The clinician noted that, while it is generally not our goal to provide skills to allow our clients to simply *feel* better, for all of the reasons we have discussed throughout treatment, there are times where "down-regulating" anger just a bit can be worthwhile, *if* it results in a values-driven course of action. In this case, it was suggested that Nicolette could have used her centering breathing techniques to not only decenter from her thoughts and feelings, but also to gently and slightly reduce the actual experience of anger so that she could have an appropriate conversation with her husband. The need to engage her husband in a discussion about this recent event, and its impact on her and their relationship, was discussed in detail. The clinician noted that Nicolette was likely to find many reasons and excuses for not having this conversation, some of which would even have some truth to them, and suggested that they would for the most part reflect a desire to avoid emotion, particularly anger. Once again, the cost of avoidance, the fact that it ultimately does not work, and that sooner or later the anger will have to be faced, was brought forth. Nicolette was asked to continue her mindfulness practice, use her centering technique as a tool to help her approach rather than avoid the necessary but difficult situation, and continue to remain present with her anger in other situations as they occur. At that point, the clinician decided that it was appropriate to move on to the next CART module.

Module 7: Commitment to Values-Based Behavior

Module 7 (session 13) began with a review of her between-session assignments, and a completion of relevant assessment measures. Nicolette reported that she engaged in all assigned tasks, and that her work environment continues to improve as she consistently responds well when experiencing anger. In addition, she reported regular and consistent practice of her mindfulness exercises. However, Nicolette sheepishly reported not having the conversation with her husband. She began reciting the reasons, and then stopped, laughed, and indicated that she knows that she found every reason possible to avoid the conversation, as predicted by the clinician. The clinician stated that, while she understood how Nicolette's history would lead her to believe that avoidance is the only option, inevitably it does not work. Nicolette pointed out (by way of agreement) that she had barely spoken to her husband, that he really didn't understand why, and that he was getting more and more "pushy" about wanting to understand. This was used as a moment to once again connect Nicolette's previously identified values (specifically related to being a good family person) and specific behaviors to be increased, such as conversations about important issues, both with her husband now, and entire family later on. This conversation also explored the notion that experiencing intense anger can (and often must) occur at the same time as the need for effective values-driven behaviors. In essence, often the most important discussions need to occur at times of greatest emotion. This idea was fully elaborated on in terms of Nicolette's own history and experiences. From this discussion, a behavioral (activation) plan was developed to record and monitor specific values-driven behaviors during two conversations that Nicolette planned to have with her husband before the next session.

Session 14 (the second session of Module 7) occurred two weeks later, as Nicolette had cancelled her appointment one week earlier at the last minute. At the outset of this session, the missed appointment was discussed. The clinician noted the fact that this missed appointment occurred at a time when Nicolette was asked to engage in a very difficult task, and that the cancellation was communicated at the very last minute.

The likelihood that both of these points suggested avoidance: (a) of the assigned task, and (b) of having to come in and talk about the assigned task, was also pointed out. Nicolette became visibly angry with the clinician for making this conclusion, and began raising her voice. The clinician patiently pointed out this behavior, and again noted that this could very well be an effort to get her (the clinician) to stop saying uncomfortable things. As noted previously, the goal of noting clinically relevant behavior, most clearly designated in Module 2, is a significant component of the CART protocol. Regardless of which phase of treatment one is in, such clinically relevant behaviors must be addressed before moving back to the content issues at hand.

After a prolonged and at times difficult discussion, Nicolette came to see the clinician's point, and acknowledged that she did in fact avoid having the conversation with her husband and "didn't want to deal with the clinician pointing it out." The clinician noted that this happened anyway, and as had been discussed, the cost of avoidance was not only the continued exacerbation of problems at home, but in addition, the conversation between the clinician and Nicolette was probably more tense than it would have been the week before. Her behaviors were also once again discussed in terms of the importance of taking the necessary actions even when faced with intense emotion (values-driven behavior), instead of engaging in emotion-driven behavior. After some additional discussion, it became clear that Nicolette wanted to have the discussion with her husband but truly had no real sense about how to proceed, what to say, and how to respond to his likely comments. Consequently, this lack of skill was directly related to her avoidance. Since Nicolette was willing to engage in emotionally charged situations in the service of her values, yet lacked some basic necessary skills, moving on to Module 8 (a skills-based module) was deemed appropriate. Nicolette was asked to continue her between-session efforts both at work and when using mass transportation in order to remain present with her internal experiences while behaving in a manner consistent with what matters to her, and was told that during the next session or two, she and the clinician would work on developing some basic conflict management and communication skills for use at home and in general life circumstances.

Module 8: Developing Effective Interpersonal Problem-Solving Skills

The primary goal of session 15 (the first session of Module 8) was to begin developing necessary conflict management and communication skills. In this regard, Nicolette and the clinician role-played a variety of necessary discussions (with respect to her husband), including both reasonable and unreasonable reactions and comments. Knowing the client's "hot buttons" and understanding the relationship and history between

Nicolette and her husband, allowed the clinician to realistically portray likely directions for these varied conversations. The focus was on: (a) mindfully listening to her husband, and not simply her mind's interpretation of her husband's words; (b) communicating her feelings clearly, while not verbally attacking her husband; and (c) engaging in these discussions with a clear reference to her own values, desired (realistic) outcomes, and the actions that would make these outcomes more likely (but never guaranteed). It was clearly communicated to Nicolette that developing these skills would be a *process* and not an event. She therefore needed to focus on small increments of improvement, with an emphasis on behaving reasonably despite the intense anger that was possible, and even likely. The clinician also noted that developing these skills was the last real skill phase of treatment, and that Nicolette's outstanding progress had brought the end of treatment within sight.

The session ended with Nicolette planning to engage her husband in several necessary and long avoided discussions.

The second session of Module 8 (session 16) consisted of a discussion of Nicolette's efforts, with reinforcement and correction as appropriate. Nicolette had made a clear effort to have some difficult conversations, and they generally went well. While the outcomes were not all that Nicolette would have hoped for, she felt good about maintaining her focus on communication, even in the face of very intense anger. Proving to herself that she could both be angry *and* act in a positive and productive fashion was important to Nicolette, and led her to be quite open to additional helpful suggestions regarding her communication style. At this point, the clinician suggested that it was time for the end of formal treatment to be discussed. After expressing some trepidation, yet feeling elated about her improvements at work and home, Nicolette and the therapist agreed to have two more sessions, the first one in two weeks, followed by an additional appointment three weeks after that. They also agreed that treatment would end at that time if all went as planned, with an understanding that the clinician would continue to be available for consultation and additional treatment in the future, if warranted.

Module 9: Integration, Relapse Prevention, and Treatment Termination

Module 9 included Nicolette's final two sessions (sessions 17 and 18). During these two sessions, Nicolette and the clinician reviewed her continued efforts to remain in contact with anger, while behaving in a values-driven way at home, at work, and in the community-at-large. In addition, Nicolette and the clinician identified and role-played potential anger-inducing triggers for the future and signs of possible lapses, and discussed ways of dealing with both of those future events. A distinction was also made between a *lapse*, which is as a predictable part of being a fallible human, and a *relapse*, which is the choice to revert back to an old way of responding to her emotions and the world around her. Finally, Nicolette and the clinician developed an ongoing action plan for continued use of CART principles and strategies in her life, including the use of regular mindfulness practice and a diary in the form of her the Between-Session Monitoring Form. Nicolette's progress was discussed, she completed a final battery of measures, and treatment was considered complete.

Final Comments About Nicolette's CART Treatment

Throughout treatment, Nicolette's progress toward her goals was continually monitored through verbal report, behavioral observations, and objective processes and outcome measures. Nicolette's treatment progress was measured through her scores on the Anger Disorders Scale (ADS), Difficulties in Emotion Regulation Scale (DERS), the Quality of Life Inventory (QOLI), and the Outcome Questionnaire (OQ-45). Behavioral observations regarding Nicolette's willingness to engage in experiential exercises and complete homework assignments were also monitored throughout treatment.

Data comparing Nicolette's scores on the utilized measures can be found in Table 7.2. As predicted, data indicate that Nicolette generally showed no reduction in the experience of anger and aggressive behavior from intake to session 4, although a slight decrease in rumination and an increase in physiological arousal and general subjective distress were noted. These findings are not unusual, as early in the CART process, the focus is on *awareness* of internal experiences (both cognitive and affective), which often results in reductions in rumination along with increases in affective and physiological sensitivity. Interestingly, as one peruses the outcome data, it appears as though increases in emotion regulation (as measured by the DERS) began by session 4 and preceded the ultimate vast improvements in behavioral responses to anger across the remainder of treatment. It is important to note that consistent with the goals of CART, improvements were noted in quality of life (as with all acceptance-based behavioral treatments) and behavioral components of anger (coercion, reactivity, etc.), while physiological arousal did not show anywhere near the same change. As the goals of treatment are awareness/acceptance/tolerance of our internal experience, and not necessarily its reduction, these outcomes are important and noteworthy, as quality of life was associated with hypothesized changes and not simply with distress reduction. Similarly, while Nicolette did manifest some reduction in cognitions related to hurt, rejection, and suspiciousness, they remained rather high, also suggesting that enhanced behavioral functioning does *not* require feeling or thinking differently, but rather understanding and reacting to thoughts and feelings differently.

This case example reflects a very typical treatment case using the CART protocol, and it is hoped that its presentation served to bring to life the treatment modules presented throughout this text. Given our fundamental belief that an empirically based profession should constantly evolve, with sound scientific research informing practice, and in turn, practice informing further research, it is our fervent hope that this text, and use of CART, will be useful for clinicians and researchers alike. Over time, as researchers and clinicians both utilize and work together to build upon this treatment approach, we envision that clients experiencing clinical anger and its vast consequences will have the opportunity to break free from this toxic experience and live the lives that they truly value.

Table 7.2 Case Outcome Data for Nicolette

	Intake	Session 4	Session 8	Session 12	Session 18
ADS-Reactivity/ Expression	93	93	80	50	40
ADS-Anger Provocation	94	94	80	60	50
ADS-Duration of Anger Problems	99	99	99	90	88
ADS-Physiological Arousal	97	99	84	70	70
ADS-Hurt/Social Rejection	98	98	80	68	68
ADS-Suspiciousness	84	80	60	66	60
ADS-Coercion	86	80	72	40	< 20
ADS-Rumination	78	64	50	40	30
OQ-45 (Distress)	54	60	58	60	58
QOLI	Average	Average	Average	Above Average	Above average
DERS	Below Average	Average	Above Average	Well Above Average	Well Above Average

Notes: ADS = Anger Disorders Scale; OQ-45 = Outcome Questionnaire-45; QOLI = Quality of Life Inventory; DERS = Difficulties in Emotion Regulation Scale.

References

Aldao, A., Nolen-Hoeksema, S., & Schweizer, S. (2010). Emotion-regulation strategies across psychopathology: A meta-analytic review. *Clinical Psychology Review, 30*, 217–237.

American Psychiatric Association (APA) (2000). *Diagnostic and statistical manual of mental disorders* (4th edn, text revision). Washington, DC: Author.

American Psychiatric Association (APA) (2013). *Diagnostic and statistical manual of mental disorders* (5th edn). Washington, DC: Author.

Anderson, C. A., & Bushman, B. J. (2002). Human aggression. *Annual Review of Psychology, 53*, 27–51.

Aquino, K., Douglas, S., & Martinko, M. J. (2004). Overt anger in response to victimization: Attributional style and organizational norms as moderators. *Journal of Occupational Health Psychology, 9*(2), 152–164.

Babcock, J. C., Green, C. E., & Robie, C. (2004). Does batterers' treatment work? A meta-analytic review of domestic violence treatment outcome research. *Clinical Psychology Review, 23*, 1023–1053.

Baer, R. A., Smith, G. T., Hopkins, J., Krietemeyer, J., & Toney, L. (2006). Using self-report assessment methods to explore facets of mindfulness. *Assessment, 13*(1), 27–45.

Bagby, R. M., Parker, J. D., & Taylor, G. J. (1994). The twenty-item Toronto Alexithymia Scale-I. Item selection and cross-validation of the factor structure. *Journal of Psychosomatic Research, 38*(1), 23–32.

Barbour, K. A., Eckhardt, C. I., Davison, G. C., & Kassinove, H. (1998). The experience and expression of anger in martially violent and martially discordant-nonviolent men. *Behavior Therapy, 29*, 173–191.

Barlow D. H. (2002). *Anxiety and its disorders: The nature and treatment of anxiety and panic* (2nd edn). New York, NY: The Guilford Press.

Barlow, D. H., Allen, L. B., & Choate, M. L. (2004). Toward a unified treatment for emotional disorders. *Behavior Therapy, 35*(2), 205–230.

Barlow, D. H., Ellard, K. K., Fairholme, C. P., Farchione, T. J., Boisseau, C. L., May, J. T. E., & Allen, L. B. (2010). *Unified protocol for transdiagnostic treatment of emotional disorders: Workbook.* New York, NY: Oxford University Press.

Baumeister, R. F., Smart, L., & Boden, J. (1996). Relation of threatened egotism to violence and aggression: The dark side of high self esteem. *Psychological Review, 103*, 5–33.

Beck, A. T. (1999). *Prisoners of hate: The cognitive basis of anger, hostility, and violence.* New York, NY: HarperCollins.

Beck, A. T. & Fernandez, E. (1998). Cognitive-behavioral therapy in the treatment of anger: A meta-analysis. *Cognitive Therapy and Research, 22,* 63–74.

Beck, A. T., & Shaw, B. F. (1977). Cognitive approaches to depression. *Handbook of rational-emotive therapy* (pp. 309–326). New York, NY: Springer.

Beck, A. T., & Steer. R. A. (1988). *Beck Hopelessness Scale.* San Antonio, TX: Psychological Corporation.

Beck, A. T., & Steer, R. A. (1991). *Manual for the Beck Scale for Suicide Ideation.* San Antonio, TX: Psychological Corporation.

Beck, A. T., & Steer, R. A. (1993). *Beck Depression Inventory manual.* San Antonio, TX: Psychological Corporation.

Beck, A. T., Steer, R. A., & Brown, G. K. (1996). *Manual for the Beck Depression Inventory, second edition (BDI-II).* San Antonio, TX: Psychological Association.

Beck, A. T., Epstein, N., Brown, G., & Steer, R. A. (1988). An inventory for measuring clinical anxiety: Psychometric properties. *Journal of Consulting and Clinical Psychology, 56,* 893–897.

Benazzi, F. (2003). Major depressive disorder with anger: A bipolar spectrum disorder? *Psychotherapy and Psychosomatics, 72*(6), 300–306.

Benson, H., & Klipper, M. Z. (1976). *The relaxation response.* New York, NY: HarperCollins.

Berking, M., Orth, U., Wupperman, P., Meier, L. L., & Caspar, F. (2008). Prospective effects of emotion-regulation skills on emotional adjustment. *Journal of Counseling Psychology, 55*(4), 485–494.

Berking, M., Wupperman, P., Reichardt, A., Pejic, T., Dippel, A., & Znoj, H. (2008). Emotion-regulation skills as a treatment target in psychotherapy. *Behaviour Research and Therapy, 46*(11), 1230–1237.

Berkowitz, L. (1983). The experience of anger as a parallel process in the display of impulsive, "angry" aggression. *Aggression: Theoretical and Empirical Reviews, 1,* 103–133.

Berkowitz, L. (1989). Frustration–aggression hypothesis: Examination and reformulation. *Psychological Bulletin, 106,* 59–73.

Berkowitz, L. (1993). Pain and aggression: Some findings and implications. *Motivation and Emotion, 17*(3), 277–293.

Berkowitz, L. (2003). Affect, aggression, and antisocial behavior. In R. J. Davidson, K. R. Scherer, & H. H., Goldsmith (eds), *Handbook of affective sciences* (pp. 804–823). New York, NY: Oxford University Press.

Bernstein, D. P., & Fink, L. (1998). *Childhood Trauma Questionnaire: A retrospective self-report manual.* San Antonio, TX: The Psychological Corporation.

Bond, F. W., Hayes, S. C., Baer, R. A., Carpenter, K. C., Guenole, N., Orcutt, H. K., . . . Zettle, R. D. (2011). Preliminary psychometric properties of the Acceptance and Action Questionnaire-II. A revised measure of psychological flexibility and acceptance. *Behavior Therapy, 42,* 676–688.

Borkovec, T. D. (1994). The nature, functions, and origins of worry. In G. C. I. Davey, & F. Tallis (eds), *Worrying: Perspectives on theory, assessment, and treatment* (pp. 5–33). New York, NY: Wiley.

Borkovec, T. D., Alcaine, O., & Behar, E. (2004). Avoidance theory of worry and generalized anxiety disorder. *Generalized anxiety disorder: Advances in research and practice* (pp. 77–108). New York, NY: Guilford Press.

Borkovec, T. D., Ray, W. J., & Stober, J. (1998). Worry: A cognitive phenomenon intimately linked to affective, physiological, and interpersonal behavioral processes. *Cognitive Therapy and Research, 22*(6), 561–576.

Brown, T. A., & Barlow, D. H. (1992). Comorbidity among anxiety disorders: Implications for treatment and *DSM-IV*. *Journal of Consulting and Clinical Psychology, 60*, 835–844.

Brown, T. A., Campbell, L. A., Lehman, C. L., Grisham, J. R., & Mancill, R. B. (2001). Current and lifetime comorbidity of the *DSM-IV* anxiety and mood disorders in a large clinical sample. *Journal of Abnormal Psychology, 110*(4), 585–597.

Bushman, B. J., & Anderson, C. A. (2001). Is it time to pull the plug on hostile versus instrumental aggression dichotomy? *Psychological Review, 108*, 273–279.

Brown, K.W., & Ryan, R.M. (2003). The benefits of being present: The role of mindfulness in psychological well-being. *Journal of Personality and Social Psychology, 84*, 822–848.

Bushman, B. J., Baumeister, R. F., & Phillips, C. M. (2001). Do people aggress to improve their mood? Catharsis beliefs, affect regulation opportunity, and aggressive responding. *Journal of personality and social psychology, 81*(1), 17–32.

Cahill, S. P., Rauch, S. A., Hembree, E. A., & Foa, E. B. (2003). Effect of cognitive-behavioral treatments for PTSD on anger. *Journal of Cognitive Psychotherapy, 17*, 113–131.

Camras, L. A. (1992). Expressive development and basic emotions. *Cognition & Emotion, 6*, 269–283.

Campbell-Sills, L., Liverant, G. I., & Brown, T. A. (2004). Psychometric evaluation of the behavioral inhibition/behavioral activation scales in a large sample of outpatients with anxiety and mood disorders. *Psychological Assessment, 16*(3), 244–254.

Carroll, C. E. (2001). Anger at work: The influence of contextual and intrapersonal factors on the evaluation of the expression of anger in a work context. *Dissertation Abstracts International, Section B. The Sciences and Engineering, 61*(10-B), 5605.

Carver, C. S., & White, T. L. (1994). Behavioral inhibition, behavioral activation, and affective responses to impending reward and punishment: The BIS/BAS scales. *Journal of Personality and Social Psychology, 67*(2), 319–333.

Castonguay, L. G., & Beutler, L. E. (eds). (2006). *Principles of therapeutic change that work*. New York, NY: Oxford University Press.

Chambers, R., Gullone, E., & Allen, N. B. (2009). Mindful emotion regulation: An integrative review. *Clinical Psychology Review, 29*, 560–572.

Chambless, D. L., & Gillis, M. M. (1993). Cognitive therapy of anxiety disorders. *Journal of Consulting and Clinical Psychology, 61*, 248.

Clark, L. A., & Watson, D. (1991). Tripartite model of anxiety and depression: Psychometric evidence and taxonomic implications. *Journal of Abnormal Psychology, 100*(3), 316–336.

Clark, L. F., & Collins, J. E. (1993). Remembering old flames: How the past affects assessments of the present. *Personality and Social Psychology Bulletin*, 19(4), 399–408.

Cloitre, M., Koenen, K. C., Cohen, L. R., & Han, H. (2002). Skills training in affective and interpersonal regulation followed by exposure: A phase-based treatment for PTSD related to childhood abuse. *Journal of Consulting and Clinical Psychology*, 70(5), 1067–1074.

Cohen, D. J., Eckhardt, C. I., & Schagat, K. D. (1998). Attention allocation and habituation to anger-related stimuli during a visual search task. *Aggressive Behavior*, 24(6), 399–409.

Davey, L., Day, A., & Howells, K. (2005). Anger, over-control, and serious violent offending. *Aggression and Violent Behavior*, 10, 624–635.

Deffenbacher, J. L., Deffenbacher, D. M., Lynch, R. S., & Richards, T. L. (2003). Anger, aggression, and risky behavior: A comparison of high and low anger drivers. *Behaviour Research and Therapy*, 41, 701–718.

Deffenbacher, J. L., Huff, M. E., Lynch, R. S., Oetting, E. R., & Salvatore, N. F. (2000). Characteristics and treatment of high-anger drivers. *Journal of Counseling Psychology*, 47(1), 5.

Deffenbacher, J. L., Richards, T. L., Filetti, L. B., & Lynch, R. S. (2005). Angry drivers: A test of state-trait theory. *Violence and Victims*, 20, 455–469.

Del Vecchio, T., & O'Leary, D. (2004). Effectiveness of anger treatments for specific problems: A meta-analytic review. *Clinical Psychology Review*, 24, 15–34.

DeMoja, C. A., & Spielberger, C. D. (1997). Anger and drug addiction. *Psychological Reports*, 81, 152–154.

Dettore, M. M., Kempel, J. & Gardner, F. L. (2010). *DSM-5 temper dysregulation disorder as a diagnosis for clinical anger*. Poster presented at the annual convention of the Association of Behavioral and Cognitive Therapies, San Francisco, CA, November.

Dettore, M. M., Lee, E. F., & Gardner, F. L. (2012). *Acceptance-based group treatment for externalizing behaviors in an urban elementary school*. Paper presented at the annual convention of the National Association of School Psychologists, Philadelphia, PA, February.

Dettore, M. M., Pabian, C., & Gardner, F. L. (2010). *Difficulties in emotion regulation as a mediator between childhood trauma and anger pathology*. Oral paper presented at the triennial conference of the World Congress of Behavioural & Cognitive Therapies, Boston, MA, June.

Dieckmann, N. F., Malle, B. F., & Bodner, T. E. (2009). An empirical assessment of meta-analytic practice. *Review of General Psychology*, 13, 101.

DiGiuseppe, R., & Tafrate, R. (2003). Anger treatment for adults: A meta-analytic review. *Clinical Psychology: Science and Practice*, 10, 70–84.

DiGiuseppe, R., & Tafrate, R. C. (2004). *Anger Disorders Scale (ADS): Technical manual*. Toronto, Ontario, Canada: Multi-Health Systems.

DiGiuseppe, R., & Tafrate, R. C. (2007). *Understanding anger disorders*. New York, NY: Oxford University Press.

DiGiuseppe, R., Fuller, R., & Fountain, T. (2006). *Diagnoses and anger symptoms*. Paper presented at the "Research on anger treatments: Beyond college students and analogue studies" symposium at the annual convention of the American Psychological Association, New Orleans, LA, July.

Donahue, J., Catella, S., Ruvo, J., Dettore, M., Peters, N., Gardner, F. L., & Moore, Z. E. (2009). *The relationship between affective-motivation systems, emotion dysregulation, anger-in and anger-out in court mandated violent offenders.* Paper presented at the annual conference of the Association for Behavioral and Cognitive Therapies, New York, NY, November.

D'Zurilla, T. J., Chang, E. C., & Sanna, L. J. (2004). *Social problem solving: Current status and future directions.* Washington, DC: American Psychological Association.

Eckhardt, C. I., & Deffenbacher, J. L. (1995). Diagnosis of anger disorders. In H. Kassinove (ed.). *Anger disorders: Definition, diagnosis, and treatment* (pp. 27–47). Philadelphia, PA: Taylor & Francis.

Edmondson, C. B., & Conger, J. C. (1996). A review of treatment efficacy for individuals with anger problems: Conceptual, assessment, and methodological issues. *Clinical Psychology Review, 16*, 251–275.

Ellis, A. (1966). *Reason and emotion in psychotherapy: A comprehensive method of treating human disturbances.* New York, NY: Citadel.

Ellsworth, J. R., Lambert, M. J., & Johnson, J. (2006). A comparison of the Outcome Questionnaire-45 and Outcome Questionnaire-30 in classification and prediction of treatment outcome. *Clinical Psychology & Psychotherapy, 13*(6), 380–391.

Erwin, B. A., Heimberg, R. G., Schneier, F. R., & Liebowitz, M. R. (2003). Anger experience and expression in social anxiety disorder: Pretreatment profile and predictors of attrition and response to cognitive-behavioral treatment. *Behavior Therapy, 34*, 331–350.

Farchione, T. J., Fairholme, C. P., Ellard, K. K., Boisseau, C. L., Thompson-Hollands, J., Carl, J. R. Barlow, D. H. (2012). Unified protocol for transdiagnostic treatment of emotional disorders: a randomized controlled trial. *Behavior Therapy, 3*, 666–668.

Fava, M., & Rosenbaum, J. F. (1998). Anger attacks on depression. *Depression and Anxiety, 8*(S1), 59–63.

Foa, E. B., Riggs, D. S., Massie, E. D., & Yarczower, M. (1995). The impact of fear activation and anger on the efficacy of exposure treatment for posttraumatic stress disorder. *Behavior Therapy, 26*, 487–499.

Frisch, M. B. (1994). *Quality of Life Inventory: Manual and treatment guide.* Minneapolis, MN: National Computer Systems.

Frisch, M. B., Cornell, J., Villanueva, M., & Retzlaff, P. J. (1992). Clinical validation of the Quality of Life Inventory. A measure of life satisfaction for use in treatment planning and outcome assessment. *Psychological Assessment, 4*(1), 92–101.

Frueh, B. C., Henning, K. R., Pellegrin, K. L., & Chobot, K. (1997). Relationship between scores on anger measures and PTSD symptomatology, employment, and compensation-seeking status in combat veterans. *Journal of Clinical Psychology, 53*, 871–878.

Gardner, F. L., Dettore, M. M., Moore, Z. E., & Foy, T. (2010). *Contributions of experiential avoidance and emotion regulation to anger symptom severity.* Paper presented at the triennial conference of the World Congress of Behavioral & Cognitive Therapies, Boston, MA, June.

Gardner, F. L., & Moore, Z. E. (2007). *The psychology of enhancing human performance: The Mindfulness–Acceptance–Commitment (MAC) approach.* New York, NY: Springer.

Gardner, F. L., & Moore, Z. E. (2008). Understanding clinical anger and violence: The Anger Avoidance Model. *Behavior Modification, 32*(6), 897–912.

Gardner, F. L., & Moore, Z. E. (2010). Collaborating with an office of probation and parole on the treatment of court-mandated violent offenders. In Z. E. Moore (Chair), *Cognitive-behavioral assessment and treatment of criminal justice populations: Implications for cross-discipline dissemination and collaboration.* Symposium presented at the annual convention of the Association for Behavioral and Cognitive Therapies, San Francisco, CA, November.

Gardner, F. L., Moore, Z. E., & Dettore, M. M. (2011). *The role of emotion regulation in domestic and non-domestic violence.* Paper presented at the annual convention of the Association for Behavioral and Cognitive Therapies, Toronto, Canada, November.

Gardner, F. L., Moore, Z. E., & Dettore, M. (2013). *The relationship between anger, early aversive history, and emotion regulation difficulties in domestic and non-domestic violent offenders.* Manuscript submitted for publication.

Gardner, F. L., Moore, Z. E., & Pess, R. (2012). *A pilot study examining the effectiveness of anger regulation therapy (ART) for the treatment of interpersonal partner violence.* Paper presented at the annual convention of the Association for Behavioral and Cognitive Therapies, National Harbor, Maryland, November.

Gardner, F. L., Moore, Z. E., Ronkowski, F., & Wolanin, A. T. (2006). New developments for clinical anger: Basic science to innovative treatment. In R. C. Tafrate (Chair), *Research on anger treatments—Beyond college students and analogue studies.* Symposium presented at the annual convention of the American Psychological Association, New Orleans, LA, July.

Gardner, F. L., Moore, Z. E., Wolanin, A. T., Alm, T., Kellog, M., & Marks, A. (2006). *Aversive history, experiential avoidance, and anger experience and expression in a clinical sample.* Paper presented at the annual conference of the Association for Behavioral and Cognitive Therapies, Chicago, IL, November.

Gardner, F. L., Moore, Z. E., Wolanin, A. T., Deutsch, V., & Marks, A. (2006). *Aversive history, experiential avoidance, and anger experience and expression in a non-clinical sample.* Paper presented at the annual conference of the Association for Behavioral and Cognitive Therapies, Chicago, IL, November.

Gardner, F. L., Ronkowski, F., Wolanin, A. T., & Moore, Z. E. (2006). *Understanding the violent offender: Early aversive history and trait anger.* Paper presented at the annual convention of the American Psychological Association, New Orleans, LA, July.

Gondolf, E. W., & Foster, R. A. (1991). Pre-program attrition in batterer programs. *Journal of Family Violence*, 6(4), 337–349.

Gortner, E. T., Gollan, J. K., Dobson, K. S., & Jacobson, N. S. (1998). Cognitive-behavioral treatment for depression: Relapse prevention. *Journal of Consulting and Clinical Psychology*, 66, 377.

Gratz, K. L., & Gunderson, J. G. (2006). Preliminary data on an acceptance-based emotion regulation group intervention for deliberate self-harm among women with borderline personality disorder. *Behavior Therapy*, 37(1), 25–35.

Gratz, K. L., & Roemer, L. (2004). Multidimensional assessment of emotion regulation and dysregulation: Development, factor structure, and initial validation of the difficulties in emotion regulation scale. *Journal of Psychopathology and Behavioral Assessment*, 26(1), 41–54.

Gray, J. A. (1981). A critique of Eysenck's theory of personality. In H. J. Eysenck (ed.), *A model for personality* (pp. 246–276). Berlin: Springer-Verlag.

Gray, J. A. (1982). *The neuropsychology of anxiety: An enquiry into the functions of the septo-hippocampal system*. Oxford: Oxford University Press.

Greenberg, L. S. (2004). Emotion-focused therapy. *Clinical Psychology & Psychotherapy, 11*(1), 3–16.

Gross, J. J. (1998). The emerging field of emotion regulation: An integrative review. *Review of General Psychology, 2*(3), 271–299.

Hansen, N. B., & Lambert, M. J. (1996). Clinical significance: An overview of methods. *Journal of Mental Health, 5*(1), 17–24.

Hayes, A. M., & Feldman, G. (2004). Clarifying the construct of mindfulness in the context of emotion regulation and the process of change in therapy. *Clinical Psychology: Science and Practice, 11*(3), 255–262.

Hayes, S. C., Strosahl, K. D., & Wilson, K. G. (1999). *Acceptance and commitment therapy: An experiential approach to behavior change*. New York, NY: Guilford Press.

Hayes, S. C., Wilson, K. G., Strosahl, K., Gifford, E. V., & Follette, V. M. (1996). Experiential avoidance and behavioral disorders: A functional dimensional approach to diagnosis and treatment. *Journal of Consulting and Clinical Psychology, 64*(6), 1152–1168.

Helmers, K. F., Posluszny, D. M., & Krantz, D. S. (1994). Associations of hostility and coronary heart disease: A review of studies. In A. Siegmen, & T. Smith (Eds.), *Anger, hostility, and the heart* (pp. 67–96). Hillsdale NJ: Lawrence Erlbaum Associates.

Higgins, E. T. (1997). Beyond pleasure and pain. *American Psychologist, 52*(12), 1280–1300.

Hofmann, S. G., Heinrichs, N., & Moscovitch, D. A. (2004). The nature and expression of social phobia: Toward a new classification. *Clinical Psychology Review, 24*, 769–797.

Howells, K., & Day, A. (2003). Readiness for anger management: Clinical and theoretical issues. *Clinical Psychology Review, 23*, 319–337.

Izard, C. E. (1991). *The psychology of emotions*. New York, NY: Plenum Press.

Izard, C. E., & Kobak, R. R. (1991). Emotions system functioning and emotion regulation. In J. Garber, & K. A. Dodge (eds), *The development of emotion regulation and dysregulation* (pp. 303–321). New York, NY: Cambridge University Press.

Jacobson, N. S., Christensen, A., Prince, S. E., Cordova, J., & Eldridge, K. (2000). Integrative behavioral couple therapy: An acceptance-based, promising new treatment for couple discord. *Journal of Consulting and Clinical Psychology, 68*, 351–355.

Jacobson, N. S., Dobson, K. S., Truax, P. A., Addis, M. E., Koerner, K., Gollan, J. K., . . . Prince, S. E. (1996). A component analysis of cognitive-behavioral treatment for depression. *Journal of Consulting and Clinical Psychology, 64*(2), 295–304.

Jakupcak, M., Lisak, D., & Roemer, L. (2002). The role of masculine ideology and masculine gender role stress in men's perpetration of relationship violence. *Psychology of Men and Masculinity, 3*(2), 97–106.

Jakupcak, M., & Tull, M. (2005). The effects of trauma exposure on anger, hostility, and aggression in a non-clinical sample of men. *Violence & Victims, 20*, 589-598.

Joorman, J., Dkane, M., & Gotlib, I. H. (2006). Adaptive and maladaptive components of rumination? Diagnostic specificity and relation to depressive biases. *Behavior Therapy*, 37(3), 269–280.

Jordan, B. K., Marmar, C. R., Fairbank, J. A., Schlenger, W. E., Kulka, R. A., Hough, R. L., et al. (1992). Problems in families of male Vietnam veterans with posttraumatic stress disorder. *Journal of Consulting and Clinical Psychology*, 60(6), 916–926.

Kashdan, T. B., Barrios, V., Forsyth, J. P., & Steger, M. F. (2006). Experiential avoidance as a generalized psychological vulnerability: Comparisons with coping and emotion regulation strategies. *Behaviour Research and Therapy*, 44, 1301–1320.

Kashdan, T. B., & Collins, R. L. (2010). Social anxiety and the experience of positive emotion and anger in everyday life: An ecological momentary assessment approach. *Anxiety, Stress, & Coping*, 23(3), 259–272.

Kassinove, H., & Sukhodolsky, D. G. (1995). Anger disorders: Basic science and practice issues. *Issues in Comprehensive Pediatric Nursing*, 18(3), 173–205.

Kassinove, H., & Tafrate, R. C. (2002). *Anger management: The complete treatment guidebook for practitioners*. Atascadero, CA: Impact Publishers, Inc.

Kohlenberg, R. J., & Tsai, M. (2007). *Functional analytic psychotherapy: Creating intense and curative therapeutic relationships*. New York, NY: Springer.

Korb, M. P., Gorrell, J., & Van De Riet, V. (1989). *Gestalt therapy: Practice and theory*. New York, NY: Pergamon Press.

Kring, A. M., & Sloan, D. M. (eds) (2009). *Emotion regulation and psychopathology: A transdiagnostic approach to etiology and treatment*. New York, NY: The Guilford Press.

Kring, A. M., & Werner, K. H. (2004). *Emotion regulation and psychopathology*. Mahwah, NJ: Lawrence Erlbaum Associates.

Langton, A., & Wenzel, A. (2004). *A naturalistic observation of anger attributions in angry, anxious, and healthy individuals*. Paper presented at the annual conference of the Association for Advancement of Behavior Therapy, New Orleans, LA, November.

Lemerise, E. A., & Dodge, K. A. (2008). The development of anger and hostile interactions. In M. Lewis, J. M. Haviland-Jones, & L. F. Barrett (eds), *The handbook of emotions* (3rd edn). New York, NY: The Guilford Press.

Linehan, M. M. (1993). *Cognitive-behavioral treatment of borderline personality disorder*. New York, NY: Guilford Press.

Longmore, R. J., & Worrell, M. (2007). Do we need to challenge thoughts in cognitive behavior therapy? *Clinical Psychology Review*, 27(2), 173–187.

Malott, R. W., Malott, M. E., & Trojan, E. A. (2000). *Elementary principles of behavior*. Upper Saddle River, NJ: Prentice Hall.

McConnaughy, E. A., Prochaska, J. O., & Velicer, W. F. (1983). Stages of change in psychotherapy: Measurement and sample profiles. *Psychotherapy: Theory, Research & Practice*, 20(3), 368–375.

McCullough, J. P., Jr. (2000). *Treatment for chronic depression: Cognitive behavioral analysis system of psychotherapy (CBASP)*. New York, NY: Guilford.

McNaughton, N., & Gray, J. A. (2000). Anxiolytic action on the behavioural inhibition system implies multiple types of arousal contribute to anxiety. *Journal of Affective Disorders*, 61(3), 161–176.

Meichenbaum, D. (1977). *Cognitive-behavior modification: An integrative approach*. New York, NY: Springer.

Mennin, D. S. (2004). Emotion regulation therapy for generalized anxiety disorder. *Clinical Psychology & Psychotherapy, 11*(1), 17–29.

Mennin, D. S., Heimberg, R. G., Turk, C. L., & Fresco, D. M. (2005). Preliminary evidence for an emotion dysregulation model of generalized anxiety disorder. *Behaviour Research and Therapy, 43*(10), 1281–1310.

Mennin, D. S., Holaway, R. M., Fresco, D. M., Moore, M. T., & Heimberg, R. G. (2007). Delineating components of emotion and its dysregulation in anxiety and mood psychopathology. *Behavior Therapy, 38*, 284–302.

Mikulincer, M. (1998). Attachment working models and the sense of trust: An exploration of interaction, goals, and affect regulation. *Journal of Personality and Social Psychology, 74*, 1209–1224.

Mineka, S., Watson, D., & Clark, L. A. (1998). Comorbidity of anxiety and unipolar mood disorders. *Annual Review of Psychology, 49*(1), 377–412.

Moore, Z. E. (2003). Toward the development of an evidence based practice of sport psychology: A structured qualitative study of performance enhancement interventions (Doctoral dissertation, La Salle University). *Dissertation Abstracts International-B, 64* (10), 5227 (UMI no. 3108295).

Moore, Z. E., & Gardner, F. L. (2007). *Understanding anger and violence: An Empirical investigation of the anger avoidance model.* Paper presented at the triennial conference of the World Congress of Behavioural & Cognitive Therapies, Barcelona, Spain, July.

Moore, Z. E., Gardner, F. L., & Wolanin, A. T. (2006). *Emotion regulation, early aversive history, and trait anger.* Paper presented at the annual convention of the American Psychological Association, New Orleans, LA, July.

Mund, M., & Mitte, K. (2012). The costs of repression: A meta-analysis on the relation between repressive coping and somatic diseases. *Health Psychology, 31*, 640–649.

Murphy, R. T., Cameron, R. P., Sharp, L., Ramirez, G., Rosen, C. S., Drescher, K., & Gusman, F. (2004). Readiness to change PTSD symptoms and other problems among veterans participating in a motivation enhancement group. *The Behavior Therapist, 27*, 33–36.

Nathan, P. E., & Gorman, J. M. (2002). *A guide to treatments that work.* New York, NY: Oxford University Press.

Nathan, P. E., & Gorman, J. M. (2007). *A guide to treatments that work* (2nd edn). New York, NY: Oxford University Press.

Neff, K. D. (2003). Self-compassion: An alternative conceptualization of a healthy attitude toward oneself. *Self and Identity, 2*, 85–101.

Neff, K. D., Kirkpatrick, K. L., & Rude, S. S. (2007). Self-compassion and adaptive psychological functioning. *Journal of Research in Personality, 41*(1), 139–154.

Neff, K. D., Rude, S. S., & Kirkpatrick, K. L. (2007). An examination of self-compassion in relation to positive psychological functioning and personality traits. *Journal of Research in Personality, 41*(4), 908–916.

Nolen-Hoeksema, S. (2000). The role of rumination in depressive disorders and mixed anxiety/depressive symptoms. *Journal of Abnormal Psychology, 109*(3), 504.

Norlander, B., & Eckhardt, C. (2005). Anger, hostility, and male perpetrators of intimate partner violence: A meta-analytic review. *Clinical Psychology Review, 25*, 119–152.

Norman, J., Oltarzewski, J., Gardner, F. L., & Moore, Z. E. (2009a). *The inter-action between gender, deficits in emotion regulation, and bulimic behavior*. Paper presented at the annual conference of the Association for Behavioral and Cognitive Therapies, New York, NY, November.

Norman, J., Oltarzewski, J., Gardner, F. L., & Moore, Z. E. (2009b). *The impact of gender on the relationship between experiential avoidance, emotional clarity, and bulimic behavior*. Paper presented at the annual conference of the Association for Behavioral and Cognitive Therapies, New York, NY, November.

Norman, S. B., Hami Cissell, S., Means-Christensen, A. J., & Stein, M. B. (2006). Development and validation of an Overall Anxiety Severity and Impairment Scale (OASIS). *Depression and Anxiety, 23*(4), 45–249.

Novaco, R. W. (1975). *Anger control: The development and evaluation of an experimental treatment*. England: Oxford Press.

Novaco, R. W. (1977). Stress inoculation: A cognitive therapy for anger and its application to a case of depression. *Journal of Consulting and Clinical Psychology, 45*, 600–608.

Novaco, R. W. (2003). *NAS-PI: The Novaco Anger Scale and Provocation Inventory: Manual*. Western Psychological Services.

Novaco, R. W., & Welsh, W. N. (1989). Anger disturbances: Cognitive mediation and clinical prescriptions. In K. Howell, & C. Hollins (eds), *Clinical approaches to violence*. Chichester: John Wiley & Sons.

Oei, T. P. S., & Baranoff, J. (2007). Young Schema Questionnaire: Review of psychometric and measurement issues. *Australian Journal of Psychology, 59*(2), 78–86.

Olatunji, B. O., Ciesielski, B., & Tolin, D. (2010). Fear and loathing: A meta-analytic review of the specificity of anger in PTSD. *Behavior Therapy, 41*, 93–105.

Olatunji, B. O., & Lohr, J. M. (2005). Nonspecific factors and the efficacy of psychosocial treatments for anger. *Scientific Review of Mental Health Practice*. Online at: http://www.srmhp.org/0302/anger.html.

Pennebaker, J. W. (1997). Writing about emotional experiences as a therapeutic process. *Psychological Science, 8*, 162–166.

Pess, R. A., Trachta, H. R., Aster, A. M., Gardner, F. L., Marks, D., & Moore, Z. E. (2012). *The mediating role of emotion regulation on the relationship between insecure attachment style and negative affect*. Paper presented at the annual convention of the Association for Behavioral and Cognitive Therapies, National Harbor, Maryland, November.

Prochaska, J. O., DiClemente, C. C., & Norcross, J. C. (1992). In search of how people change: Applications to addictive behaviors. *American Psychologist, 47*(9), 1102–1114.

Ridker, P. M., Hennekens, C. H., Buring, J. E., & Rifai, N. (2000). C-reactive protein and other markers of inflammation in the prediction of cardiovascular disease in women. *New England Journal of Medicine, 342*, 836–843.

Roemer, L., & Orsillo, S. M. (2009). *Mindfulness- and acceptance-based behavioral therapies in practice*. New York, NY: Guilford Press.

Rothbart, M. K., & Sheese, B. E. (2007). Temperament and emotion regulation. In J. J. Gross (ed.), *Handbook of emotion regulation* (pp. 331–350). New York, NY: Guilford Press.

Rottenberg, J., & Gross, J. J. (2003). When emotion goes wrong: Realizing the promise of affective science. *Clinical Psychology: Science and Practice*, 10(2), 227–232.

Saarni, C., Campos, J. J., Camras, L. A., & Witherington, D. (2006). Emotional development: Action, communication, and understanding. In W. Damon, & N. Eisenberg (eds), *Handbook of child psychology: Social, emotional, and personality development* (5th edn, vol. 3, pp. 237–309). New York, NY: John Wiley & Sons.

Saini, M. (2009). A meta-analysis of the psychological treatment of anger: Developing guidelines for evidence-based practice. *Journal of the American Academy of Psychiatry and the Law*, 37, 473–488.

Segal, Z. V., Williams, J. M. G., & Teasdale, J. D. (2012). *Mindfulness-based cognitive therapy for depression*. New York, NY: Guilford Publication.

Segerstrom, S. C., Tsao, J. C. I., Alden, L. E., & Craske, M. G. (2000). Worry and rumination: Repetitive thought as a concomitant and predictor of negative mood. *Cognitive Therapy and Research*, 24, 671–688.

Siegel, J. M. (1986). The Multidimensional Anger Inventory. *Journal of Personality and Social Psychology*, 51, 191–200.

Smith, T. W., & Ruiz, J. M. (2002). Psychosocial influences on the development and course of coronary heart disease: Current status and implications for research and practice. *Journal of Consulting and Clinical Psychology*, 70, 548.

Smith, T. W., Glazer, K., Ruiz, J. M., & Gallo, L. C. (2004). Hostility, anger, aggressiveness, and coronary heart disease: An interpersonal perspective on personality, emotion, and health. *Journal of Personality*, 72, 1217–1270.

Smits, D. J., & Kuppens, P. (2005). The relations between anger, coping with anger, and aggression, and the BIS/BAS system. *Personality and Individual Differences*, 39(4), 783–793.

Smyth, E. J., Dettore, M., Gardner, F. L., & Moore, Z. E. (2010). *Emotion dysregulation as a mediator between early maladaptive schemas and anger*. Paper presented at the annual convention of the Association for Behavioral and Cognitive Therapies, San Francisco, CA, November.

Spielberger, C. D. (1999). *STAXI-2: State Trait Anger Expression Inventory-2*. Odessa, FL: Psychological Assessment Resources, Inc.

Stokols, D., Novaco, R. W., Stokols, J., & Campbell, J. (1978). Traffic congestion, type A behavior, and stress. *Journal of Applied Psychology*, 63, 467–480.

Stover, C. S., Meadows, A. L., & Kaufman, J. (2009). Interventions for intimate partner violence: Review and implications for evidence-based practice. *Professional Psychology: Research and Practice*, 40(3), 223–233.

Straus, M. A., Hamby, S. L., Boney-McCoy, S., & Sugarman, D. B. (1996). The revised Conflict Tactics Scales (CTS2) development and preliminary psychometric data. *Journal of Family Issues*, 17(3), 283–316.

Suls, J., & Bunde, J. (2005). Anger, anxiety, and depression as risk factors for cardiovascular disease: The problems and implications of overlapping affective dispositions. *Psychological Bulletin*, 131, 260–300.

Tafrate, R. C. (1995). Evaluation of treatment strategies for adult anger disorders. In H. Kassinove (ed.), *Anger disorders: Definition, diagnosis, and treatment*. Philadelphia, PA: Taylor & Francis.

Tafrate, R. C., Kassinove, H., & Dundin, L. (2002). Anger episodes in high- and low-trait-anger community adults. *Journal of Clinical Psychology*, 58, 1573–1590.

Teasdale, J. D. (1999a). Emotional processing, three modes of mind and the prevention of relapse in depression. *Behaviour Research and Therapy, 37,* 553–577.

Teasdale, J. D. (1999b). Metacognition, mindfulness and the modification of mood disorders. *Clinical Psychology and Psychotherapy, 6,* 146–155.

Tedeschi, J. T., & Nesler, M. S. (1993). Grievances: Development and reactions. In R. B. Felson, & J. T. Tedeschi (eds), *Aggression and violence: Social interactionist perspectives* (pp. 13–45). Washington, DC: American Psychological Association.

Tull, M. T., Barrett, H. M., McMillan, E. S., & Roemer, L. (2007). A preliminary investigation of the relationship between emotion regulation difficulties and posttraumatic stress symptoms. *Behavior Therapy, 38,* 303–313.

US Department of Transportation National Highway Traffic Safety Administration (2005). *Traffic Safety Facts, 2005.* Online at: http://www.-nrd.nhtsa.dot. gov.

Watson, D., Clark, L. A., & Tellegen, A. (1988). Development and validation of brief measures of positive and negative affect: The PANAS scales. *Journal of Personality and Social Psychology, 54*(6), 1063–1070.

Wenzel, A., & Lystad, C. (2005). Interpretation biases in angry and anxious individuals. *Behaviour Research and Therapy, 43,* 1045–1054.

Williams, J. E., Paton, C. C., Siegler, I. C., Eigenbrodt, M. L., Nieto, F. J., & Tyroler, H. A. (2000). Anger proneness predicts coronary heart disease risk: Prospective analysis from the atherosclerosis risk in communities (ARIC) study. *Circulation, 101*(17), 2034–2039.

Williams, R. B., Barefoot, J. C., & Shekelle, R. B. (1985). The health consequences of hostility. In M. A. Chesney, & R. H. Rosenman (eds), *Anger and hostility in cardiovascular and behavioral disorders* (pp. 173–185). New York, NY: Hemisphere.

Wilson, K. G., & Dufrene, P. D. T. (2008). *Mindfulness for two: An acceptance and commitment approach to mindfulness in psychotherapy.* Oakland, CA: New Harbinger.

Young, J. E., Klosko, J. S., & Weishaar, M. E. (2003). *Schema therapy: A practitioner's guide.* New York, NY: The Guilford Press.

Index